THE PRACTICAL ENCYCLOPEDIA OF

FENG SHUI

THE PRACTICAL ENCYCLOPEDIA OF FENG SHUI

GILL HALE

HERMES HOUSE

This edition published by Hermes House
an imprint of
Anness Publishing Limited
Hermes House
88-89 Blackfriars Road
London SE1 8HA

A CIP catalogue record for this book is available from the British Library

Publisher: Joanna Lorenz
Senior Editor: Joanna Rippin
Designer: Nigel Partridge
Special Photography: John Freeman
Stylist: Claire Hunt
Illustrator: Geoff Ball
Production Controller: Julie Hadingham
Editorial Reader: Richard McGinlay

Printed and bound in China

3 5 7 9 10 8 6 4 2

CONTENTS

INTRODUCTION 6

FENG SHUI IN THE HOME 30

The Outside World 32

Inside the Home 46

Putting the Principles into Practice 82

FENG SHUI IN THE GARDEN 128

Feng Shui Principles in the Garden 132

Garden Features 154

Creating the Garden 168

THE FENG SHUI OFFICE 192

External Factors 196

The Working Office 208

Office Energies 236

Acknowledgements 252

Bibliography and Useful Addresses 253

Index 254

INTRODUCTION

Feng Shui is basically an environmental science and its origins are simple. It is based on an interpretation of the natural world which enabled the Chinese to create efficient agricultural systems, and also the study of the movement of heavenly bodies in order to determine the passage of time. Over the centuries, the interpretation grew more complex and became removed from its original purpose. As its exponents spread out from China across the world, their beliefs altered to fit into local beliefs and customs and, inevitably, folklore and superstition grew up around them. Fortunately, the ancient Chinese preserved the information in written form. In essence, all societies retain the knowledge contained in Feng Shui, but it has become absorbed into different disciplines. In China it underlies all aspects of life, from nutrition and medicine to exercise and the arts. By understanding the basic concepts, we can choose designs, meaningful images and symbols from our own culture to support us in our lives.

As practised today, Feng Shui gives us advice on how to create environments in which we feel comfortable and supported. Some of these environments are common sense. Others may not make sense until we understand that by recognizing problem areas in our lives and taking positive steps to improve them, we can connect to the energy of the spaces around us and bring about desired changes.

There is currently much discussion about which is the correct way to practise Feng Shui in the West. Should we stick strictly to what is now called Traditional Chinese Feng Shui or should we allow for other interpretations? Is Feng Shui Chinese, or have we in the West adopted a term which means something else for us? This book aims to set what we have come to understand as Feng

Shui in context and, by using modern examples alongside ancient ones, explore what the basic principles are.

Modern lifestyles leave us little time to stop and consider the effect our surroundings have on us. There is increasing awareness that some aspects of modern technology, the materials we use and the substances we release into the atmosphere can create lasting damage to our health and to the planet. Although this is not Feng Shui in its purest form, concern for our environment and an awareness of the damage we inflict on it must form part of Feng Shui for the present age. We have reached a stage where the human race has become capable of the most amazing feats on the one hand and the most amazing follies on the other. We have the capacity to cure hereditary diseases but also to let genetically-engineered organisms loose into the environment in the most dangerous form of warfare humankind has ever known. We send people into space to collect information never dreamed of half a century ago, yet at the same time we allow the planet we inhabit to become increasingly polluted and less able to sustain the life forms on which we depend for our survival.

These anomalies of modern living are becoming increasingly destructive and more and more people are turning to different approaches to living, in order to attempt to redress the balance. Feng Shui offers us the opportunity to achieve health, happiness and well-being through living in harmony with our environment.

The intention of this book is to interpret Feng Shui for modern times without straying from the underlying principles. While it cannot teach the interpretive skills and understanding which come with many years of study and practice, it is possible to give an insight into how we can interpret the principles to create nurturing and life-enhancing supportive spaces in our homes, gardens and offices. This knowledge will enable us to make an impact on the wider environment so that we can preserve it for future generations.

WHAT IS FENG SHUI?

The Chinese have a saying, "First, luck; second, destiny; third, Feng Shui; fourth, virtues; fifth, education": although Feng Shui can be a powerful force in shaping our lives, it is not a cure for all ills. Luck plays a major role, and personality, or karma, is almost as important. What we do with our lives and how we behave towards others will play a part, and education gives us the tools to make sense of the world. Feng Shui is just one part of the complete package.

▲ *In China the dragon symbolizes good fortune. Its presence is felt in landforms and watercourses.*

▲ *The Dragon Hills which protect Hong Kong are believed to be responsible for its prosperity.*

The single factor which sets Feng Shui apart from other philosophical systems is that it has the capacity for change built into it. Most systems evolved from similar principles; understanding the natural world played a major role and natural phenomena were believed to be imbued with a spirit or deity, recognition of which would give people some benefit in their lives. Where these systems became established as religions, the deities were worshipped, but Feng Shui has remained a philosophy and can be used in any culture and alongside any belief system.

► *Much of the symbolic imagery in Feng Shui is taken from landscapes such as this in Guilin, southern China.*

Feng Shui uses formulae which determine the rising and falling energy in a given time span of an individual or a house. Other formulae indicate a person's best location within a home or office, and can suggest the best placing of beds and desks. Many Chinese people consult astrologers annually to further refine this, so that every activity within the year can be pinpointed accurately and undertaken at an auspicious time. This can be as precise as the best time to conceive or even when to wash your hair.

The philosophy of Feng Shui is embraced by people who are aware of the impact their surroundings have on them and feel the need to take action to improve their lives, but using Feng Shui correctly is a skill and its principles cannot be adapted simply to suit the circumstances of a place or an individual.

▼ *Our surroundings affect us. Fresh air, natural products and a healthy environment enhance our mental and physical well-being.*

Feng Shui enables us to position ourselves within our environment to our best advantage. The positioning of our houses and offices as well as their internal design affects each of us positively or negatively. Feng Shui helps us to determine the most favourable positions for us and the layouts, colours and designs which will support us. In the garden we can determine the best locations for the different activities we intend to pursue there, but we also have to take account of the plants in the garden and their needs, which are equally important if the environment is to thrive.

▲ *Water energy plays a significant role in Feng Shui. Here a fountain brings life to an office courtyard.*

The following chapters provide information on those aspects of this complex and fascinating subject that can be utilized by everyone in their own space. When we introduce Feng Shui into our lives we can only benefit, even where we only touch the surface. As we become more aware of our surroundings, and actively begin to change those factors with which we feel uncomfortable, we begin to gain a deeper insight into ourselves and our part in the wider picture.

▼ *The T'ung Shui almanac, produced for centuries, details the best times to move house, conceive and even wash your hair.*

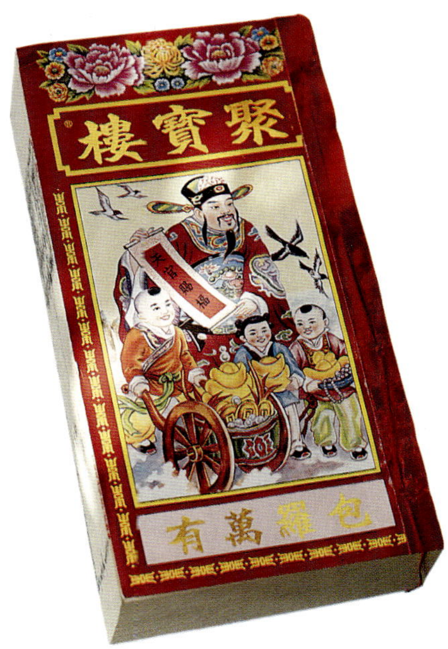

APPROACHES TO FENG SHUI

Feng Shui is about interpreting environments. Practitioners use a number of different approaches to connect with the energy or "feel" of a place, and fine-tune it to make it work for those living or working there. Provided the principles are understood, the different approaches will be effective. More often than not, practitioners use a mixture of methods to create the effects they want.

The Environmental Approach

In ancient times, people lived by their wits and knowledge of local conditions. Their needs were basic: food and shelter. Observation would tell them from which direction the prevailing winds were coming and they would build their homes in protective sites. They needed water in order to grow and transport their crops so rivers were important, and the direction of the flow and the orientation of the banks would determine the type of crops which could be grown. This branch of Feng Shui is known as the Form or Landform School and was the earliest approach to the subject.

▼ *The Form School regards this as the ideal spot on which to build. The Black Tortoise hill at the rear offers support while the White Tiger and Green Dragon give protection from the wind, with the all-powerful dragon slightly higher than the Tiger. The Red Phoenix marks the front boundary, and the river irrigates the site and enables crops to be transported for trade.*

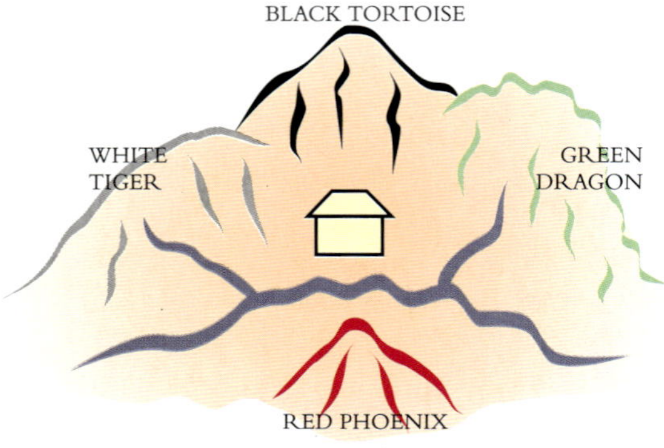

▲ *These "Karst" limestone hills in China symbolically protect an area of rich agricultural land.*

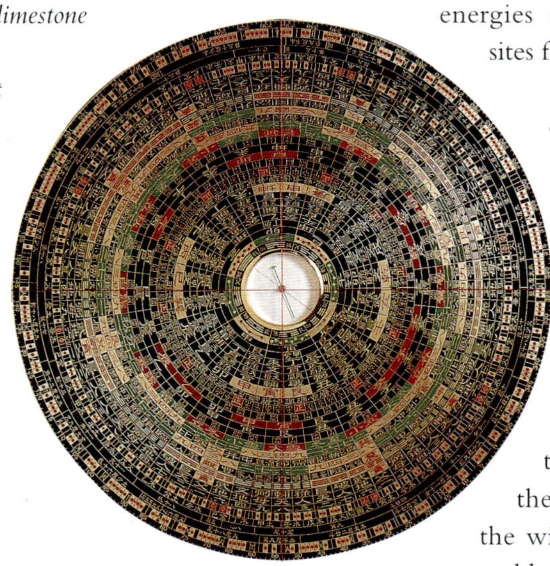

► *A luo pan or compass, used by geomancers in ancient China. Much of the information it records is regularly used by Feng Shui consultants.*

The Compass Approach

In ancient China, geomancers investigated earth formations and watercourses while astronomers charted the skies. Those who understood the power of the information they possessed recorded their knowledge on an instrument called a luo pan, or compass. The luo pan illustrates not only direction, but also investigates the energy of each direction, depending on the landform or heavenly body to be found there. Interpreting these energies suggests suitable sites for human beings. Feng Shui is based on the *I Ching*, a philosophical book which interprets the energies of the universe. Its 64 images from the yearly nature cycle form the outer ring of the luo pan. With the wisdom of ancient sages added to it over the centuries, the *I Ching* offers us a means to connect to the natural flow of the universe. Its built-in time factor allows individuals to connect to it in different ways at different times in their lives.

The Intuitive Approach

Ancient texts illustrate every shape of mountain and watercourse. The names illustrate concepts significant to the Chinese psyche. "Tiger in Waiting" suggests a negative place, where residents will never be able to relax, whereas "Baby Dragon Looking at its Mother" indicates a much more restful environment.

The ancient text of the *Water Dragon Classic* provides more information on the best places to build, showing flow direction and position within the tributaries, with the names again indicating the type of environment. The sensibilities of people living and working on the land were finely tuned and their knowledge of the natural world endowed them with an instinct for suitable sites to grow crops.

▶ *Mountain sites (1 & 2) and river sites (3 & 4); the dots represent buildings. All except for "Tiger in Waiting" are auspicious positions to build a new home.*

▼ *This prime site is protected by mountains, with healthy watercourses.*

Building Positions

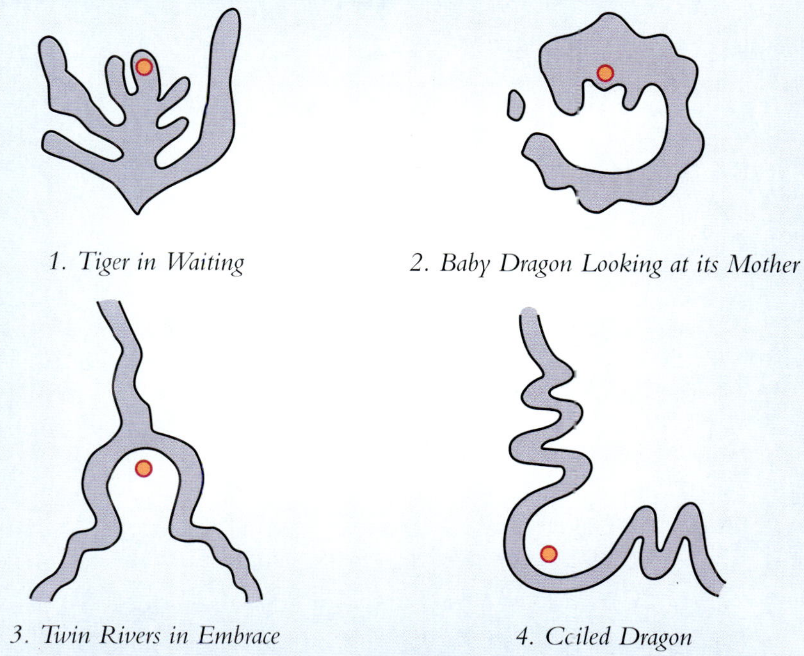

THE PRINCIPLES OF FENG SHUI

Ancient peoples regarded the heavens, the earth and themselves as part of one system. This holistic view of life persists in many cultures, where health and medicine, food and lifestyle, and the route to salvation are all interconnected in one ecological system.

The Way

The Tao, or the Way, the philosophy of which underlies Feng Shui, shows how to order our lives to live in harmony with ourselves, each other and the natural world. We can use Feng Shui to help us work towards achieving this.

Yin and Yang

Positive and negative forces act together in order to create energy – in electricity, for instance. Yin and yang represent these two forces which are in constant movement, each attempting to gain dominance. Where one achieves dominance, an imbalance occurs, so when one force becomes too strong its influence subsides and the other takes over. Still water, for example, is yin; a raging torrent is yang. Imagine a slow-moving yin river. When it hits rocks and descends, turbulence occurs, it speeds up and becomes yang. When it flows into a lake, it slows down and becomes yin once more. Yin and yang are opposing but interdependent concepts – without the idea of cold we would not be able to describe heat. At their extremes they

▲ *The T'ai Chi symbol illustrates the concept of yin and yang, the opposite yet interdependent forces that drive the world.*

◀ *Circle, Square, Triangle – signifying Heaven, Earth, human beings – the universal cosmological symbol.*

▼ *"The Dragon Breathing on the Lake" – the lake is a powerful Chinese image, symbolizing a light-reflective surface harbouring a dark and deep interior.*

Yin	**Yang**
Moon	Sun
Winter	Summer
Dark	Light
Feminine	Masculine
Interior	Exterior
Low	High
Stillness	Movement
Passive	Active
Odd numbers	Even numbers
Earth	Heaven
Cold	Heat
Soft	Hard
Valleys	Hills
Still water	Mountains
Gardens	Houses
Sleep	Wakefulness

change into each other; ice can burn and sunstroke sufferers shiver. The aim is to achieve a balance between them. There are examples throughout the book of how we can achieve this in our own environments. Some of the more common associations are listed left.

Chi

Chi is a concept unknown in Western philosophy but figures repeatedly in the philosophies of the East. It is the life force of all animate things, the quality of environments, the power of the sun, the moon and weather systems, and the driving force in human beings. In China, the movements in T'ai Chi encourage chi to move through the body. Acupuncture needles are used to unblock its flow when stuck. Chinese herbal medicine uses the special energetic qualities of herbs to correct chi when it becomes unbalanced. Meditation helps to establish a healthy mind: every brush stroke of the Chinese artist or sweep of the calligrapher's pen is the result of trained mental processes and the correct breathing techniques, which ensure that each carefully composed painting or document is infused with chi.

▲ *Chinese people practising T'ai Chi. The exercises are designed to aid the flow of chi in the body.*

▼ *An acupuncturist at work. The needles unblock the energy channels and enable chi to flow round the body.*

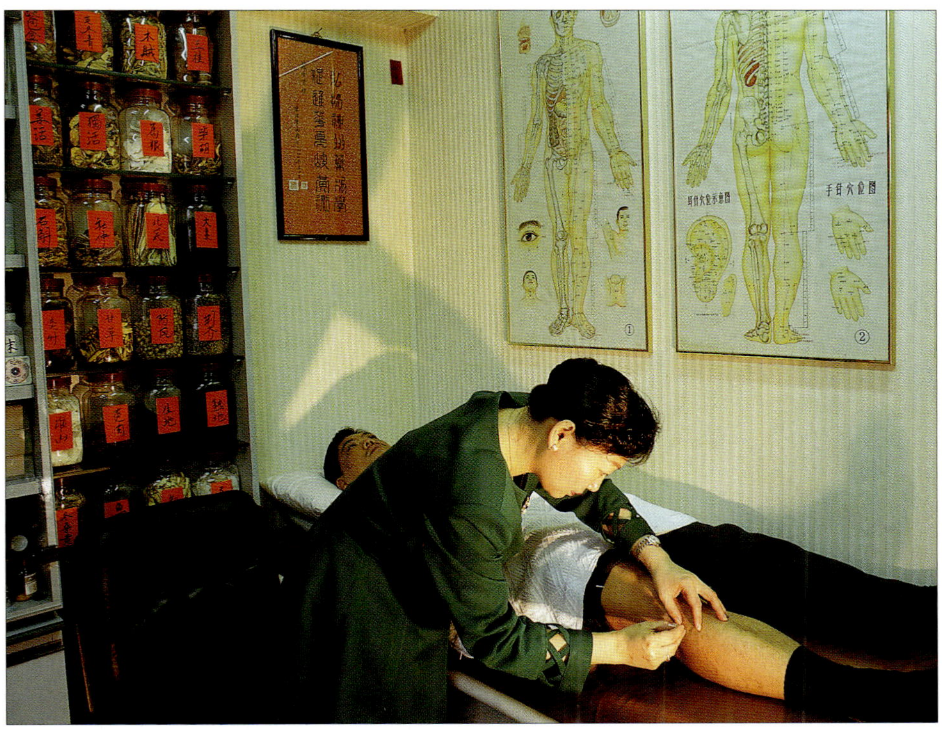

The purpose of Feng Shui is to create environments in which chi flows smoothly to achieve physical and mental health. Where chi flows gently through a house, the occupants will be positive and will have an easy passage through life. Where chi moves sluggishly or becomes stuck, then the chances are that problems will occur in the day-to-day life or long-term prospects of those living there.

Where chi flows smoothly in the garden, the plants will be healthy and the wildlife there will flourish. Animals, birds, insects and the myriad of unseen micro-organisms that live there will regulate themselves and create a balanced and supportive environment. Where chi cannot flow unimpeded and becomes sluggish or stuck, an area may become dank or there may be an imbalance which creates, say, a plague of aphids.

In an office where chi flows freely, employees will be happy and supportive, projects will be completed on time and stress levels will be low. Where the chi is stuck, there will be disharmony and the business will not flourish.

FIVE TYPES OF ENERGY

Some of the latest scientific theories enable us to make sense of the ancient formulae on which Feng Shui is based. It is accepted that everything in the universe vibrates. All our senses and everything we encounter are attuned to certain frequencies, which react with us in a positive or negative way. We are all familiar with sound waves, which bring us radio, and electromagnetic waves, which bring us television. Colours, shapes, food, weather conditions – everything in our lives affects us on a vibrational level for good or ill and, in turn, we react in various yet predictable ways, depending on our individual traits.

The concept of elements exists throughout the world. The Chinese recognize five which arise out of the interplay of yin and yang and represent different manifestations of chi. They represent a classification system for everything in the universe, including people, some of these are shown in the "Relationships of the Five Elements" table.

Ideally, there should be a balance of all the elements. Where one dominates or is lacking, then difficulties occur. Interpreting and balancing the elements plays a major part in the practice of Feng Shui. The elements move in a predetermined way, illustrated as a cycle in which they all support each other. A useful way of remembering this is by looking at the cycle in the following way. Water enables Wood to grow, Wood enables Fire to burn resulting in ashes or Earth, in which forms Metal, which in liquid form resembles Water. Another cycle indicates how the elements control each other and can be memorized as follows: Water extinguishes Fire, and in turn is soaked up by the Earth, which is depleted of energy by Wood in the form of trees, which can be destroyed by Metal tools. the "Relationships of the Five Elements" table introduces another aspect – how in supporting another element, an element can itself be weakened. The applications of the five elements are illustrated throughout this book.

▲ *Storms are nature's way of restoring a balance. They replenish negative ions in the atmosphere, which improves air quality.*

▼ *The heavenly bodies are essential to our lives and their movements lie at the heart of Feng Shui.*

The Relationships of the Five Elements

Element	Helped by	Harmed by	Weakened by	Weakens
Wood	Water	Metal	Fire	Earth
Fire	Wood	Water	Earth	Metal
Earth	Fire	Wood	Metal	Water
Metal	Earth	Fire	Water	Wood
Water	Metal	Earth	Wood	Fire

The Five Elements

Element	Characteristics	Personalities	Associations
WOOD 	Symbolizes spring, growth and plant life. In its yin form, it is supple and pliable, in its yang form as sturdy as an oak. Positively used, it is a walking stick; negatively used, a spear. Bamboo is cherished in China for its ability to sway in the wind yet be used as scaffolding. Viewed as a tree, Wood energy is expansive, nurturing and versatile.	Wood people are public-spirited and energetic. Ideas people, their outgoing personalities win them support. They visualize rather than committing themselves to plans. *Positively* – they are artistic and undertake tasks with enthusiasm. *Negatively* – they become impatient and angry and often fail to finish the tasks they have begun.	Trees and plants Wooden furniture Paper Green Columns Decking Landscape pictures
FIRE 	Symbolizes summer, fire and heat. It can bring light, warmth and happiness or it can erupt, explode and destroy with great violence. Positively, it stands for honour and fairness. Negatively, it stands for aggression and war.	Fire people are leaders and crave action. They inspire others to follow, often into trouble, as they dislike rules and fail to see consequences. *Positively* – they are innovative, humorous and passionate people. *Negatively* – they are impatient, exploit others and have little thought for their feelings.	Sun symbols Candles, lights and lamps Triangles Red Man-made materials Sun or fire pictures
EARTH 	Symbolizes the nurturing environment that enables seeds to grow, which all living things emanate from and return to. It nurtures, supports and interacts with each of the other elements. Positively, it denotes fairness, wisdom and instinct. Negatively, it can smother or represent the nervous anticipation of non-existent problems.	Earth people are supportive and loyal. Practical and persevering, they are a tower of strength in a crisis. They do not rush anything, but their support is enduring. Patient and steady, they possess inner strength. *Positively* – earth people are loyal, dependable and patient. *Negatively* – they are obsessional and prone to nit-picking.	Clay, brick and terracotta Cement and stone Squares Yellow, orange and brown
METAL 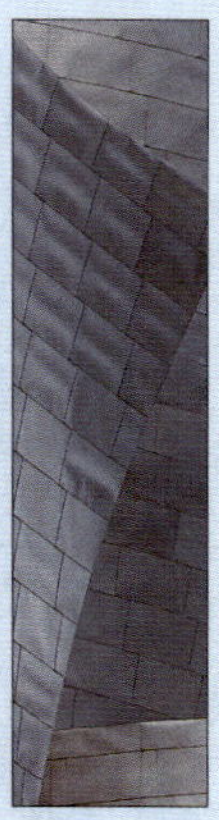	Symbolizes autumn and strength. Its nature represents solidity and the ability to contain objects. On the other hand, metal is also a conductor. Positively, it represents communication, brilliant ideas and justice. Negatively, it can suggest destruction, danger and sadness. Metal can be a beautiful and precious commodity, or the blade of a weapon.	Metal people are dogmatic and resolute. They pursue their ambitious aims single-mindedly. Good organizers, they are independent and happy in their own company. Faith in their own abilities inclines them towards inflexibility although they thrive on change. They are serious and do not accept help easily. *Positively* – they are strong, intuitive and interesting people. *Negatively* – they are inflexible, melancholic and serious.	All metals Round shapes Domes Metal objects Door furniture and doorsteps Kitchenware White, grey, silver and gold Coins Clocks
WATER 	Symbolizes winter and water itself, gentle rain or a storm. It suggests the inner self, art and beauty. It touches everything. Positively, it nurtures and supports with understanding. Negatively, it can wear down and exhaust. Associated with the emotions, it can suggest fear, nervousness and stress.	Water people communicate well. They are diplomatic and persuasive. Sensitive to the moods of others, they will lend an ear. They are intuitive and make excellent negotiators. Flexible and adaptable, they view things holistically. *Positively* – water people are artistic, sociable and sympathetic. *Negatively* – water people are sensitive, fickle and intrusive.	Rivers, streams and lakes Blue and black Mirrors and glass Meandering patterns Fountains and ponds Fish tanks Water pictures

CHINESE ASTROLOGY

An analysis of an environment using a luo pan compass looks at the energetic qualities of the various compass points. The Earthly Branches on the compass represent 12 of these points and also correspond to the 12 animals which relate to Chinese astrology. We often find ourselves in situations at home, or at work, when we canot understand how another person can view the same situation so differently from us, or can make us feel uncomfortable, or find different things irritating or amusing. Looking at the animals enables us to explore these differences by allowing us an insight into the make-up of our natures and personalities.

With this knowledge, we can come to know ourselves better and to accept the personalities of others. At home, it may encourage us to think twice, for instance, before launching into a tirade on tidiness or punctuality. It also has an important use in the workplace in keeping warring factions apart and ensuring a harmonious balance between productive output and socializing.

The Cycles

The Chinese calendar is based on the cycle of the moon, which determines that each month is approximately 29½ days long, beginning with a new moon. The years progress in cycles of 12 and it is helpful to appreciate the subtleties of Chinese symbology since each year is represented by an animal and the characteristics of each animal and its way of life are used to identify different types of people. Cultural differences are apt to get in the way if we attempt this identification ourselves; whereas Westerners would describe the Rat's character, for example, as sly and crafty, the Chinese respect its quick mind and native cunning.

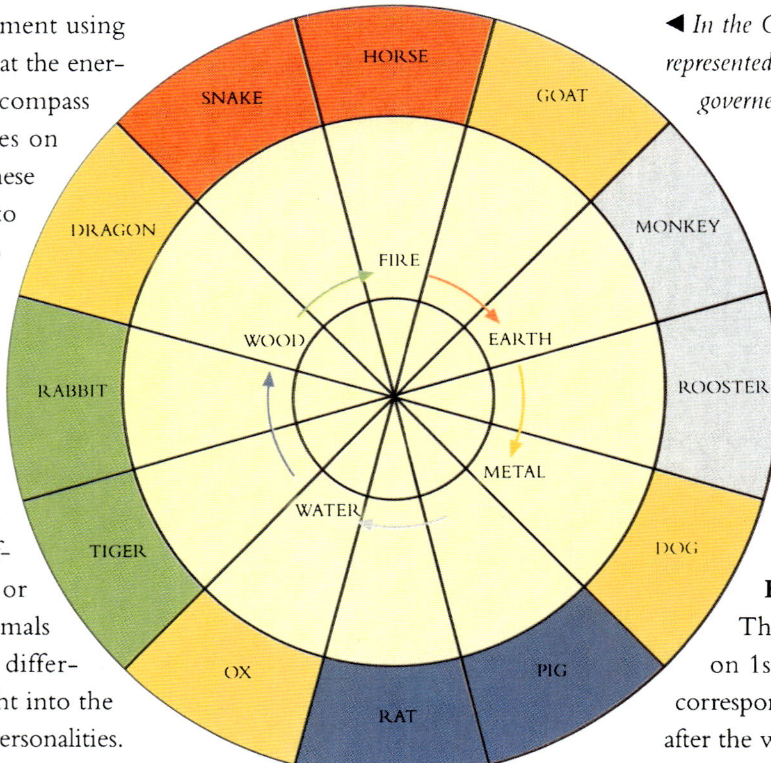

◀ *In the Chinese calendar each year is represented by an animal and each animal is governed by an element.*

Each animal is governed by an element which determines its intrinsic nature. The cycle of 12 is repeated five times to form a larger cycle of 60 years and in each of these cycles, the animals are ascribed an element with either a yin or yang characteristic, which determines their characters. Thus in 60 years, no two animals are the same. We begin by investigating the basic animal characteristics.

The Nature of the Animals

Rat	Water
Ox	Earth
Tiger	Wood
Rabbit	Wood
Dragon	Earth
Snake	Fire
Horse	Fire
Goat	Earth
Monkey	Metal
Rooster	Metal
Dog	Earth
Pig	Water

If we do not get on with someone, it may be that the animals associated with us in the Chinese calendar are not compatible. Alternatively, it may be that the elements that represent the time of our birth are not in harmony with the elements of the other person.

Finding your Animal

The Chinese year does not begin on 1st January but on a date which corresponds with the second new moon after the winter equinox, so it varies from year to year. Thus someone born on 25th January 1960 according to the Western calendar would actually be born in 1959 according to the Chinese calendar. The "Chinese Animals Table" opposite gives the exact dates when each year begins and ends, as well as its ruling animal and element. Their outer characteristics are identified by the element of the year they were born, as shown in "The Nature of the Animals" box (left). The ways in which the elements affect an animal's personality are described in "The Five Elements" table.

Animal Cycles

One of the 12 animals represents each lunar month, each with its own element governing its intrinsic nature. Over 60 years, the Five Elements cycle spins so that each animal can be Wood, Fire, Earth, Metal or Water, which determines its character.

In a full analysis by an experienced Feng Shui consultant, each of us will have a collection of eight elements that together make up not only our character, but also our destiny.

Chinese Animals Table

Year	Year Begins	Year Ends	Animal	Element
1920	20 February 1920	7 February 1921	Monkey	Metal +
1921	8 February 1921	27 January 1922	Rooster	Metal –
1922	28 January 1922	15 February 1923	Dog	Water +
1923	16 February 1923	4 February 1924	Pig	Water –
1924	5 February 1924	24 January 1925	Rat	Wood +
1925	25 January 1925	12 February 1926	Ox	Wood –
1926	13 February 1926	1 February 1927	Tiger	Fire +
1927	2 February 1927	22 January 1928	Rabbit	Fire –
1928	23 January 1928	9 February 1929	Dragon	Earth +
1929	10 February 1929	29 January 1930	Snake	Earth –
1930	30 January 1930	16 February 1931	Horse	Metal +
1931	17 February 1931	5 February 1932	Goat	Metal –
1932	6 February 1932	25 January 1933	Monkey	Water +
1933	26 January 1933	13 February 1934	Rooster	Water –
1934	14 February 1934	3 February 1935	Dog	Wood +
1935	4 February 1935	23 January 1936	Pig	Wood –
1936	24 January 1936	10 February 1937	Rat	Fire +
1937	11 February 1937	30 January 1938	Ox	Fire –
1938	31 January 1938	18 February 1939	Tiger	Earth +
1939	19 February 1939	7 February 1940	Rabbit	Earth –
1940	8 February 1940	26 January 1941	Dragon	Metal +
1941	27 January 1941	14 February 1942	Snake	Metal –
1942	15 February 1942	4 February 1943	Horse	Water +
1943	5 February 1943	24 January 1944	Goat	Water –
1944	25 January 1944	12 February 1945	Monkey	Wood +
1945	13 February 1945	1 February 1946	Rooster	Wood –
1946	2 February 1946	21 January 1947	Dog	Fire +
1947	22 January 1947	9 February 1948	Pig	Fire –
1948	10 February 1948	28 January 1949	Rat	Earth +
1949	29 January 1949	16 February 1950	Ox	Earth –
1950	17 February 1950	5 February 1951	Tiger	Metal +
1951	6 February 1951	26 January 1952	Rabbit	Metal –
1952	27 January 1952	13 February 1953	Dragon	Water +
1953	14 February 1953	2 February 1954	Snake	Water –
1954	3 February 1954	23 January 1955	Horse	Wood +
1955	24 January 1955	11 February 1956	Goat	Wood –
1956	12 February 1956	30 January 1957	Monkey	Fire +
1957	31 January 1957	17 February 1958	Rooster	Fire –
1958	18 February 1958	7 February 1959	Dog	Earth +
1959	8 February 1959	27 January 1960	Pig	Earth –
1960	28 January 1960	14 February 1961	Rat	Metal +
1961	15 February 1961	4 February 1962	Ox	Metal –
1962	5 February 1962	24 January 1963	Tiger	Water +
1963	25 January 1963	12 February 1964	Rabbit	Water –
1964	13 February 1964	1 February 1965	Dragon	Wood +
1965	2 February 1965	20 January 1966	Snake	Wood –
1966	21 January 1966	8 February 1967	Horse	Fire +
1967	9 February 1967	29 January 1968	Goat	Fire –
1968	30 January 1968	16 February 1969	Monkey	Earth +
1969	17 February 1969	5 February 1970	Rooster	Earth –
1970	6 February 1970	26 January 1971	Dog	Metal +
1971	27 January 1971	15 February 1972	Pig	Metal –
1972	16 February 1972	2 February 1973	Rat	Water +
1973	3 February 1973	22 January 1974	Ox	Water –
1974	23 January 1974	10 February 1975	Tiger	Wood +
1975	11 February 1975	30 January 1976	Rabbit	Wood –
1976	31 January 1976	17 February 1977	Dragon	Fire +
1977	18 February 1977	6 February 1978	Snake	Fire –
1978	7 February 1978	27 January 1979	Horse	Earth +
1979	28 January 1979	15 February 1980	Goat	Earth –
1980	16 February 1980	4 February 1981	Monkey	Metal +
1981	5 February 1981	24 January 1982	Rooster	Metal –
1982	25 January 1982	12 February 1983	Dog	Water +
1983	13 February 1983	1 February 1984	Pig	Water –
1984	2 February 1984	19 February 1985	Rat	Wood +
1985	20 February 1985	8 February 1986	Ox	Wood –
1986	9 February 1986	28 January 1987	Tiger	Fire +
1987	29 January 1987	16 February 1988	Rabbit	Fire –
1988	17 February 1988	5 February 1989	Dragon	Earth +
1989	6 February 1989	26 January 1990	Snake	Earth –
1990	27 January 1990	14 February 1991	Horse	Metal +
1991	15 February 1991	3 February 1992	Goat	Metal –
1992	4 February 1992	22 January 1993	Monkey	Water +
1993	23 January 1993	9 February 1994	Rooster	Water –
1994	10 February 1994	30 January 1995	Dog	Wood +
1995	31 January 1995	18 February 1996	Pig	Wood –
1996	19 February 1996	6 February 1997	Rat	Fire +
1997	7 February 1997	27 January 1998	Ox	Fire –
1998	28 January 1998	15 February 1999	Tiger	Earth +
1999	16 February 1999	4 February 2000	Rabbit	Earth –
2000	5 February 2000	23 January 2001	Dragon	Metal +
2001	24 January 2001	11 February 2002	Snake	Metal –
2002	12 February 2002	31 January 2003	Horse	Water +
2003	1 February 2003	21 January 2004	Goat	Water –
2004	22 January 2004	8 February 2005	Monkey	Wood +
2005	9 February 2005	28 January 2006	Rooster	Wood –
2006	29 January 2006	17 February 2007	Dog	Fire +
2007	18 February 2007	6 February 2008	Pig	Fire –
2008	7 February 2008	25 January 2009	Rat	Earth +
2009	26 January 2009	13 February 2010	Ox	Earth –
2010	14 February 2010	2 February 2011	Tiger	Metal +
2011	3 February 2011	22 January 2012	Rabbit	Metal –
2012	23 January 2012	9 February 2013	Dragon	Water +
2013	10 February 2013	30 January 2014	Snake	Water –

THE ANIMAL SIGNS

Using characteristics that are perceived to be an inherent part of the natures of the 12 animals, Chinese astrology attributes certain aspects of these to the characteristics and behaviour of people born at specific times. This system operates in much the same way as Western astrology.

The Rat

The Rat is an opportunist with an eye for a bargain. Rats tend to collect and hoard, but are unwilling to pay too much for anything. They are devoted to their families, particularly their children. On the surface, Rats are sociable and gregarious yet underneath they can be miserly and petty. Quick-witted and passionate, they are capable of deep emotions despite their cool exteriors. Their nervous energy and ambition may lead Rats to attempt more tasks than they are able to complete successfully. Rats will stand by their friends as long as they receive their support in return. However, they are not above using information given to them in confidence in order to advance their own cause.

鼠

▼ *Sociable and family-minded, rats are quick witted and opportunistic.*

▲ *Dynamic and generous, Tigers are warm-hearted unless they are crossed.*

▼ *Dependable and loyal, the Ox displays endless patience until pushed too far.*

The Ox

The Ox is solid and dependable. Oxen are excellent organizers and systematic in their approach to every task they undertake. They are not easily influenced by others' ideas. Loyalty is part of their make-up, but if crossed or deceived they will never forget. Oxen do not appear to be imaginative though they are capable of good ideas. Although not demonstrative or the most exciting people romantically, they are entirely dependable and make devoted parents. They are people of few words but fine understated gestures. Oxen are renowned for their patience, but it has its limits – once roused, their temper is a sight to behold.

牛

The Tiger

The Tiger is dynamic, impulsive and lives life to the full. Tigers often leap into projects without planning, but their natural exuberance will carry them through successfully unless boredom creeps in and they do not complete the task. Tigers do not like failure and need to be admired. If their spirits fall, they require a patient ear to listen until they bounce back again. They like excitement in their relationships and static situations leave them cold. Tigers are egotistic. They can be generous and warm, but will also sometimes show their claws.

虎

The Rabbit

兔

The Rabbit is a born diplomat and cannot bear conflict. Rabbits can be evasive and will often give the answer they think someone wishes to hear rather than enter into a discussion. This is not to say they give in easily: the docile cover hides a strong will and self-assurance. It is difficult to gauge what Rabbits are thinking and they can often appear to be constantly daydreaming, though in reality they may be planning their next strategy. The calmest of the animal signs, Rabbits are social creatures up to the point when their space is invaded. Good communication skills enable Rabbits to enjoy the company of others and they are good counsellors. They prefer to keep away from the limelight where possible and to enjoy the finer things of life.

▲ *Good counsellors and communicators, Rabbits also need their own space.*

▲ *Powerful leaders, Dragons prefer to follow their own path in life.*

The Dragon

龍

The Dragon will launch straight into projects or conversations with a pioneering spirit. Dragons often fail to notice others trying to keep up or indeed those plotting behind their backs. Authority figures, they make their own laws and cannot bear restriction. They prefer to get on with a job themselves and are good at motivating others into action. They are always available to help others, but their pride makes it difficult for them to accept help in return. Although they are always at the centre of things, they tend to be loners and are prone to stress when life becomes difficult. Hard-working and generous, Dragons are entirely trustworthy and are loyal friends. They enjoy excitement and new situations. When upset, they can be explosive, but all is soon forgotten.

The Snake

The Snake is a connoisseur of the good things in life. Inward-looking and self-reliant, Snakes tend to keep their own counsel and dislike relying on others. They can be ruthless in pursuing their goals. Although very kind and generous, Snakes can be demanding in relationships. They find it hard to forgive and will never forget a slight. Never underestimate the patience of a snake, who will wait in the wings until the time is right to strike. They are elegant and sophisticated and although they are good at making money, they never spend it on trifles. Only the best is good enough for them. Very intuitive, Snakes can sense the motives of others and can sum up situations accurately. If crossed, Snakes will bite back with deadly accuracy. They exude an air of mystery, ooze charm and can be deeply passionate.

▼ *Mysterious and passionate, Snakes have endless patience.*

▲ *Active and excitable, the Horse's nervous energy often runs away with them.*

The Horse

馬

The Horse is ever-active. Horses will work tirelessly until a project is completed, but only if the deadline is their own. Horses have lightning minds and can sum up people and situations in an instant, sometimes too quickly, and they will move on before seeing the whole picture. Capable of undertaking several tasks at once, Horses are constantly on the move and fond of exercise. They may exhaust themselves physically and mentally. Horses are ambitious and confident in their own abilities. They are not interested in the opinions of others and are adept at side-stepping issues. They can be impatient and have explosive tempers although they rarely bear grudges.

The Goat

羊

The Goat is emotional and compassionate. Peace-lovers, Goats always behave correctly and they are extremely accommodating to others. They tend to be shy and vulnerable to criticism. They worry a lot and appear to be easily put upon, but when they feel strongly about something they will dig their heels in and sulk until they achieve their objectives. Goats are generally popular and are usually well cared for by others. They appreciate the finer things in life and are usually lucky. They find it difficult to deal with difficulties and deprivation. Ardent romantics, Goats can obtain their own way by wearing their partners down and turning every occasion to their advantage. They will do anything to avoid conflict and hate making decisions.

▼ *Peace-loving Goats are kind and popular, they hate conflict and will try to avoid it.*

The Monkey

猴

The Monkey is intelligent and capable of using its wits to solve problems. Monkeys often wriggle out of difficult situations and are not above trickery if it will further their own ends. Monkeys tend to be oblivious of other people and of the effect their own actions may have on them. In spite of this, they are usually popular and are able to motivate others by their sheer enthusiasm for new projects. Monkeys are constantly on the look out for new challenges and their innovative approach and excellent memories generally make them successful. They are full of energy and are always active. They have little sympathy for those who are unable to keep up with them, but will soon forget any difficulties.

▼ *Energetic Monkeys use their intelligence to push their own ideas forward.*

▲ *The flamboyant Rooster can be easily won over by flattery and admiration.*

The Rooster

雞

The Rooster is a very sociable creature. Roosters shine in situations where they are able to be the centre of attention. If a Rooster is present, everyone will be aware of the fact because no Rooster can ever take a back seat at a social gathering. They are dignified, confident and extremely strong-willed, yet they may have a negative streak. They excel in arguments and debates. Incapable of underhandedness, Roosters lay all their cards on the table and do not spare others' feelings in their quest to do the right thing. They never weary of getting to the bottom of a problem and are perfectionists in all that they do. Roosters can usually be won over by flattery. Full of energy, Roosters are brave, but they hate criticism and can be puritanical in their approach to life.

The Dog

犬

The Dog is entirely dependable and has an inherent sense of justice. Intelligent, Dogs are loyal to their friends and they always listen to the problems of others, although they can be critical. In a crisis, Dogs will always help and they will never betray a friend. They can be hard workers, but are not all that interested in accumulating wealth for themselves. They like to spend time relaxing. Dogs take time to get to know people but have a tendency to pigeon-hole them. When they want something badly they can be persistent. If roused they can be obstinate and occasionally they lash out, although their temper is usually short-lived. Some Dogs can be rather nervous and they may be prone to pessimism.

▼ *Dogs are loyal and hard-working, but enjoy relaxing too.*

▲ *Peace-loving Pigs are sociable and popular and are able to organize others well.*

The Pig

豬

The Pig is everybody's friend. Honest and generous, Pigs are always available to bail others out of difficulties. Pigs love the social scene and are popular. They rarely argue and if they do fly off the handle, they bear no grudges afterwards. They abhor conflict and very often will not notice when others are attempting to upset them. They prefer to think well of people. Over-indulgence is their greatest weakness and Pigs will spend heavily in pursuit of pleasure. They always share with their friends and trust that, in return, their friends will make allowances for their own little weaknesses. Great organizers, Pigs like to have a cause and will often rally others to it as well.

COMPATIBILITY OF SIGNS

The saying, "You can choose your friends but not your family", is often heard from those who do not have harmonious family relationships, and we all find that we are drawn more to some people than to others. Chinese astrology uses the year, month, day and time of birth (each of which is represented by an animal and the yin or yang attributes of its accompanying element) to analyse characters and predict fortunes. Analyses of relationships depend upon the interaction of the elements on each person's chart. We can gain some insight into our own characters and those of our family and colleagues by using the "Chinese Animals Table" and then looking at the associated elements with their yang (+) (positive characteristics) or yin (–) (negative characteristics) in "The Five Elements" table.

▲ *We function well at work when we are compatible with our colleagues. The man on the right looks uncomfortable.*

▼ *We are drawn to people for a variety of reasons. Compatibility of animal signs and elements can certainly help.*

▼ *This table shows which of our family, friends and colleagues we relate to best according to Chinese astrology.*

Compatibility Table

	Rat	Ox	Tiger	Rabbit	Dragon	Snake	Horse	Goat	Monkey	Rooster	Dog	Pig
Rat	+	=	+	–	★	=	–	–	★	–	+	+
Ox	=	+	–	=	+	★	–	–	+	★	–	+
Tiger	+	–	+	–	+	–	★	+	–	=	★	=
Rabbit	+	+	–	+	=	+	–	★	–	–	=	★
Dragon	★	–	+	=	–	+	–	+	★	+	–	=
Snake	+	★	–	+	=	+	–	=	–	★	+	–
Horse	–	–	★	–	=	+	–	=	+	+	★	+
Goat	–	–	=	★	+	+	=	+	+	–	–	★
Monkey	★	+	–	–	★	–	–	+	=	+	+	=
Rooster	–	★	+	–	=	★	+	=	–	–	+	+
Dog	+	–	★	=	–	+	★	–	+	–	=	+
Pig	=	+	=	★	+	–	–	★	–	+	+	–

Key: ★ Excellent = Good + Workable – Difficult

THE ANIMAL YEARS

As we have seen, each year is ruled by an animal and its character is said to denote the energetic quality of the year.

The animal which rules each year and the date of the Chinese New Year for around a hundred-year period are shown on the "Chinese Animals Table". For ease of reference, 1999–2010 are shown below. Our fortunes in each year are indicated by whether or not we are compatible with the animal ruling that year, which can be checked by referring back to the "Compatibility Table".

1999	Rabbit	2005	Rooster
2000	Dragon	2006	Dog
2001	Snake	2007	Pig
2002	Horse	2008	Rat
2003	Goat	2009	Ox
2004	Monkey	2010	Tiger

Year of the Rabbit
A respite from the past year and a breather before the next, rest is indicated here. This is a time for negotiations and settlements, but not for new ventures. Women's and family concerns are considered important.

Year of the Dragon
The time for new business ventures and projects. Euphoric and unpredictable, this is the year for outlandish schemes and taking risks. Dragon babies are considered lucky.

Year of the Snake
Peace returns and allows time to reflect. Care should be taken in business matters as treachery and underhand dealings are indicated. Money is made and communication is good. A fertile year, in which morality becomes an issue.

Year of the Horse
An energetic and volatile year in which money will be spent and borrowed. Some impulsive behaviour will bring rewards, while some will fail. A year for marriage and divorce.

Year of the Goat
A quiet year in which family matters are to the fore. A year for consolidating and for diplomatic negotiations, rather than launching new projects.

Year of the Monkey
An unpredictable year when nothing goes according to plan. Only the quick-witted will prosper. New ideas abound and communication will flourish.

Year of the Rooster
A year for making feelings known and letting grievances out. This may cause disharmony in families so tact is required.

Year of the Dog
Worthy causes abound – human and animal rights and environmental issues are in the public eye. Security should be checked, by governments and at home. A year for marriage and the family.

▼ *Family relationships are usually harmonious if the animal signs are compatible and the elements do not clash.*

Year of the Pig
The last year of the cycle and unfinished business should be concluded. Optimism abounds and the pursuit of leisure is indicated. Family concerns will go well.

Year of the Rat
This is a lucky year, a good time to start a new venture. The rewards will not come without hard work, but with careful planning they will arrive.

Year of the Ox
Harvest is the symbol for this year so we will reap what we have sown. Decisions should be made now and contracts signed. This is a conservative year so grand or outrageous schemes are not considered appropriate.

Year of the Tiger
Sudden conflicts and crises arise in this year and will have an impact for some time. The year for grand schemes for the courageous, but underhand activities may suffer from repercussions.

THE BAGUA AND THE MAGIC SQUARE

The compass directions and their associations are fundamental to the practice of Feng Shui. Astronomical and geomantic calculations and the place of human beings within them are plotted on a luo pan, an instrument so powerful that, it has been likened to a computer. The luo pan can indicate, to those who know how to interpret it, which illness someone in a certain location might be suffering from, or the fortunes of a person living in a certain room in a house.

This vast amount of information has been reduced to a shorthand form incorporated in a "Magic Square". In cultures worldwide, this was used as a talisman. Many formulae based on the magic square are used to discover whether a place is auspicious, in itself and for the people living there, and the simplest of these are introduced in this book. The diagram on the right shows how the energies represented by the Magic Square always move in a fixed pattern. These patterns are repeated over time and can indicate the fortunes of a person or building in a certain year.

THE BAGUA

The information contained in the luo pan is condensed into the Magic Square, which forms the basis of the Bagua, or Pa Kua, a tool we can use to investigate our homes and offices. The Bagua below holds some of the images which describe the energies of the eight directions and the central position. The Bagua represents the journey of life, the Tao, and we can use it to create comfortable living, working and leisure spaces.

When applying Feng Shui principles to your house, garden or office you will need a tracing of the Bagua with the colours, compass points and directions all added on.

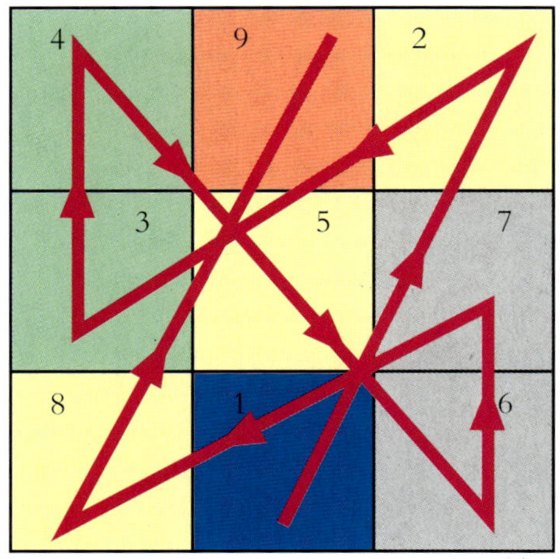

▲ *The Magic Square: the "magic" lies in the fact that every line adds up to 15. Magic squares exist all over the world. In ancient cultures, such symbols were a source of power to their initiates. In Hebrew culture, the pattern formed by the movement of energies is known as the seal of Saturn and is used in Western magic. In Islamic cultures, intricate patterns are based on complex magic squares.*

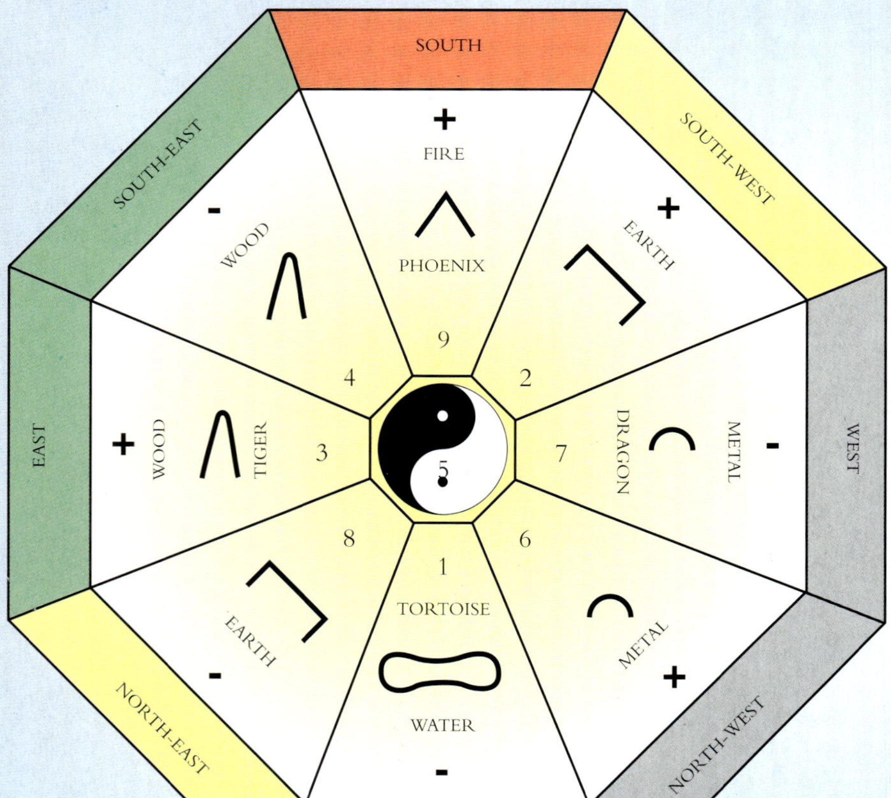

THE BAGUA, OR PA KUA

This diagram shows the energies associated with each of the eight directions. The outer bar shows the colours and directions associated with the five elements. The symbols indicate the yin (-) or yang (+) quality of the element associated with each direction. Also shown are the shapes associated with each element. The four symbolic animals which represent the energy of each of the four cardinal directions – north, south, east, west – are indicated, and the numbers of the Magic Square are shown in their associated directions. We take on the characteristics of a number and the energies associated with it, which are thought to shape who we are, where we feel comfortable, and our fortunes. The Chinese compass is always drawn facing south since this is the favoured direction for houses to face in parts of China. This does not affect the actual magnetic north-south directions.

FINDING YOUR MAGIC NUMBER

To complete the picture, it is necessary to discover how human beings fit into the scheme. Each person is allocated a "magic" number that enables them to position themselves to their best advantage. Before finding our number from the tables opposite, we must check the date of the Chinese New Year from the "Chinese Animals Table". The previous year is used if our birthday falls before the start of the new year.

▼ *Each of the magic numbers represents a particular type of energy suggested by the annual nature cycle. Find your number on the table and discover your energy below.*

Energy of Numbers

1: Water. Winter. Independent. Intuitive
2: Earth. Late Summer. Methodical.
3: Thunder. Spring. Progressive
4: Wind. Late Spring. Adaptable.
5: Earth. Central Force. Assertive.
6: Heaven. Late Autumn. Unyielding.
7: Lake. Autumn. Flexible. Nervous.
8: Mountain. Late Winter. Obstinate. Energetic.
9. Fire. Summer. Impulsive. Intelligent.

Using the Magic Numbers

Some Feng Shui consultants use only the male, or yang, numbers in their calculations, some use both male and female, or yin, numbers. Others regard the yin (female) numbers as depicting the inner self, while the yang (male) numbers represent the image a person presents to the world. Traditional male and female stereotypes are no longer the norm. Modern men and women, with more interchangeable roles, tend to have both yin and yang characteristics.

East-west Directions

People tend to fare better in some directions than in others. They fall into two groups, the east group or the west group. Those who fall into the east group should live in a house facing an east group direction, those in the west group a west group direction. If this is not possible, your bed and/or your chair should face an appropriate direction.

▼ *Once you have found your magic number, you can identify which group you are in, east or west, which directions suit you. and whether your house is compatible.*

Group	Numbers	Directions
East	1, 3, 4, 9	N, E, SE, S
West	2, 5, 6, 7, 8	SW, NW, W, NE, CENTRE

The Magic Numbers

YEAR	M	F	YEAR	M	F	YEAR	M	F	YEAR	M	F
1920	8	7	1952	3	3	1984	7	8	2002	7	8
1921	7	8	1953	2	4	1985	6	9	2003	6	9
1922	6	9	1954	1	5	1986	5	1	2004	5	1
1923	5	1	1955	9	6	1987	4	2	2005	4	2
1924	4	2	1956	8	7	1988	3	3	2006	3	3
1925	3	3	1957	7	8	1989	2	4	2007	2	4
1926	2	4	1958	6	9	1990	1	5	2008	1	5
1927	1	5	1959	5	1	1991	9	6	2009	9	6
1928	9	6	1960	4	2	1992	8	7	2010	8	7
1929	8	7	1961	3	3	1993	7	8	2011	7	8
1930	7	8	1962	2	4	1994	6	9	2012	6	9
1931	6	9	1963	1	5	1995	5	1	2013	5	1
1932	5	1	1964	9	6	1996	4	2	2014	4	2
1933	4	2	1965	8	7	1997	3	3	2015	3	3
1934	3	3	1966	7	8	1998	2	4	2016	2	4
1935	2	4	1967	6	9	1999	1	5	2017	1	5
1936	1	5	1968	5	1	2000	9	6	2018	9	6
1937	9	6	1969	4	2	2001	8	7	2019	8	7
1938	8	7	1970	3	3						
1939	7	8	1971	2	4						
1940	6	9	1972	1	5						
1941	5	1	1973	9	6						
1942	4	2	1974	8	7						
1943	3	3	1975	7	8						
1944	2	4	1976	6	9						
1945	1	5	1977	5	1						
1946	9	6	1978	4	2						
1947	8	7	1979	3	3						
1948	7	8	1980	2	4						
1949	6	9	1981	1	5						
1950	5	1	1982	9	6						
1951	4	2	1983	8	7						

Key: M = male F = female

▼ *A Chinese Feng Shui expert studies the luo pan (compass).*

PERCEPTION AND THE SYMBOLIC BAGUA

Much of the skill in undertaking a Feng Shui survey of our immediate environment is in reading the signals there. If we are healthy and happy, this may prove to be a comparatively easy process. If we are not, our perception may be coloured by our emotional or physical state and we may not be able to see things clearly.

The Chinese phrase "First, luck; second, destiny; third, Feng Shui; fourth, virtues; fifth, education" is worth repeating, as it shows that to some extent our fortunes and personalities are out of our hands. If we embrace Feng Shui, think and act positively, and make use of the knowledge the universe has to offer, then we can begin to take charge of the parts of our lives that we can control and make the best of them.

Part of the process of Feng Shui is to awaken our senses and sensibilities to our environment. Among other things, each of the Five Elements governs different senses, and our aim is to create a balanced environment in which all our senses are satisfied and none is allowed to predominate over the rest to create an imbalance.

We can heighten our perception of the world if we introduce ourselves to different experiences. Take an objective look at your weekly routine and decide on a new experience or activity which will add something different to your life.

A Magical Template

When Feng Shui began to take off in the West several years ago, the workings of the compass were known only to a handful of scholars. Those early days were distinguished by the creation of, and endless discussions on, the workings of the Bagua. It was used then, as it is now, by the Tibetan Black Hat practitioners, as a magical template that is aligned with a front door, the entrance to a room, the front of a desk or even a face.

This template is then used to supply information which can enable us to understand our energy and make corrections to create balance and harmony. Some Chinese practitioners have since

A Healthy Lifestyle and a Healthy Mind

Stuck energy in our homes is often a reflection of our lifestyle and state of mind. A healthy daily regime will make us receptive to the powers of Feng Shui.

Ideally, we should take time out each day to meditate – or just to escape from stress. Often a short walk, gardening or a few minutes sitting quietly will help us to relax. Holidays and new experiences can help our mental energy.

Chi Kung and T'ai Chi are part of the same system. Their exercise programmes help to keep the energy channels in the body unblocked, while also releasing the mind.

Eating a healthy balanced diet of food-stuffs, produced without chemical interference, is another way of ensuring that harmful energies, or toxins, do not upset our bodily balance.

If we do become ill, acupuncture and acupressure and Chinese herbal medicine can balance the energies in our bodies and help to keep us fit.

◀ *Meditation (left), hiking in the mountains (bottom left) or a daily session of T'ai Chi (bottom right) will all benefit our mental energy and help to heighten our perceptions.*

▲ *Mountains afford protection to the rear and sides of this village, while a lake in front accumulates chi – all that remains is to arrange the inside of the house to create a supportive environment.*

sought to use the Bagua alongside the compass method. They place it over the plan of a home so that it is positioned with the Career area in the north, irrespective of where the front door lies.

Other traditional Chinese approaches concentrate on interpreting the energies indicated by the Five Elements and by the rings of the luo pan. Such is the "magic" of Feng Shui that, in the right hands, all approaches appear to work.

Newcomers to Feng Shui may find it difficult to connect to a compass. Hopefully, they will use either method to experience for themselves the magic of the early days of discovery, and will be drawn deeper into this amazing philosophy, gaining an insight into its power.

▼ *The Three Gates Bagua. This may be entered through "Career" (back), "Knowledge" (bottom left) or "Helpful People" (bottom right). The compass Bagua with associated colours is shown inside to help you balance the elements of your home.*

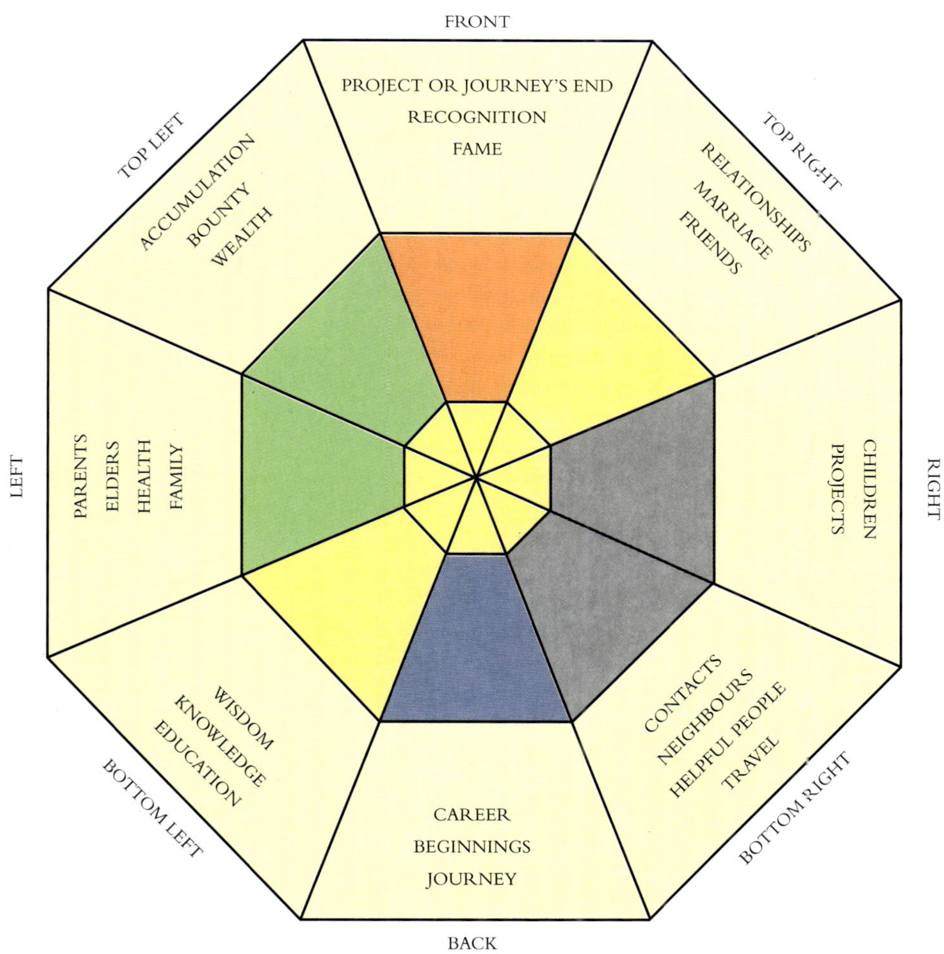

The Symbolic Bagua

Throughout this book we will see how various images are connected to each of the eight points of the Magic Square or the Bagua, which is based on it. The symbolic Bagua uses the energies of each direction to relate to the journey of life. The journey begins at the entrance to our home – the mouth of chi – and moves in a predetermined way through the home until it reaches its conclusion. By focusing on an aspect of our lives which we want to stimulate or change, we can use the energies of the universe and make them work for us. Psychologically, focusing on an area enables us to create the circumstances to bring about change.

So far, a traditional compass approach has been used, but the diagram to the left allows us to use either approach. From now on readers should feel free to connect with the Bagua as they wish, and through it to the intangible forces which make this such a fascinating subject. Most people who have used Feng Shui have experienced changes in their circumstances. These often correspond to the actual energy around a relationship or situation rather than our desires. The results will ultimately serve our best interests, but the outcome is often unexpected.

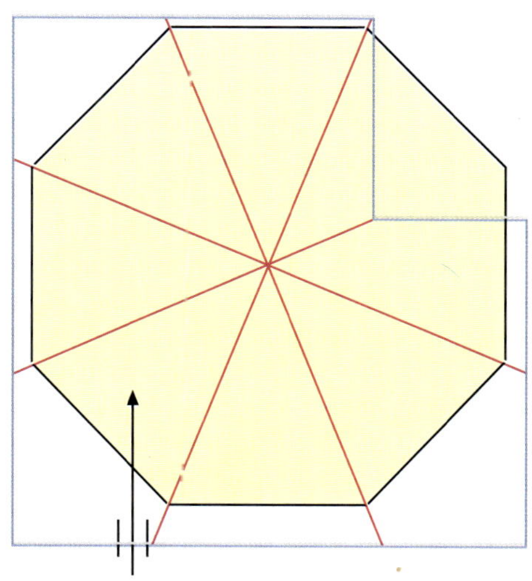

▲ *The Three Gates Bagua is flexible. If a home has an irregular shape, the corresponding area of the Bagua is also considered to be missing. In this house, the front entrance is in the "Knowledge" area and the "Relationships" part of the house is missing.*

FENG SHUI IN THE MODERN WORLD

▲ *Night-time in Mexico City. The 23 million inhabitants are denied a view of the stars because of neon lighting and pollution.*

▶ *The rice harvest in traditional regions of China has used many of the same processes for the past thousand years.*

Modern lifestyles are far removed from those of our ancestors. For them, charting the progress of the moon and sun, and interpreting the different weather conditions and other activities occurring in the natural world in relation to the movement of the stars and planets, was essential. These peoples depended on the land to provide them with the means to survive. The modern city-dweller may never see food growing naturally and may not even be able to view the night sky because of pollution and neon lighting. However, we still depend on the natural world for our well-being. We can be at the mercy of hurricanes, or bask on sun-drenched beaches; mountains may erupt, or provide sustenance for livestock; human beings can pollute the air and contaminate the land, or create sanctuaries for wildlife species.

▼ *There are still thriving cultures in which ancient skills and lifestyles remain such as this village in Chad.*

Ancient peoples, through necessity, regarded the heavens, the earth and themselves as part of one system. This holistic view of life has persisted in many cultures, where health and medicine, food and lifestyle are all interconnected. In the West, scientific development created different disciplines which advanced in isolation from each other. Through recent movements in health and food production, we are seeking to correct the imbalances caused by this approach. The Tao, or the Way, the philosophy which underlies Feng Shui, shows how it is possible to order our lives to exist in harmony with each other and the natural world. We can use Feng Shui to help us work towards achieving this.

The traditional concept of Gaia, the Greek earth goddess, was used by James Lovelock and Lynne Margulis in the 1970s to encourage us to perceive the world as a biosphere in which each constituent part has a role to play. In order to understand Feng Shui we need to expand this concept of ecosystems further to include human beings and the impact of the cosmos, and to expand our awareness so that we can predict the consequences of our actions.

▲ *In 1948 science writer Fred Hoyle predicted: "Once a photograph of the Earth taken from the outside world is available … a new idea as powerful as any other in history will be let loose." The environmental awareness movement began at the time human beings landed on the moon.*

Working with the Natural World

A good example of working with the natural world is provided by an apparently admirable scheme to plant 300 oak forests in Britain to celebrate the millennium. But in the natural world oak trees grow singly and not in rows in large groups, and recent research has indicated that where many oaks grow together there is a higher incidence of Lyme disease, a debilitating illness which attacks the nervous system. The reason for this is that mice and deer feed on acorns and also carry the ticks which transmit the disease. Thus, where there are many oaks, there is also a high incidence of Lyme disease. Mixed planting, which mirrors the natural world, would be preferable.

In order to save money, one forest was planted with Polish oak trees that came into bud two weeks later than the native trees. This meant there were no caterpillars feeding on the buds to provide food for newly-hatched fledglings. These mistakes might have been avoided if Taoistic principles had been applied to the scheme.

▼ *Native trees act as the Tortoise, Dragon, Tiger formation to protect these buildings.*

As we investigate the ideas behind Feng Shui and consider practical ways of introducing them into our lives, we also need to shift our perception. Feng Shui in the modern world incorporates intuition. Maori warriors navigate hundreds of miles by the feel of a place and by observing signs. The Inuit language incorporates many words to describe the complexities of different types of snow. Similarly, we can heighten our awareness of our environment by adopting the principles of Feng Shui.

Until recently navigators used the stars to steer by, and in some parts of the world those who work with the land still use the stars to determine planting times for their crops. These people recognize patterns in the interrelationship between different parts of the natural world, noticing which plants are in flower or when birds return from migration and comparing them to the weather. Many customs are firmly based in natural wisdom.

犬

雞

鼠

龍

猴

FENG SHUI IN THE HOME

WHEREVER WE LIVE, IN THE TOWN OR THE COUNTRY, WE CAN ARRANGE OUR IMMEDIATE ENVIRONMENT SO THAT WE RECEIVE MAXIMUM SUPPORT. SOME HOUSES INSTINCTIVELY "FEEL" RIGHT AND A LUO PAN READING WILL USUALLY CONFIRM THIS. OTHER HOMES MAY NOT, AND SOMETIMES EXTERNAL INFLUENCES CAN ADVERSELY AFFECT BENEFICIAL ENERGY. THIS SECTION OF THE BOOK OFFERS SOLUTIONS TO HELP US TO BE NOURISHED BY OUR HOMES.

豬

THE OUTSIDE WORLD

We need to feel comfortable inside our homes but sometimes the external environment impinges upon us. Perhaps the view from the windows is unattractive or the traffic is noisy. We are aware of such things but there may also be other influences that affect us psychologically over a period of time. Our physical health can also be harmed by more subtle forces that we cannot see. Feng Shui can identify these influences and forces for us, and can help us to take precautionary measures. When we move house, we can use the information we have gained to show us what to look for.

CHOOSING A LOCATION

Whether we own our own home or apartment or live in rented accommodation, we can use the principles which follow to create a living space in which we feel comfortable. If we are on the verge of moving, or are in the fortunate position of having acquired a piece of land to design and build our own home upon, there are some important considerations to make. You will probably already have a location in mind, but within the area there will be choices you can make which will affect your well-being in your new home.

When choosing a property we normally investigate the immediate environment. We use certain criteria to judge it according to our individual requirements – the appearance of neighbouring properties, proximity to schools, efficient transport for travel to work, green spaces, sports facilities and so on.

Some moves are dictated by new jobs in different areas, some when people give up their hectic urban lifestyles and relocate to rural areas. Many older people retire to the coast. Young people leaving home for the first time might be attracted by the hurly-burly of city living. The decline of heavy industry in many countries has seen a rise in the regeneration of dockland and riverside areas with large warehouses being developed as spacious apartments for these new city dwellers. Whatever the reason for the move, few people remain where they were born, or retain the extended support networks which prevailed only a generation or two ago. Our choice of home as a nurturing space is therefore important. With a little foresight and a knowledge of Feng Shui principles, we can select prime positions for our homes.

▲ *The modern city of Durban in South Africa is full of young energy.*

► *A seaside location is very attractive in summer but can be inhospitable in winter.*

▼ *Living on a remote farm will suit some people perfectly, but not others.*

Think Before You Move

There are certain things to consider when selecting an area to which to move before we even consider choosing a house. Ideally we should know the area well. An idyllic bay in summer may be cold and windswept in winter, and a woodland glade at the end of an unmade track may be inaccessible after heavy winter snows.

Neighbours can prove to be a problem. They may resent a new house which spoils a view, or may erect screens that maintain their privacy but deprive you of

Assessing a Location

Natural phenomena	Immediate environment	Positive aspects	Negative aspects
Wind direction	Proposed road developments	Local amenities	Factories
Sun direction	Proposed building developments	Trees	Petrol stations
Rainfall	Land use plans	Street lighting	All-night cafés
Flood areas	Previous land use	Good street maintenance	Pubs and discos
Geological faults	Tree preservation orders	Good schools	Police stations
Soil type	Local architecture	Community spirit	Fire stations
Height above sea level	Neighbours, predecessors	Local shops	Airports
		Clubs and classes	Cemeteries and crematoriums
		Playgroups and nurseries	Motorways and highways
			Electricity sub-stations and pylons

◀ *This sheltered village is a delightful location to return home to after a day in the bustling city.*

▶ *High-rise flats in Hong Kong – financially the sky is the limit and young people are attracted there, but few of them stay to put down roots.*

light. It is important to determine the ownership of boundaries. Previous owners are another consideration. Earlier occupants may have tipped chemicals just where you want to grow strawberries, or you may learn that all the previous owners got divorced or mysteriously contracted a similar illness. Feng Shui may be able to offer an explanation. The box above indicates some things to check before moving to a new area.

The modern world has problems that did not exist in the ancient world and these must be taken into consideration when we apply Feng Shui today. It is no use selecting a site with the classic Tortoise, Dragon, Tiger formation if the Tortoise is an electricity pylon, which may be linked to childhood leukemia, the Dragon is a chemical factory leaking its waste into the river, and the Tiger is a poorly managed petrol station. In modern times we have to apply the formulae to contemporary life and the ancient sages were wise enough to allow us the leeway to do this by building in formulae for change.

Our environment makes a psychological impact on us: whatever we see, hear or smell will make an impression. We also have to look at ourselves and what type of people we are in order to understand our needs in terms of living spaces. There is no point moving to a remote country area if you enjoy street life and love shopping because you will never feel comfortable. A Rabbit who retires to the seaside will, at best, be tired and drained and, at worst, become ill. With a new insight into our own natures and increased awareness of the effect our environment has on us, we can use Feng Shui principles to find harmonious spaces for ourselves and our families.

When you are ready to sell your home and move on, Feng Shui can help to speed up this often lengthy and stressful process. The tip below combines the energy of the Five Elements to give a powerful boost to the sale.

▼ *Pavement cafés are part of metropolitan life in many cities around the world.*

Feng Shui Tip for Speeding up a House Sale

Take a red envelope and place in it:

- A piece of metal from the kitchen
- Some earth from the garden
- Some wood from a skirting board

Throw the envelope into a fast-moving river.

UNSEEN ENERGIES

Before finally deciding on a location, it is wise to check if there are any underground water sources, geological faults or other earth disturbances. These all create unseen energies which could affect your well-being.

Geopathic Stress

The word "geopathic" comes from the Greek *geo*, meaning "Earth", and *pathos*, meaning "disease". It covers naturally occurring phenomena that cause problems for us and our homes. The Earth and living organisms vibrate at complementary frequencies, which are negatively affected by geopathic faults. Dowsers are able to detect these problems, which a property surveyor may miss.

Underground Streams

Just as water erodes rocks on the coast, underground streams have had the same effect beneath the Earth's surface. This process alters the electromagnetic frequency of the Earth so that it is out of our frequency range. Fast-moving and polluted underground water produces the same effect.

Underground streams produce energy spirals, the effects of which are felt inside any buildings directly overhead. Where a clockwise spiral meets an anti-clockwise spiral, ill health may be experienced by people situated above them. Where spirals meet other forces, such as leys, the problems are accentuated.

▲ *If trees lean for no reason, they may be situated on a geopathic stress line.*

Leys

Leys, or ley lines, are a network of surface energy lines running across the countryside. Our distant ancestors may have built their churches and standing stones on these lines, performing an "acupuncture of the Earth" as they tapped into its energy. It is believed the leys also provided routes for travellers.

▲ *Underground water creates magical places, but it is not desirable near a house as it can undermine the foundations.*

◀ *Stone circles are extremely powerful places. They harness the Earth's energies and respond to those of the Cosmos.*

▲ *The Chinese believe that quarrying damages the Dragon – the spirit of a place.*

▲ *Nearby railway lines can cause land disturbance and create instability.*

RADON

We are exposed to radiation throughout our lives, mainly from the sun. Exposure over long periods to higher than normal levels may make us ill. Leukemia and birth defects have been linked to exposure to radon, which occurs naturally in uranium in the Earth. As the uranium breaks down, it forms radioactive ions which attach themselves to air particles that become trapped inside houses. Some regions in the world have recorded levels of radioactivity in excess of those recorded after the Chernobyl disaster. Pockets of high incidence have been found in Sweden and the United States as well as in Derbyshire and Cornwall in Great Britain. Local authorities are aware of the problem and assistance is available to eradicate it from buildings.

EARTH GRIDS

Two German doctors, Hartmann and Curry, have advanced the theory that the earth is covered by a series of force lines which are activated by the interaction of the Earth's magnetic field and the gravitational pull of the sun and moon. It is thought that these lines shift as a result of their interaction with the movement of charged particles trapped in the atmosphere as the sun blasts the Earth with radiation. The point where these lines cross may adversely affect the human body.

HUMAN ACTIVITY

Human beings can also disturb the Earth's energies. Quarries, tunnels, mines, polluted water and railways have all been found to contribute negative effects. Before erecting or buying a house, check for any mining or tunnelling that may have taken place in the area.

STRESS INDICATORS

Leaning trees
Cankers on tree trunks
Elder trees
Illness shortly after moving
Uneasy atmosphere
Tunnelling activity
Cold, damp rooms

CLEARING THE ENERGIES

If there is no apparent reason for feeling unwell for a long period of time, then geopathic stress is a possible cause. Experienced dowsers are able to detect Earth energies and, in some instances, divert negative energies, albeit often only on a temporary basis. Many people can detect water with rods or pendulums, but experience is needed to deal with Earth energies and protection is needed to minimize ill effects. It is best, if possible, to move away from such energies, and it may be a question of simply moving a bed 60 cm–1 m (2–3 ft). The effect of clearing energies can be dramatic and can even cause shock. When dealing with heart patients, for example, the work should be done slowly.

▲ *Dowsing rods are part of a Feng Shui consultant's tools. Metal coat hangers also work for dowsing.*

▲ *Dowsing rods cross when they detect underground water. They are used to locate landmines and to find pipes.*

THE URBAN ENVIRONMENT

▲ *An enticing night scene in Villefranche, Cote d'Azur, France. Summer in the city can be envigorating and exciting.*

Urban environments are very diverse. Living in an apartment above a shop in a city centre throbbing with nightlife is quite different to the tranquillity of a house in a leafy suburb or the vast buildings in a redeveloped docklands area.

City and Town Centres

The centres of large cities, where clubs and restaurants are open through the night, are full of yang energy and lifestyles will reflect this. City centres attract younger people with no roots, who can move about freely. Homes tend to be apartments and inside we should aim for some yin energy – muted colours, natural flooring and a large plant or two to create a quiet haven. Smaller town centres, particularly where there are shopping precincts, tend to close down at night and the atmosphere is yin and rather spooky. If you live here, make sure you have plenty of lights on the perimeter of your property and bright colours inside to prevent feeling closed in.

Parks and Spaces

These green oases are somehow apart from the bustling city centre. Homes are usually expensive and sought after, since they provide tranquil spaces and fresh air while still connected to the life of the city. People residing here will have more stable lifestyles as they have the yin-yang balance. Their homes should reflect this with a mixture of stimulating shapes, colours and materials, plus restful spaces.

Docklands

The energy of docklands is interesting. The yang energy of the large converted warehouses contrasts with the daytime yin energy when the occupants, usually young executives, are at work. At weekends this changes as café life and boating activities take over. Docklands are usually on main traffic routes, so on weekdays there is often stuck energy. Large trees should be planted to help cope with the pollution, and also to bring yin energy into the area. Rooms tend to be huge and it is difficult to ground the energy. Cosy yin spaces need to be created within the vast expanse to offer support. Large plants will also help the yin-yang balance.

Suburbs

The energy in the suburbs is mainly yin, with little nightlife. People tend to hide and become insular in suburbs, and often a yang balance is required. Imaginative use of colour is often all that is required to raise the energy of suburban homes.

▼ *Suburban living at its best in Sag Harbour, New York; wide streets, mature trees and no parked cars.*

Roads

Roads conduct chi through an environment and transport patterns can affect the nature of a neighbourhood. Living close to urban highways is an obvious health risk, but so too is living on narrow suburban "rat runs". Chi travels fast on straight urban roads and thus residents will not relax easily. In the United States, where suburban roads are built on a grid system, large gardens compensate and help to maintain a balance. Check the transport patterns before purchasing a new home and visit at different times of the day. Well-designed cul-de-sacs have excellent chi, but those where car movement has not been well planned create stuck energy and danger for children playing there.

The visual impact of a flyover in a residential area can be devastating. The fast-moving traffic conducts chi away from the area and will greatly affect the fortunes of those living at eye level or underneath the flyover.

Railways

The effect of a railway is similar to a motorway in that trains carry chi away from an area, particularly if they are at the end of the garden. Trains also create slight unease in the expectation of their arrival. Underground trains are destabilizing if they pass immediately below houses. If systems are old and poorly maintained the Chinese saying "Angry Dragons waiting to erupt" applies.

▼ *Parks and green areas are an important part of city life. This park is located in Adelaide, Australia.*

Roads and Chi

Today roads serve as conductors of chi. Steadily moving traffic on curving roads near our homes is beneficial. Fast traffic and roads pointing at us are not.

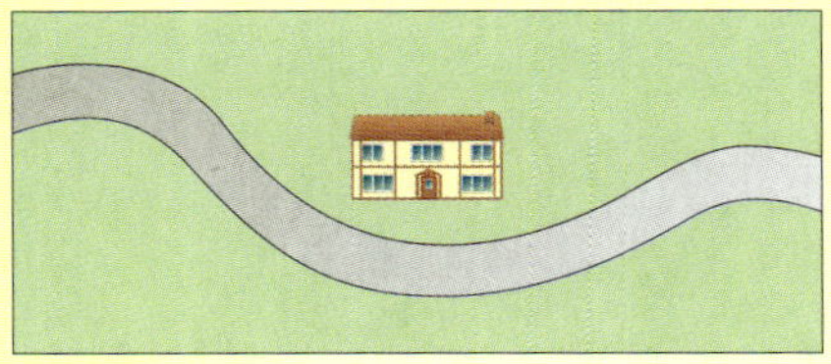

The Curving Road The road gently curves and appears to "hug" this house. This is a very auspicious Feng Shui position for a dwelling.

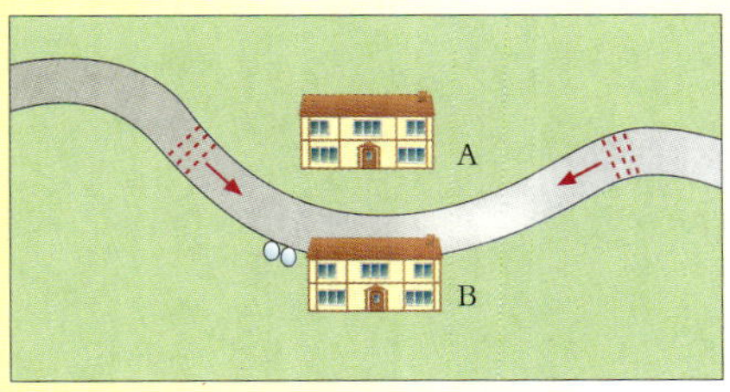

The Bending Road House B is in an inauspicious position. Traffic from both directions may break suddenly at the bend and could hit the house. At night, car beams will illuminate the rooms. There will always be a negative air of expectancy here. Convex mirrors on the outer bend would be the usual solution, but they would deflect and deplete the energy of the auspicious house A. Instead, a better solution would be to have traffic-calming measures in place as shown.

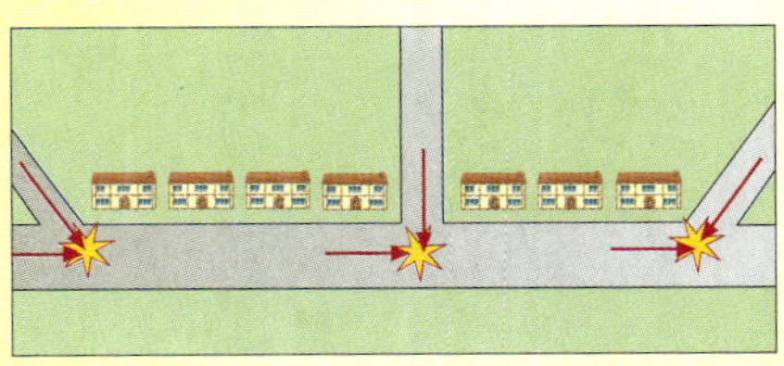

The Fast Road This creates a visual and psychological barrier. Waist-high shrubs and plants on the boundary of the garden and plants on the windowsill inside the houses will slow down the chi. Those living at the junction of such roads are likely to be jumpy. Screeching brakes and even crashes are common at such points.

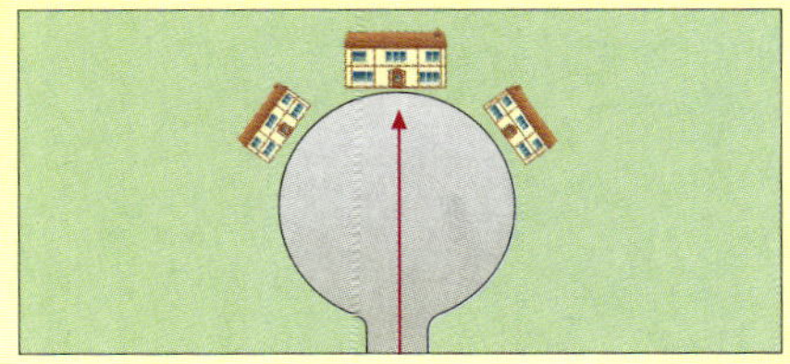

The Dead-end Road The house facing the entrance is at risk since the chi seems to hurtle towards it, as at a T-junction. Deflection is needed, and a hedge would help. An alternative would be to build a porch with the door at the side. Mirrors are often used to return the harmful influence back on itself. If the path to the door faces the road, it would be better to move and curve it. The effect is the same where a bridge points at a house. Residents will feel exhausted in such a location.

The Knife The road appears to cut into the apartments like a knife. The constant flow past the window will leave residents tetchy. A mirror outside will symbolically deflect the problem. Coloured glass in the windows facing the road would block the unattractive view whilst allowing light in.

The Flyover Residents here will feel overwhelmed and apprehensive. Lights on the corners of the house will symbolically lift the flyover, but this is not a good house to live in. Residents will feel oppressed and have no energy.

RURAL LOCATIONS

The energies found in the countryside are quite different to those of urban areas, but just as powerful. By carefully positioning our homes within the natural features of the landscape we can draw on their protection to nourish us.

Country Living

A sheltered position contained by trees or hills is ideal, especially in remote areas where protection from the elements is very important in winter. The classical arrangement of the four animals is the perfect site but if there are no woods or mountains where you wish to live, large trees and buildings can also act as protectors. Road access is vital in rural areas but, as in towns, it is preferable not to live close to major roads or through routes.

Beneficial Locations

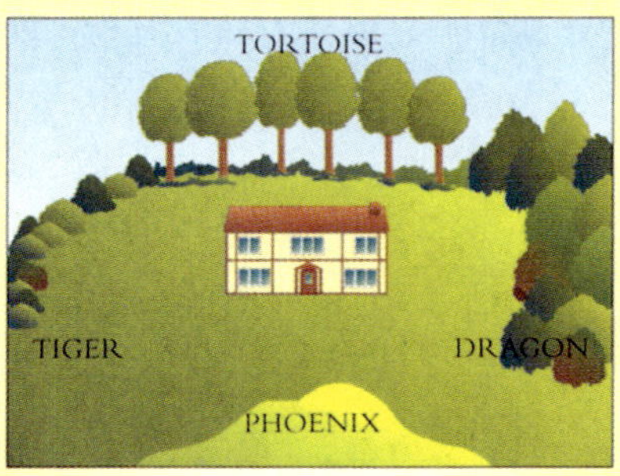

A tree belt behind acts as the Tortoise, and hedges represent the Dragon and Tiger. The Dragon is higher to keep the unpredictable Tiger in its place. A small hill in the foreground acts as the Phoenix.

A stream feeding a healthy pond is auspicious. Shrubs hide the water's exit from the property.

▲ *This lovely Mediterranean-style house is positioned in a supportive rural setting.*

Even if you live out in the wild, it is important to have a social centre within reach. Out-of-town superstores have knocked the heart out of many country towns and villages, and have made an impact on the chi of these places, but those that continue to thrive usually have an excellent yin-yang balance. They provide sport and leisure facilities for young people and a good community life, which are the yang activities in the yin setting of the countryside.

In the fields and woods, chi is good and there are many opportunities to restore the balance in our busy modern lives. Intensive farming methods can be harmful, however, so look out for telltale signs such as few songbirds or no hedges before purchasing a property.

Positive Aspects	Possible Negative Aspects
Natural smells	Agrochemicals
Leisurely pace of life	Isolation
Walks	Flooding
Trees	Travel distances & access
Wildlife	Limited public transport
Fresh food	Landfill
Air quality	Military training areas
Relaxed lifestyle	Bad weather
Outdoor life	Effluent pipes
Happy people	Amenities closed in winter

Rivers and Lakes

Energy is usually very good near water, especially near slow-flowing rivers that meander through the countryside. Proportion is important, so if the water is balanced by an undulating landscape and plenty of green vegetation it will feel comfortable. A stream feeding into a healthy pond is ideal as it will accumulate chi and also attract wildlife to visit your garden. The energy near lakes is different, reflecting the breathless movement of the wind across the water and the sudden appearance and disappearance of water sports activities at weekends.

If you decide to live in a flood plain you will need to make enquiries about the likelihood of floods in the area, especially following those of recent years.

Coastal Areas

Being beside the sea gives most of us a sense of well-being. This is partly due to the beneficial effects of negative ions in the air, which create an invigorating atmosphere. Waves can, however, adversely affect some people, depending on their animal sign – Rabbits, for example, tend to feel uneasy near the sea.

▲ *A house situated next to a slow-moving river will benefit from good chi flow.*

In the summer, the teeming beaches full of holiday-makers are yang. In winter the towering seas are also yang, but the deserted seaside towns and isolated bays are yin. It is a good idea to visit the area in both seasons as they are so different. The elements of wind and water are never so much in evidence as when the storms lash the sea against the rocks. A peninsula is difficult to live on because the chi there dissipates in the winter when it is hammered by the elements.

▶ *A tranquil bay in summer looks very different in winter.*

Roads to Home

Living in rural areas may mean that you have to commute to work and spend quite some time in the car. The daily journey you make, and the roads on which you travel, will have a considerable impact on your life, so check both when considering your new home.

Where trees overhang a road they can afford a welcome relief from the glaring sun. However, long stretches may cause nausea and headaches brought on by the flickering, dappled light.

Travelling to work in an easterly direction in the morning and returning in a westerly direction with the sun glaring on the windscreen could affect our moods considerably. This can be particularly dangerous on narrow roads.

Wonderful views can make us feel euphoric and energized, although care must be taken not to lose concentration when driving. Scenic roads can be tricky in adverse weather conditions.

Narrow country lanes with high banks or hedges funnel chi and afford no relief for the driver. Where they twist and turn, the driver's vision is extremely limited. Regular use will become a strain.

HOUSE STYLES

▲ *A balance of Metal, suggested by the circular lawn, and Water in the curved path.*

The position of our homes within their environment and how they fit in with the surrounding buildings can affect how comfortable we are living there. At a simple level, if our home is a big detached house in a road of smaller terraced houses, then we will be set apart from the rest of the community. Similarly, if the house is very different in style from its neighbours it will not fit into its environment. Strict planning laws in some areas have preserved the "spirit" or chi of towns and villages, and such places tend to have a sense of community. On the other hand, where building has been unrestricted and tall blocks spring up between two-storey houses with no regard for the character of the environment, then the area's chi dissipates and its sense of community is lost.

When we make alterations to our houses or decorate them, we should be mindful of the impact on the neighbourhood. If ours is the only stucco house in a row of brick houses, we isolate ourselves and change the chi of the area. If all the houses in the neighbourhood are of a certain era and we decide

▼ *This painted house is not in sympathy with its neighbours.*

Balancing the Elements

Element	Helped by	Harmed by	Weakened by	Weakens
Wood	Water	Metal	Fire	Earth
Fire	Wood	Water	Earth	Metal
Earth	Fire	Wood	Metal	Water
Metal	Earth	Fire	Water	Wood
Water	Metal	Earth	Wood	Fire

▲ *The intrusive tower blocks have completely changed the nature of this area.*

to change the style of the windows or substantially alter the architectural detail, we again damage the energy of the environment. Doors, chimney stacks and porches all add to the character and overall proportion not only of our house, but of the neighbourhood.

House Shapes

The best-shaped house is square. It is well proportioned and is the symbolic shape for Earth, which gathers, supports and nourishes. Rectangular buildings are also well regarded. An L-shaped building is considered inauspicious since it is said to resemble a meat cleaver and the worst position to have a room is in the "blade". If a teenager has a room in this position, they may feel isolated and may get up to all sorts of things undetected. An older relative with such a room may feel unwanted. Where houses are not a uniform shape, we need to make them more regular, as we will investigate later.

Orientation

The direction in which a building faces will also affect its chi. North-facing buildings with the main windows at the front will feel cheerless since they will not receive any sun. The energy can become stagnant and it is important to warm the house with colour. Houses with the main windows facing south and south-west will receive strong yang energy and will need cool colours to compensate. Houses facing east receive early morning sun and vibrant energy. In the west, the energy is falling. Directions determine room placement within the house.

Buildings and the Five Elements

Wood: Tall thin apartment blocks and offices are often Wood-shaped.

Earth: Earth-shaped buildings are long and low such as bungalows.

Fire: Fire buildings have pyramid-shaped or pointed roofs.

Fire: Wood-shaped windows and Earth-shaped lines give balance.

Metal: Metal buildings have domed roofs; the shape of these African homes is mirrored in Western churches.

Water: Water buildings are those which have had sections added to them over the years in a random pattern.

Five Element Cures for Correcting Imbalances

Wood: Posts, pillars, tower-shaped plant supports, green walls, trees

Fire: Pyramid-shaped finials, wigwam-shaped plant supports, garden buildings with Fire-shaped roofs, red walls, lights

Earth: Straight hedges, rectangular garden buildings, flat-topped trellis, terracotta troughs, or terracotta walls

Metal: Round finials, round weather vanes, metal balls, white walls

Water: Wavy hedges, water features, black or blue walls

ENTRANCES, PATHS AND FRONT DOORS

The entrance to our home is very important. It represents the image we present to the world and can indicate the view we have of ourselves. When we return to our home, we need to be drawn into our own nurturing space through a pleasant environment, however small. If we live in an apartment, we need to distinguish our own special part of the block and make it unique, by using a colourful doormat, introducing plants or by other means.

Entrances

Front gardens can fill up with an accumulation of stagnant energy unless we are careful. In house conversions where the grounds are not managed, the situation can be difficult since no-one is in overall charge of the garden. As a result, packaging, old furniture, chunks of wood and other assorted rubbish can pile up. Often, dustbins are sited in the front garden and can seriously affect how we feel when we return home. Bins should be placed away from the front entrance, preferably behind a hedge or fencing. If one resident clears up, others may follow suit.

▲ *Tree guardians mark the entrance to this attractive house. The effect that is created is very welcoming.*

Paths

These should gently meander through the garden to enable us to unwind at the end of a long day, or to welcome us back from a trip. Straight paths from the street to the front door carry chi too quickly and we do not have time to change gear. Ideally there should be an open space in front of the entrance where the chi can gather, but often these are filled with parked cars and there is no distinction

▼ *A meandering path enables us to shed the cares of the day before arriving home.*

Entrances

◀ This tree is overpowering the house. A convex mirror on the front door or a polished door knob will disperse its energy. Gateposts symbolically reverse the flow and send it back to the tree.

▼This tree blocks the gap between the two opposite houses. Such gaps symbolically represent money escaping.

▼ This house illustrates a situation known as "long eye", which can cause health problems.

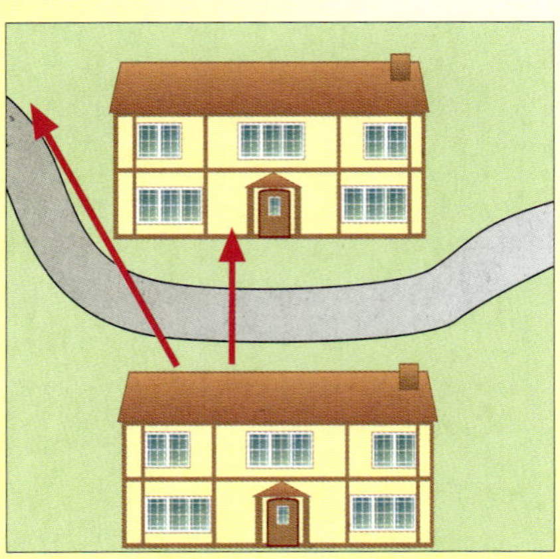

▼ Counteract "long eye" by ensuring both eyes have the same focal length. Placing trees as shown is one way.

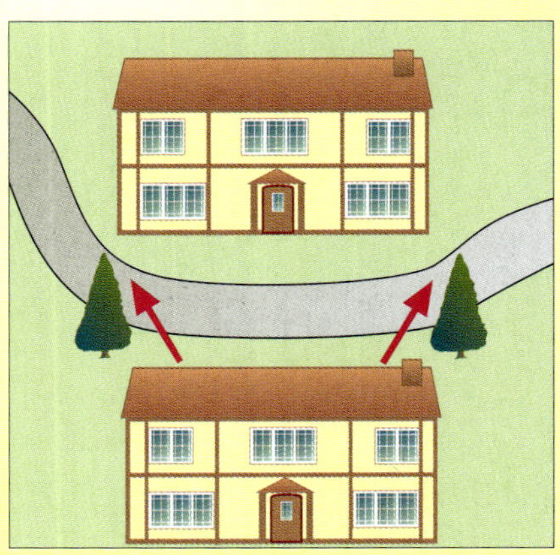

Paths

▲ Straight paths to the front door funnel chi too quickly to and from the house.

▲ Ideally, garden paths should meander to the front door to slow down the energy.

▲ Narrowing paths of this shape funnel chi too quickly into our homes.

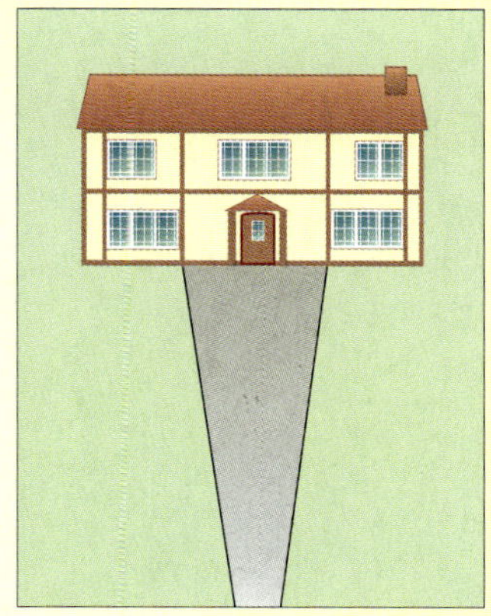

▲ Paths this shape resemble a jug pouring away from the house and disperse chi.

between home and work. Squeezing past a car to enter the house is claustrophobic, as are very small enclosed porches, creating restriction which may be mirrored in our approach to life.

Front Doors

These should be well-maintained and clean. A tub of plants on either side is welcoming but they should not restrict the space. House numbers should be visible by day and night and doorbells should be in working order to maintain harmonious relationships with callers. The chi of an area can be severely depleted if visitors whistle, shout or use their car horns. Door colours should reflect the compass direction they face and be balanced according to the Five Elements.

◀ *Plants either side of the poles would improve these well-maintained apartments.*

Departing

What we see when we leave our homes can also colour our day. Large objects like telegraph poles and trees directly in line with the front door send "poison arrows" of chi at the house, as do the corners of other buildings. If tall hedges or fences restrict our vision from the house we may become insular or feel depressed.

▼ *A balance of the Five Elements, but taller plants would improve the proportion.*

▼ *A plant pot on the left would help to balance this front entrance.*

▼ *The Metal-shaped pot plants on either side of this door are full of energy.*

INSIDE THE HOME

Once you have found a suitable location, make sure that your house is facing a supportive direction and then turn your attention to the interior. Even if the external environment is less than perfect, you can still maximize the potential of your home by choosing suitable rooms for different activities and decorating them appropriately. Using Feng Shui, you can enhance specific areas of your home and thus improve certain aspects of your life that you are not satisfied with.

BENEFICIAL POSITIONS

Having selected a protected site in which to live, it is desirable that the house is orientated in what is considered in Feng Shui to be an auspicious direction which will support its occupants. Those who fall into the east category should face their houses toward the east directions; west group people should face the west directions. It is very likely that there will be a mixture of east and west group people within a family or others sharing a house. The people who are compatible with the house will feel most comfortable in it. Others should ensure that principle rooms fall into their favoured directions or at least that beds, desks and chairs are positioned correctly.

Positioning Yourself

Once you know your "magic" numbers, it is possible to design the interior of your house so that you position yourself in directions which are beneficial to you. Beds should be orientated so that the top of your head when lying down faces one of the four beneficial locations. In the same way chairs that you sit in should also face one of your beneficial locations.

► *We need to relax at the end of the day. A room with windows facing west is good, or a position favoured by our "magic" number.*

▼ *We aim to locate our rooms in good directions and decorate to suit the elements.*

▲ *The compass direction your house faces is dependent on where the main entrance is, and is the starting point for positioning yourself inside the house.*

Find Your Best and Worst Directions

1. Check your magic number on "The Magic Numbers" table.
2. Check the "Best and Worst Directions" table to determine prime places for you to sit, sleep and work.

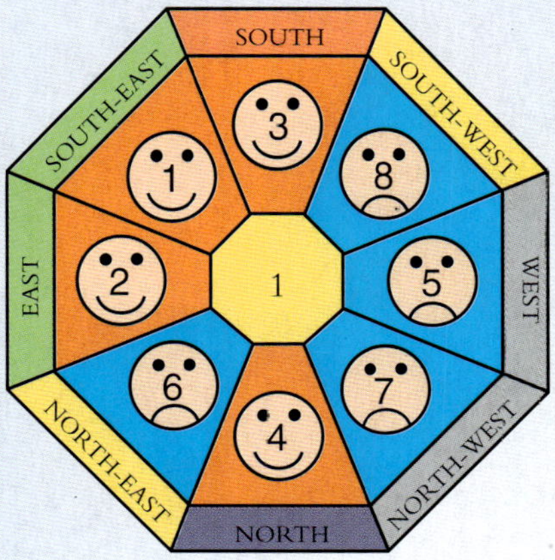

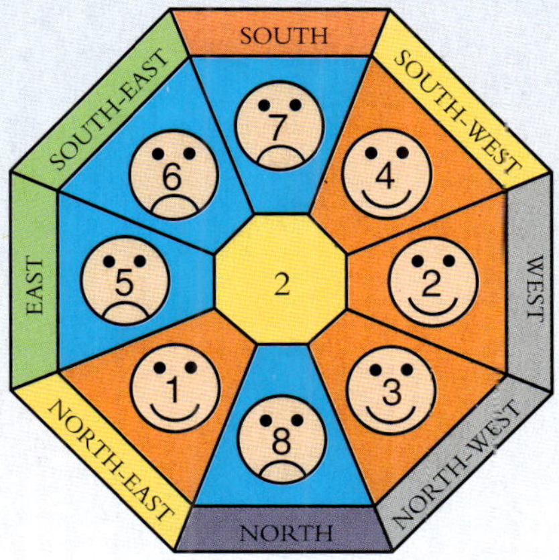

Best and Worst Directions

Numbers on the faces indicate:

1. Abundance and happiness, if all other aspects are in order. This is the place to site the main door and as many of the principal rooms as possible; also the top of the bed.

2. Health. The place for the bedroom and the top of the bed when ill.

3. Family harmony. This is the best position for the family rooms.

4. The self. This position aids perception and thought processes. The place for a study or for a desk.

5. Mishaps. In this position, things will not go according to plan. The study should not be here.

6. Arguments at home and work. Not the place for family rooms.

7. Legal and health problems. Do not site principal rooms here.

8. Disaster. Avoid this direction. Site storerooms and toilets here.

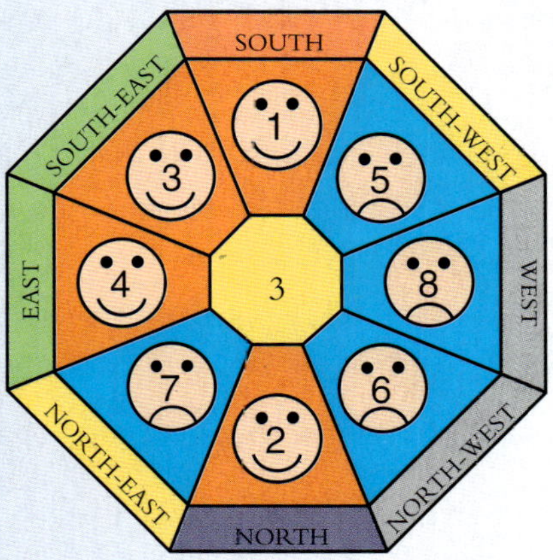

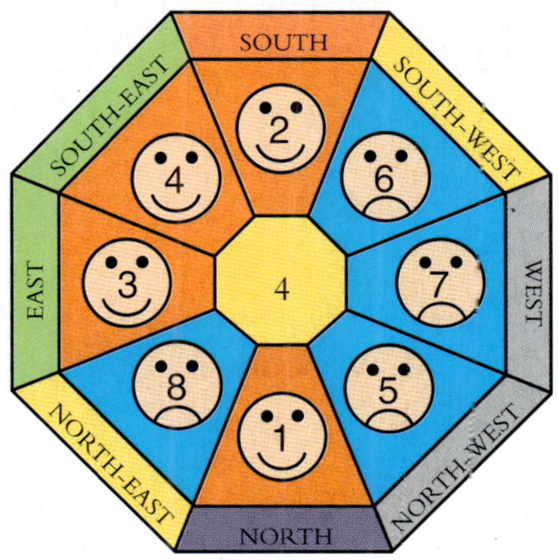

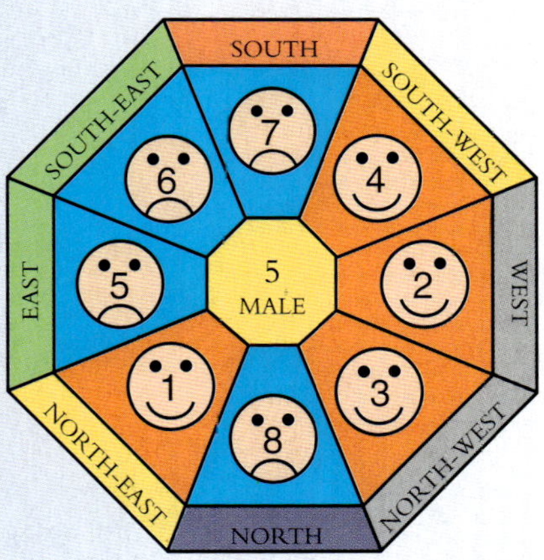

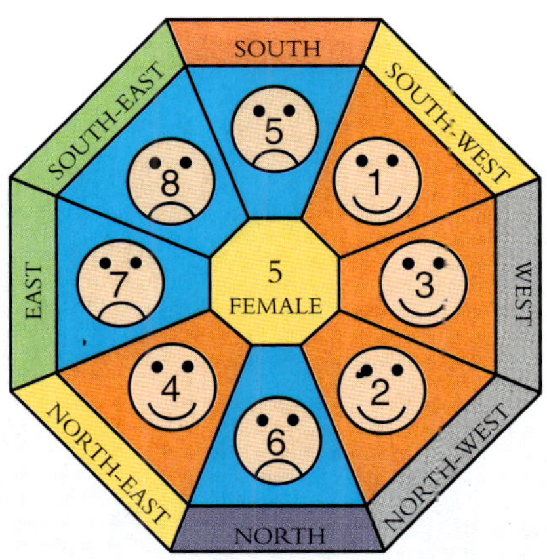

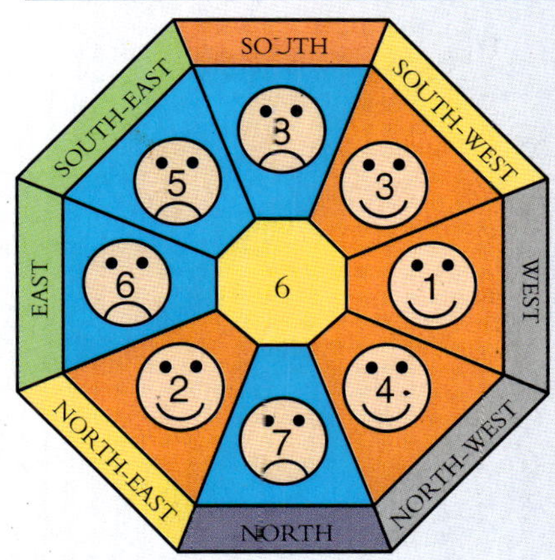

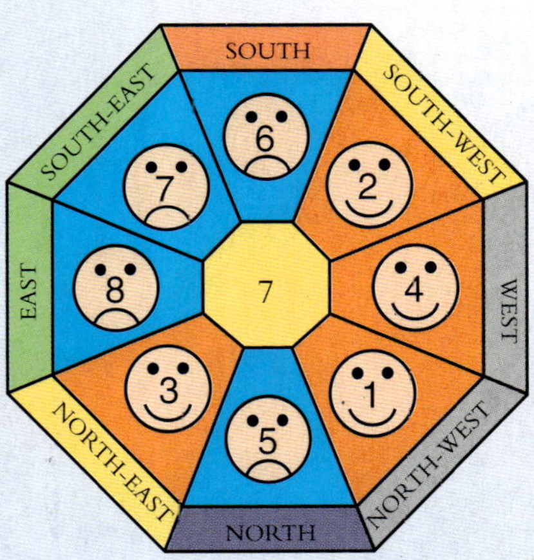

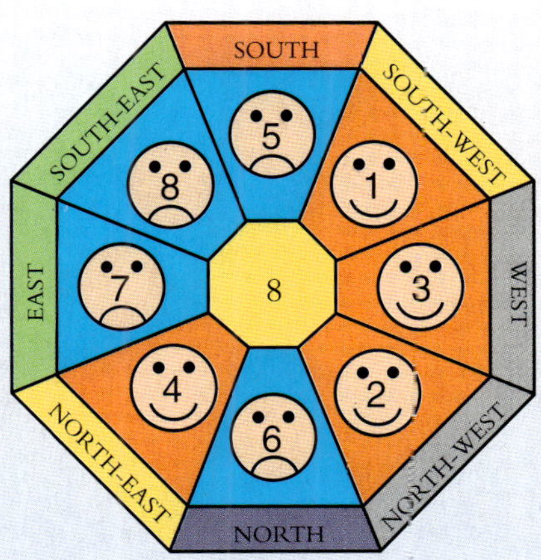

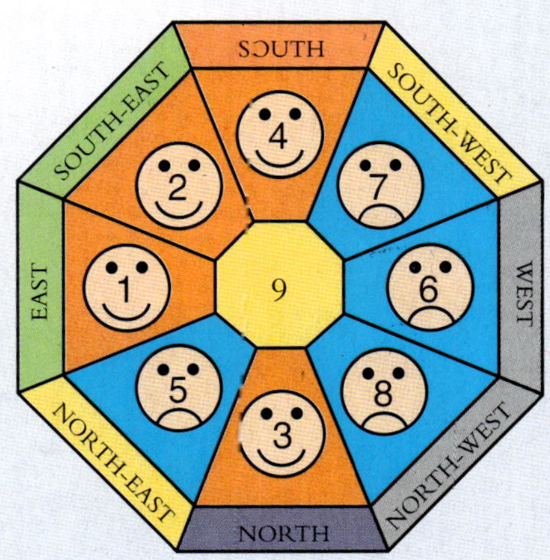

DRAWING THE PLAN

It is now possible to begin to apply the principles we have learned. In order to position ourselves to our best advantage, we need to determine the compass readings for our homes.

You Will Need

- A compass with the eight directions clearly marked
- A protractor – a circular one is best
- A scale plan of your home. If you own your home you will already have one. If not, it will be necessary to draw one, in which case you will also need a tape measure and graph paper
- A ruler
- A lead pencil and five coloured pencils – green, red, yellow, grey, dark blue
- A tracing of the Bagua with the suggested information marked on

To Draw a Plan

Using graph paper, take measurements for each floor, marking external walls, internal walls, alcoves, staircases, doors, windows and permanent fixtures such as baths, toilets, kitchen units and equipment, and fireplaces.

Take a Compass Reading

1. Remove watches, jewellery and metal objects and stand clear of cars and metal fixtures.

2. Stand with your back parallel to the front door and note the exact compass reading in degrees.

3. Note the direction, eg 125° SE, on to your plan as shown in the diagram. You are now ready to transfer the compass readings on to your Bagua drawing.

► *Use this table to double check that your heading in degrees corresponds with the direction your front door faces, since it is possible to misread the protractor.*

Directions and Degrees	
North	337.5–22.5°
North-east	22.5–67.5°
East	67.5–112.5°
South-east	112.5–157.5°
South	157.5–202.5°
South-west	202.5–247.5°
West	247.5–292.5°
North-west	292.5–337.5°

▼ *Draw a scale plan of your home and mark on it the positions of windows, doors, alcoves and all internal fixtures and fittings as well as bed and desk positions.*
A compass, protractor, ruler, coloured pencils and a tracing of the Bagua diagram will allow you to survey your home.

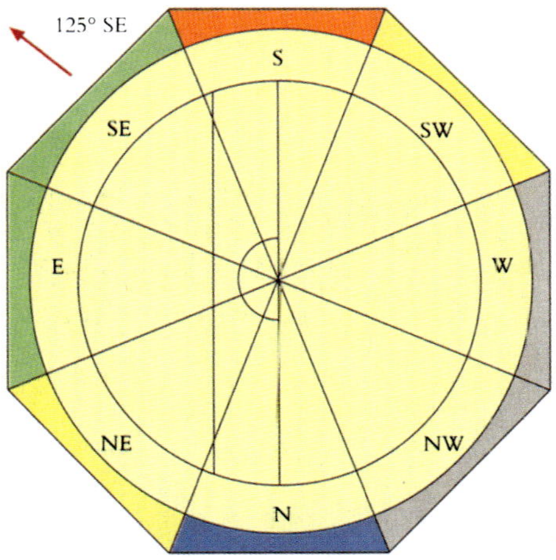

Transfer the Compass Reading to the Bagua

1. Place the protractor on the Bagua diagram so that 0° is at the bottom at the north position and mark the eight directions.

2. Having found the compass reading for your home, ie the direction faced by your front door, check it matches the direction; if not you may be reading the wrong ring. Mark the position of your front door.

3. Double-check the direction by looking at the "Directions and Degrees" table. When you have done this you will end up with a Bagua diagram such as the one above, with the front door position marked. You are now almost ready to place this template on to your home plan.

East West Directions

Just as people fit into east or west categories, so too do houses. Determine whether your house belongs to the east or west group of directions by checking the direction in which the front door faces.

Eastern directions: north-east, south-east, south

Western directions: south-west, north-west, west, north-east

East group people should preferably live in east group houses and west group people in west group houses.

Transfer the Directions to the Plan

1. Find the centre of the plan. Match the main walls across the length of the plan and crease the paper lengthways.

2. Match the main walls across the width and crease the paper widthways. Where the folds cross is the centre of your home. If your home is not a perfect square or rectangle, treat a protrusion of less than 50% of the width as an extension to the direction. If the protrusion is more than 50% of the width, treat the remainder as a missing part of the direction.

3. Place the centre of the Bagua on the centre point of the plan and line up the front door position.

4. Mark the eight directions on the plan and draw in the sectors.

5. Transfer the colour markings.

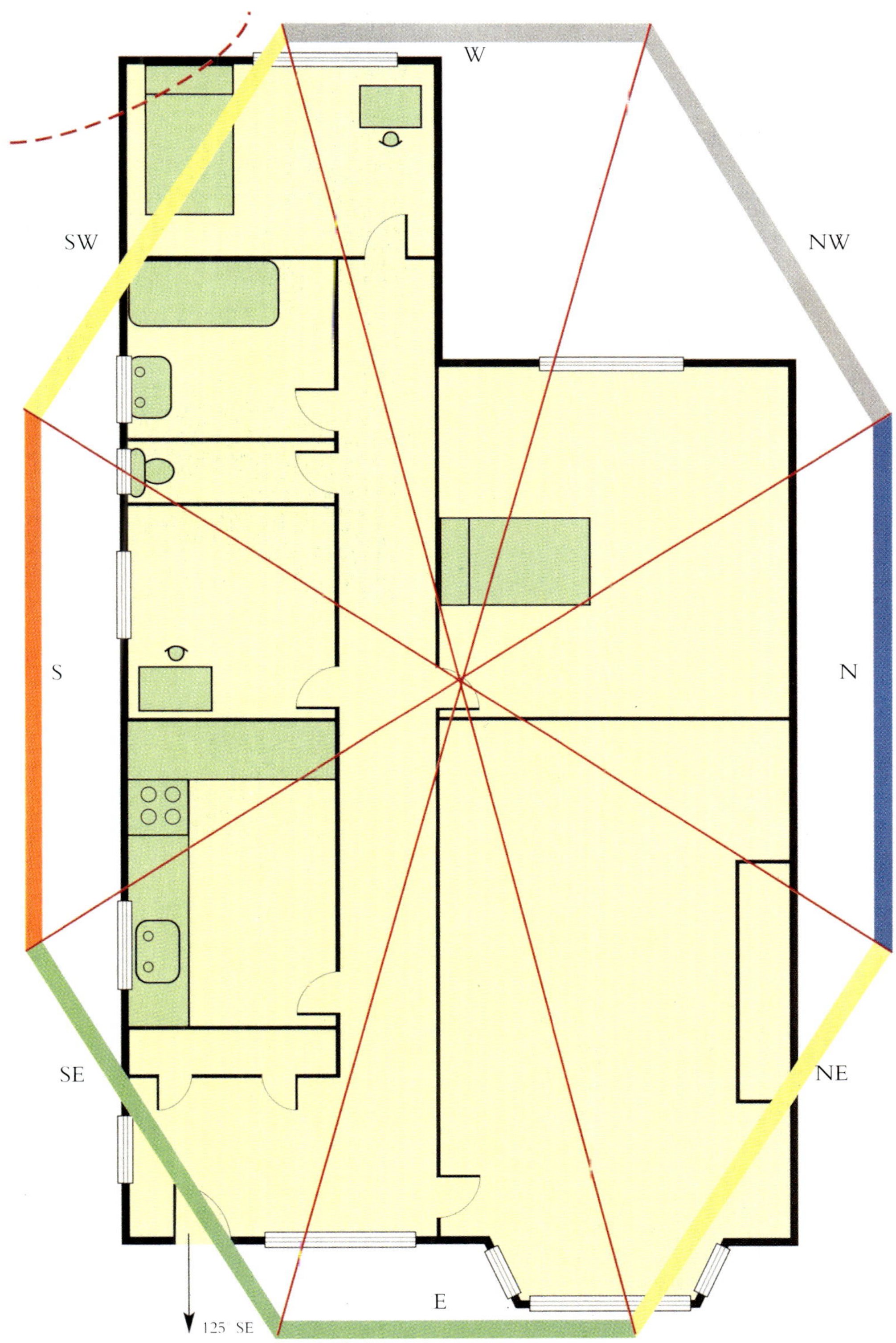

EDGES, CORNERS AND SLANTING WALLS

Certain structural details are problematic in Feng Shui. Often the result of conversions, they affect chi and can cause discomfort for the occupants of the house.

EDGES

Wherever the chi flow in a room is disrupted, difficulties occur. Anyone who has ever walked down a windy street flanked by high buildings will know that the gusts are always worse at the corners of buildings where the wind whips up into a spiral. Where major structural work has been undertaken and walls have been knocked down, a room is often left with supporting pillars. These are not conducive to the free flow of chi because they are usually square and have four corners which point, knife-like, into the room, and they can also interfere with vision.

If there are edges we should aim to soften them. Plants are one solution and fabrics are another. Wherever possible, make columns rounded as this creates an entirely different feel.

Having the edges of furniture pointing at us can make us feel uncomfortable, as can the edges of shelves and fireplaces. Keeping books in cupboards is a solution, but the pleasure of plucking a book from a shelf would be lost and the cupboards would become harbingers of tired energy. Instead, we can use plants to soften shelf edges near where we sit.

▲ *Round pillars are less obtrusive than square ones. The plant softens the effect.*

▲ *A plant will enliven an awkward corner and move the chi on.*

◀ *Plants can be used to soften shelf edges near to where we sit.*

CORNERS

The corners of rooms are often dark, so it is a good idea to place something colourful there, like a vase of silk flowers for example. Alternatively, you can use something that moves such as a lava lamp or a water feature. Putting plants in dark corners where stagnant chi accumulates will help the chi to move on. Spiky plants are particularly good provided they are away from chairs where they could direct "poison arrows" towards the occupants. Uplighters or round tables with lamps on them are other options for dark corners.

Alcoves on either side of a fireplace are often filled with shelves, which help to prevent stagnant areas provided they are not crammed full and some gaps are left.

▲ *Here, in one place, we have several methods of introducing movement into a dark corner – an octagonal table, a plant, a corner cupboard and a little shelf.*

The Flow of Chi in a Living Room

1. These chairs need to be repositioned as the corners of the fireplace will shoot "poison arrows" at people sitting in them.
2. The edges of these built-in shelves will affect anyone sitting here unless the offending edges are softened with plants.
3. A round table with a plant or lamp will move the chi on in this dark corner.
4. The corner of this pillar will send a "poison arrow" at the occupant of the chair; the chair can be moved or the edge of the pillar softened in some way.
5. Anybody who chooses to sit in this seat will be unaffected by this pillar as it is a safe distance away.
6. Uplighters in these corners of the room will lift the energy.

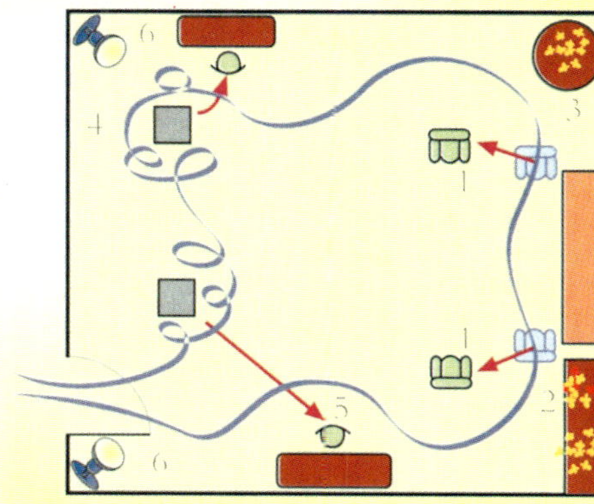

▼ *This slanting wall will not adversely affect anyone sleeping in this room as there is plenty of headroom.*

Slanting walls

These are becoming increasingly common as expanding families in small houses convert attic space into rooms. Attic rooms with sloping ceilings are often turned into children's bedrooms or home offices. Sleeping or working under a slope depresses personal chi and these areas do nothing to aid the regenerative process of sleep nor creative processes during the day. Sloping ceilings also create a visual imbalance in a room. Mirrors and lights may help to create the illusion of lifting the slope and paint can achieve the same effect Such rooms are far better used as hobby or play rooms or for any activity of a temporary nature.

If possible, it is preferable to have a smaller room of a conventional shape created instead of a room with sloping walls. A good solution is to fill the sloping walls in with built-in cupboards for storage. Where roof windows are installed to let light into attic conversions, make sure it is possible to see more out of them than just a patch of sky.

▼ *Placing storage cupboards under the eaves gives an attic room a more regular shape.*

BEAMS

Beams are not recommended in Feng Shui because they can be oppressive when positioned over a bed, stove or desk and suppress the chi of the people living beneath them. Proportion, however, is everything. In a barn conversion or in some of the eco-houses now being built, the ceilings are high and often vaulted so the beams do not seem to press down on the occupants. The reverse problem occurs when people and small-scale furniture rattle around in vast spaces and are unable to gather chi around them. However, beams in normally proportioned houses do tend to upset the flow of chi in a room, especially if we position ourselves in unsuitable places under them. Simply by moving the dining table, desk or bed, we can often overcome any difficulties.

Many people dream of owning a country cottage, complete with roses round the door, log fires and beams. Traditionally it has been the custom to paint beams black so that they stand out, but when these cottages were built it is highly unlikely that this was their original colour. In the same way that pollution and time turn pale sandstone buildings in cities to a tobacco brown, so cooking and fires down the ages have transformed pale oak beams into charcoal-coloured wood. Interior fashions change, however, and it is now more common for beams to be painted the same colour as the ceiling, a welcome trend which makes all the difference to low-ceilinged rooms.

Another way of reducing the effect of beams is to use uplighters underneath them, which give the illusion of "lifting" the beam. Small, light-coloured hanging objects will lighten a beam. Do not hang large, dark or heavy objects below a beam, or anything that collects dust. False ceilings can be attached to beams, either

▲ *These beams are unobtrusive because the roof is so high. Avoid sitting under the low crossbeam running across the room.*

▼ *The oppressive effect of these beams is reduced by painting them a light colour.*

▼ *Sloping walls and a beam across the bed make this an inauspicious bedroom. The insecurity of the window behind the bed adds to the effect.*

the conventional type or translucent ones with light behind. In larger spaces, such as restaurants, beams have been successfully mirrored, but this would not look good in most homes. Muslin or other fabrics will hide them, but these will harbour dust and create stagnant chi unless washed regularly. Traditionally, bamboo flutes tied with red ribbon were hung from the beam to create an auspicious octagon shape. Beams over a bed are believed to cause illnesses to occupants at

◀ *This modern living room is made inauspicious by the sloping walls and the dark beam running down the centre of the room.*

▲ *Imagine this room with dark beams – the light beams create quite a different effect.*

the points where they cross. A beam that runs along the length of the bed can cause a rift between the couple that shares it. When beams are situated over the stove or dining room table, they are thought to hamper the fortunes of the family. If they are over a desk, they may hinder the creative flow of the person who works there, and may even be a cause of depression. It is certainly better not to sleep under a beam, and sitting in a chair under a beam or under a gallery is not a comfortable experience either.

DOORS AND WINDOWS

Doors represent our freedom and our access to the outside world; they are also a barrier, acting as protection, supplying support and comfort. Windows act as our eyes on the world. Both play an important role in Feng Shui and if our access or vision through them is impeded in any way we may suffer problems as a consequence.

Doors

Open doors allow us access to a room or to the outside world. Closed doors shut off a room or our entire home. If either of these functions is impeded, then the chi flow around the house will suffer. Doors which squeak, stick, have broken latches, or handles too close to the edge so we scrape our knuckles whenever we open them, should all be repaired. Keep a wedge close to doors that might slam irritatingly in the breeze.

Ideally, a door should not open to a

► *The uplifting view from this window has not been restricted by curtains or blinds.*

Cures for Problem Doors

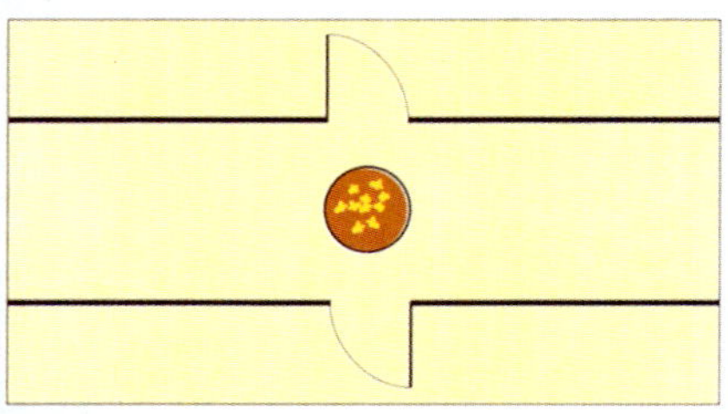

▲ If doors are located opposite each other, place an obstruction such as a table or a bookcase to slow down the chi.

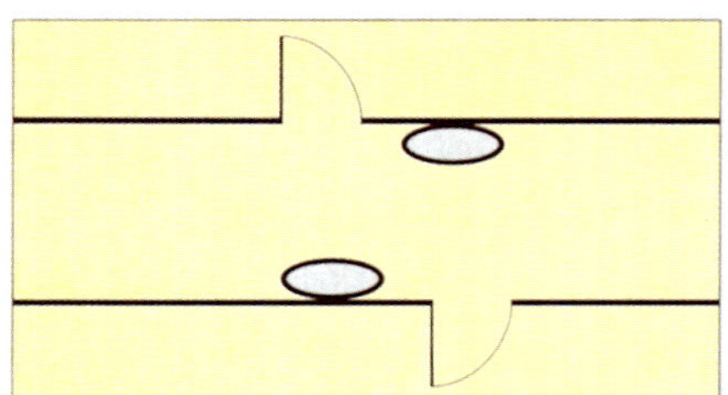

▲ Where doors are out of alignment, create a balance by positioning mirrors or pictures on each side.

▲ Where there are three or more doors in a row, break up the perspective by hanging low lights or positioning semi-circular tables to slow down the chi.

▲ Where an opened door restricts the view into a room, position a mirror to correct this. Doors were traditionally hung in this way to prevent draughts. This practice may also have arisen because of the desire to preserve modesty in Victorian times.

▼ *Stained glass panels in doors permit light and lift the energy in dark spaces.*

restricted view of the whole room on entering, but doors in old houses used to be hung in this way to prevent draughts or, some speculate, to preserve modesty during the decorous Victorian era.

Windows

Sash windows which only open halfway restrict the amount of chi that can enter a room. Some double-glazed units only open halfway, with the same result. Ideally, all windows should open fully, and outwards. Beware of windows which have fixed double-glazed panels with only a small opening section at the top. These can cause fatal accidents if fire breaks out; they are usually fitted with safety glass, so it is virtually impossible to smash them.

▲ *Adding an attractive stained-glass hanging can offer some privacy while creating a lively energy in the room.*

▼ *This stencilled decoration allows privacy in a bathroom, while at the same time letting in as much daylight as possible.*

▲ *Tied-back curtains are ideal here as they do not restrict the pleasant view.*

If these have been fitted in your home, it is advisable to remove them as soon as possible, particularly in children's rooms.

Safety is, of course, paramount in children's rooms and measures should be taken to ensure that they cannot fall out of windows.

The top of a window should be as tall as the tallest person in the house. Everyone should have a view of the sky through the seasons or they will lose their connection with the natural world. Drooping blinds which prevent this view lower the chi of a room considerably, and slatted blinds send cutting chi into the room.

If you keep your curtains closed during the day, the chances are that you are depressed and feel vulnerable. Net curtains, although necessary in some areas, blur the view out of the window. Experiment with other solutions, such as large plants, coloured glass or window stickers to prevent the outside world looking in. The aim should be to see out as much as possible. South-west-facing windows will, however, need some screening in summer, particularly in a study or kitchen.

Too many windows can create excessive yang since they blast the house with chi, while too few windows restrict its flow and are yin. Windows too near the

▲ *The seating in this room impedes access to the window, and can be easily rearranged.*

floor in attic rooms feel unstable and a solid object or low table should be placed in front. It is preferable for bathrooms to have windows with an air flow. If this is not available, a water feature containing aromatic oils should be used and an extraction unit installed.

Too many windows in the dining room are considered to be especially inauspicious since the aim is to gather chi around the dining table and the food prepared for friends and family.

▼ *This lovely etched bathroom window allows the occupants privacy, but still permits the maximum amount of light.*

MATERIALS

The materials with which we surround ourselves affect us on a physical level by how they feel and what they look like. They also affect us on a psychological level through their energy. Like everything else, materials have elemental qualities which affect the chi of the part of the home in which they are used, and they can also have a profound effect on our health and well-being.

▼ *A wooden floor makes the room look attractive and warm.*

▲ *Natural materials such as wood, wicker and cotton fabrics look fresh and inviting.*

Hard, reflective surfaces such as those used in the kitchen have a yang energy and chi moves across them quickly. Soft materials and those with depth of colour or texture are yin and tend to slow chi movement down.

HARMFUL CHEMICALS ARE FOUND IN

- *Wood preservation treatments:* use safe alternatives
- *Cavity wall foam*
- *Paint:* use natural pigments
- *Vinyl wallpaper and paints:* use untreated papers and paints
- *Synthetic carpets and treated woollen carpets:* use natural untreated materials
- *Plastic floor tiles and coverings:* use linoleum or rubber
- *Adhesives:* use non-chemical and acrylic alternatives
- *Upholstery foam:* use natural fibres
- *Processed wood products:* use solid or recycled wood
- *Cleaning materials:* use natural alternatives
- *Food:* Select organic food
- *Fuels:* keep consumption to a minimum
- *Water supply:* dispose of hazardous chemicals safely

MATERIALS AND HEALTH

Our choice of materials for fabrics and soft furnishings, furniture, decorating materials, and cleaning and washing agents can play a part in our health and well-being. Each of us takes responsibility for our own health and that of our families whenever we choose materials for use inside our homes. Many substances present in the products we select can cause life-threatening illnesses over time and many are known to be responsible for allergies.

PLANTS WHICH CLEAN THE AIR

Lady Palm – *Rhapis excelsa*
Anthurium – *Anthurium andraeanum* (below right)
Rubber Plant – *Ficus robusta*
Dwarf Banana – *Musa cavendishii*
Peace Lily – *Spathiphyllum*
Ivy – *Hedera helix*
Heart Leaf Philodendron
Croton – *Codiaeum variegatum pictum*
Kalanchoe – *Kalanchoe blossfeldiana* (below left)
Golden Pothos – *Epipremnum aureum*
Ficus alii
Boston Fern – *Nephrolepis exaltata* 'Bostoniensis'

While investigating the air quality inside spacecraft, scientists at NASA discovered that some plants are useful in extracting harmful substances from the atmosphere. This is a very good reason for introducing plants into our homes, in addition to their other virtues. The list above shows plants which have been found useful in cleaning the air.

◀ *Wicker furniture is strong and comfortable, and it is also biodegradable.*

Materials and the Five Elements

Materials and their colours and shapes can be used to enhance, weaken or support the energy of an area according to the relationships of the elements.

Wood

Wood plays a crucial role in most houses. Its strength can support the structure of a house, yet its grain suggests fluidity and movement. Highly polished woods conduct chi quickly but stripped pine seems to absorb it. Wood is ideal for use on floors as it is easy to clean and does not harbour dust and mites, which can cause allergies.

Bamboo, Wicker and Rattan

These natural products fall into the Wood element category. In contrast to the yang characteristics of highly polished wood, these materials tend to be yin and thus slow down chi.

Coir, Sisal, Sea Grass and Rush Matting

These are popular because they are natural products. They make attractive floor coverings but are difficult to clean; this must be done regularly or they will harbour dirt and insects.

Fabrics

These can be made of natural fibres, like cotton and linen which belong to the Wood element, or from man-made fibres. Provided they are not treated with chemicals for fire or stain resistance, natural fibres are preferred since man-made fibres create static electricity and deplete the beneficial negative ions in the home. Fabrics can encourage stagnant chi if they become faded and dirty.

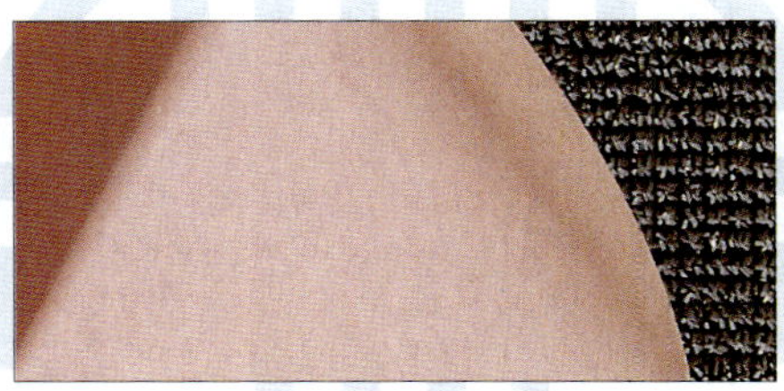

Plastics

Plastics and other man-made materials generally fall into the Fire element category as they have usually been produced using heat processes. They can block chi and produce harmful vapours and chemicals which may affect health, so they should be kept to a minimum.

Metal

Metal objects – steel, chrome and other metals – speed up chi flow. The reflective surfaces suggest efficiency and action, and metal is therefore useful in the kitchen and in stagnant areas such as bathrooms. Being smooth and reflective, glass is often classified in the Metal element and some of its qualities are similar.

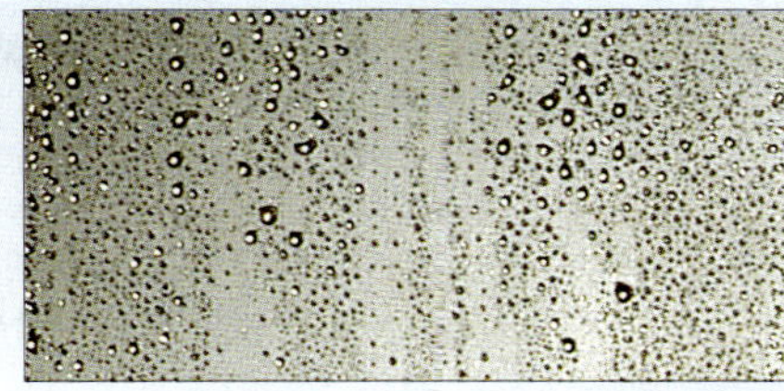

Glass

Glass is often classified as the Metal element and shares some of its qualities. However, glass has depth, and light reflecting on it suggests patterns which flow like Water. Sand is used in the production of glass, so sometimes it also suggests Earth. It depends on the energetic quality of the particular glass and the use to which it is put.

Clay and Ceramics

These two related materials fall into the Earth element category. They can be yin or yang in nature, depending on whether or not their surfaces are shiny. Glazed surfaces such as china and vases are more yang and they conduct chi quickly.

Stone and Marble

Stone floors and walls fall into the Earth element category. They tend to be yin since their surfaces are non-reflective and the natural patterning on them gives them depth. Stone floors are stable and are particularly useful in kitchens. Marble, on the other hand, is yang because it is smooth, hard and polished. The natural patterns in marble also suggest the flow of the Water element.

MIRRORS

Mirrors have been described as "the aspirin" of Feng Shui and they have many curative uses. They should always reflect something pleasant, such as an attractive view or a landscape, which will bring the vibrant energy of a garden or scene into the house. When placing a mirror to enhance a space or "cure" an area, be aware of what is reflected in it or a problem may be created elsewhere. Mirrors should never distort or cut into the image of a person as this symbolically distorts or cuts their chi. They should always have frames to contain the chi of the image.

Mirrors are useful in small spaces where they apparently double the size of the area. Don't hang them opposite a door or a window since they merely reflect the chi back at itself and do not allow it to flow around the home. Mirrors opposite each other indicate restlessness and are not recommended. Other reflective objects can be used in the same way as mirrors; for example, highly polished door furniture, metal pots, glass bowls and shiny surfaces.

▲ *This hallway is already light but the mirror makes it positively sparkle. Mirrors create an illusion of space and depth.*

▼ *A mirror will make a small space seem much larger. Do not position it directly opposite a door or window.*

Irregular Spaces

Where part of a house is "missing", in other words irregularly shaped, mirrors can be used to effectively recreate the missing space and make a regular shape.

Stagnant areas

Use mirrors in dark corners and at bends in passages to help the chi to circulate around these awkward places.

Long Corridors

In long corridors the chi moves too fast. Mirrors offer one method of slowing the chi down. Position several mirrors in a staggered manner to reflect pleasant images placed on the opposite wall.

Mirrors to Deflect

Convex mirrors are used in Feng Shui to deflect fast-moving chi or the influences

The Do's and Don'ts of Mirrors

Do

- ✔ Have frames around mirrors
- ✔ Keep them clean
- ✔ Replace broken ones
- ✔ Reflect your whole image

Don't

- ✘ Have joins or mirror tiles
- ✘ Hang mirrors opposite each other
- ✘ Place them opposite the bed
- ✘ Place them opposite doors
- ✘ Place them directly opposite windows
- ✘ Hang Bagua mirrors indoors

The Bagua Mirror

The markings on the Bagua mirror are a kind of shorthand, representing the energies of the Cosmos.

of uncomfortable features outside the house, for example, corners of buildings, telegraph poles and trees which overpower the front of the house. They will also deflect unwanted influences indoors, but because they distort images position them where they will not reflect people.

Bagua Mirrors

Bagua mirrors are used to protect a house from malign energies which may attack the occupants. They can often be seen outside Chinese homes and shops. They are used on front doors to deflect the influences of negative energy sources – harsh corners, tall objects and other features. Bagua mirrors represent a yin energy cycle and, as such, should never be hung inside the house or they will affect the energies of the occupants.

▲ *If a house is not of a perfect shape, a mirror hung inside will symbolically reflect the missing area.*

The Wealth area of this house is missing. Place mirrors to symbolically repair the shape and energize the missing space.

Use a mirror to repair the shape of an L-shaped room by symbolically drawing in the missing area.

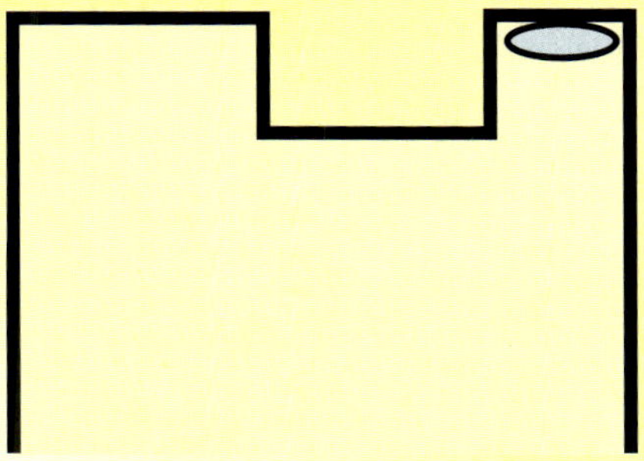

A mirror placed in this gloomy corner, reflecting a view or plant, will enliven a dark space and prevent energy stagnating.

Place a mirror to reflect a bright picture on the opposite wall and thus bring energy to this dark area.

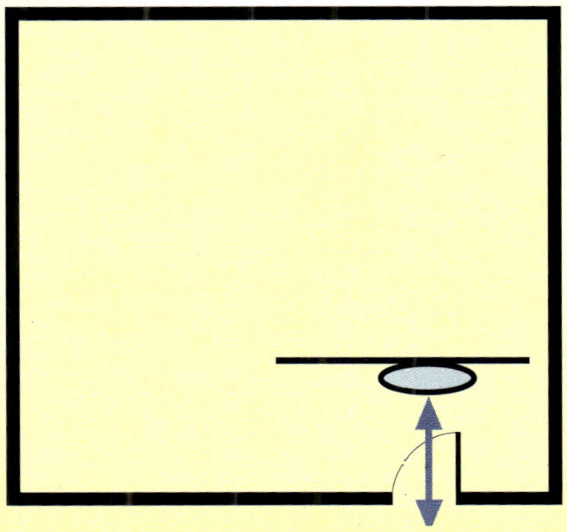

A mirror in this position will not allow the chi into the house or room and will reflect it back through the door.

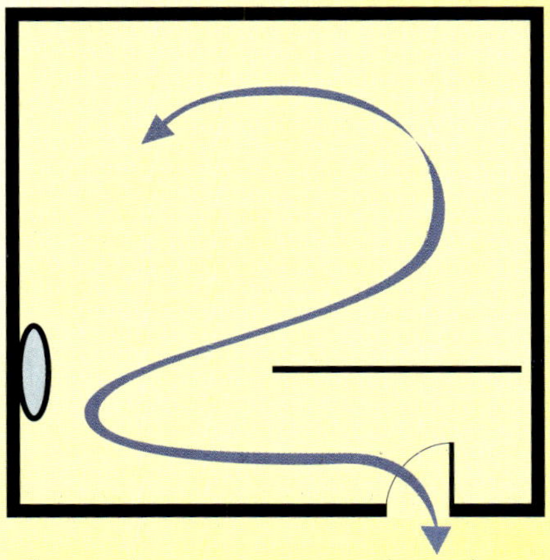

This is a better position as it draws the chi into and through the living area and does not act as a barrier.

PLANTS

Plants play an important role in Feng Shui because they bring a life force into the home and help to keep the air fresh. Depending on their shape, plants create different types of energy. Upright plants with pointed leaves are yang, and are useful in the south and in corners to move energy. Round-leaved and drooping plants are more yin and calming, and best placed in the north. Plants should be healthy – sick plants and those which shed leaves and flowers profusely will create stagnant energy.

Colour and Shape

Plants with shapes and colours that correspond to the Five Elements are ideal. Care should be taken when siting spiky plants to ensure that they are not directing harmful energy towards a chair where someone may sit.

Indoor Bulbs

Spring: Dwarf tulip, Dwarf narcissus, Crocus, Hyacinth (above)
Summer: *Scilla peruviana, Albuca humulis, Calochortus subalpinus, Rocoea humeana*
Autumn: Nerine, Autumn crocus, Cyclamen, *Liriope muscari*
Winter: *Iris reticulata, Chionodoxa luciliae*, Muscari, Cymbidium

▲ *Colourful plants will brighten any area and increase Wood energy. Plants in these colours will benefit an Earth area.*

▲ *The money plant has been adopted as the Feng Shui plant. Its leaves resemble coins and Metal energy.*

► *This trained ivy plant brings a lively energy to a room. It would look best in the west or north-west.*

Plants that Represent the Five Elements

▲ *Geraniums are easy to grow on a sunny windowsill and represent Fire.*

FIRE: Geranium, Cordyline, Begonia, Bromeliad, Poinsettia, Aspidistra.
EARTH: Slipper flower, Marigolds, Sunflowers and other yellow plants.
METAL: Money plant, Jasmine, Fittonia, Oleander, Calathea.

▲ *All the elements are here, captured in both the colours and the shapes of this attractive pot of lillies.*

▲ *Summer jasmine is often grown in an arch shape. Its delicate white flowers have a beautiful scent.*

WATER: The Water element can be introduced by standing plant pots on blue or clear glass nuggets.
WOOD: All plants are representative of the Wood element.

Flowers

Flowers look beautiful in a vase but, once cut, they are technically dead and often stand forgotten in stagnant water. The cut-flower industry uses vast amounts of energy in heating greenhouses, transportation and the manufacture of chemicals to feed their products and keep them pest-free. Choose potted plants instead. You could grow pots of bulbs through the seasons and plant them afterwards in the garden.

Dried flowers are also technically dead and have a stagnant energy, particularly when their colours fade and they gather dust. As an alternative, pictures of flowers, brightly painted wooden replicas and silk flowers are all acceptable to symbolize growth and stimulate energy in the house.

▼ *Use a pretty flowering plant in the house like this Cymbidium, instead of cut flowers.*

The Feng Shui Plant

The money plant (*Crassula ovata*) has been adopted as the Feng Shui plant. The name helps, but the round succulent leaves are representative of Metal energy. Use them in the west and north-west. If used in the south-east (the Wealth area), their Metal energy will be in conflict with the Wood energy of that direction.

▶ *This bright arrangement would do well in the south-west – an Earth area.*

Use Plants To:

- Hide a jutting corner
- Move energy in a recessed corner
- Harmonize Fire and Water energy in kitchens
- Slow down chi in corridors
- Drain excess Water energy in the bathroom
- Bring life into the house
- Enhance the east and south-east, and support the south

LIGHTING

Life on Earth depends directly or indirectly on the sun. Our bodies are attuned to its cycles and in every culture the daily rhythms of light and dark are built into the mythology. In China, the yin-yang or T'ai Chi symbol reflects the daily and annual cycles of the sun: the white yang side representing daytime and

▼ *Stained glass is very decorative and provides privacy in a room which is overlooked.*

▲ *Our bodies need plenty of sunlight in order to stay healthy.*

▶ *Muslin filters the light in rooms where the sun's glare is too strong, or offers privacy.*

the dark yin side night-time. In the modern world, many of us spend a lot of time inside buildings and our rhythms become out-of-tune with the natural cycle of the sun. In northern countries, which have little sunlight, a condition known as SAD (Seasonal Affective Disorder) is prevalent. It is treated with light that imitates the ultraviolet and infra-red rays of the sun.

The correct type and level of light are very important to our general health and well-being. In our homes, natural light is important but its quality varies throughout the day according to the way our houses face. Natural light can cause glare or create shadows and we often have to subdue it or enhance it by artificial means. Light can be reflected off shiny surfaces or filtered by net or muslin curtains, blinds or frosted or tinted glass. Being aware of how natural light comes into our homes enables us to position our furniture and arrange our activities to make the best use of it.

Artificial Lighting

In rooms where we are active, such as kitchens, offices and workrooms, and where safety is important, for example on staircases, direct lighting is necessary. In rooms we relax in – living rooms and bedrooms – we can use softer lighting which can be reflected or diffused. To highlight particular areas, such as a picture, chopping board or desk, task lighting can be used.

The position of lighting has a profound effect on the occupants of a house. If shadows are cast where we read or prepare food, or the lights flicker, or light glares on to the computer or TV screen, we will constantly be irritated. Harsh lighting can also affect our moods.

The quality of light is important. Ordinary light bulbs produce light which veers towards the red end of the spectrum, with little blue or green light. Fluorescent light is the opposite; it emits higher electromagnetic fields than other sources and its flicker can cause headaches. Full spectrum lighting was designed to copy natural daylight as much as possible, but unfortunately contains slightly higher levels of ultraviolet radiation than ordinary light sources.

Energy production is a drain on the world's natural resources. Recent developments designed to reduce this include CFL (compact fluorescent lamp) bulbs, which not only last longer but also use less electricity. Tungsten-halogen lamps give a bright, white light that is close to daylight. The high-voltage varieties are too bright for task lighting but are useful as uplighters; the low-voltage varieties can be used for spotlights. These bulbs are also energy-efficient.

▲ *Glass bricks have been used here instead of a solid wall. They can be very useful if you want to open up dark areas.*

▼ Soft wall lighting helps us to relax at the end of a stressful day.

▶ *Use uplighters to transform dark corners. Placed under heavy beams, they serve to lighten their negative effect.*

ELECTROSTRESS

We are becoming increasingly aware of the negative effects of electromagnetic radiation on the human body. The effects of exposure to ionizing radiation in X-rays and ultraviolet rays in sunlight are now well-known. The low-frequency radiation which surrounds power lines has also been linked to childhood illness. Such radiation also exists around electrical appliances. Non-ionizing radiation emitted by household appliances can be equally harmful over time. Cathode ray tubes in televisions and computer monitors are particularly harmful because both adults and children now spend so much time in front of them. It is wise to sit as far away as possible from the screen. Lap-top computers should not be used on our laps as we would then be connected to an electric circuit. The electromagnetic field around ionizers has a particularly large range so it is not a good idea to place them in bedrooms.

▲ *Placing a Boston fern next to the television screen has been shown to absorb some of the radiation it emits.*

◀ *Round-the-clock working and satellite links to the rest of the world have resulted in Hong Kong having higher-than-average electromagnetic activity.*

▼ *Mobile phones are convenient and allow us to conduct business outside, but pose a health risk if used constantly. A laptop computer should not be used on our laps.*

We live in an electrical "soup". Radio, TV and microwave emissions pass around and through us wherever we live. There are few places left on Earth where this is not the case. Satellites connect continents instantly and we can communicate with people across the world, but at a price. Recent research into the use of mobile telephones indicates that frequent use can affect us. The radiation from the appliances we use every day of our lives has been linked to various cancers, allergies, Parkinson's disease, Alzheimer's disease, cataracts, ME and even the total breakdown of the immune system.

Despite our awareness of the effects of radiation, we are so dependent on appliances and communication technology that we are unwilling, or unable, to live without them. We should therefore take precautions. At night, electric blankets should never be left on when we are in bed; if we must use them, they should be unplugged from the mains before we get into bed. Water beds are connected to the electricity supply, so in Feng Shui terms they display the conflict of Fire (electricity) and Water. We need to feel secure when we sleep and the constant motion of a water bed is not a natural way for us to rest.

Microwave ovens are potentially the most dangerous of all household appliances and should be used with care. They have been found to emit low-frequency radiation far in excess of that known to cause lymphatic cancer in children.

Apartments that have under-floor or overhead heating systems should be avoided as they can create the effect of living in an electromagnetic box.

◀ *Microwave ovens can damage your health if they leak. Have them checked annually as you would other household fixtures. They are not well regarded in Feng Shui.*

▶ *A gadget-free bedroom is essential for a healthy body and peace of mind. While we sleep, our body cells can regenerate naturally, a process which works best if unimpeded by any harmful external influences.*

Precautions

- Use mobile phones as little as possible
- Make lengthy social calls from a conventional telephone
- Fit screen filters to VDUs
- Sit, and make sure children sit, at least 2 m (6 ft) away from the television
- Sit as far away from the computer as possible when not working
- Limit children's use of the computer
- Do not use the computer and television as substitute babysitters
- Do not stand near a microwave when it is on
- Dry your hair naturally instead of using electrical appliances
- Choose gas or wood-burning stoves and heaters rather than electric
- Keep all electrical appliances away from the bed
- Do not have wiring under the bed
- Do not use storage heaters in bedrooms

▲ *Children sleep better if they are not surrounded by stimulating equipment.*

▼ *A wood-burning stove lends an attractive focus to a room.*

▼ *Storing electrical equipment out of sight will help us to relax.*

THE SENSES: SIGHT

What we see affects us positively or negatively, or even subconsciously so we may not even be aware of the effect. If we surround ourselves with wonderful views, bright colours, interesting food and a clean and clear environment we are more likely to lead full and happy lives, because our surroundings will reflect a positive attitude to life. The reverse is equally true.

Most homes have problem areas – dark corners which would benefit from light, rooms with columns or L-shaped rooms where the corners point at us – but we can disguise them with plants and materials to soften the edges. There may be things outside which affect us and we may want to keep their influence out.

▲ *Skyscapes are so beautiful that we should make sure we can capture a view of them in our homes.*

We can attempt to deflect the problem with mirrors and other reflective objects, or create a barrier, such as a hedge or shrub, to keep it at bay. There is a difference between this type of positive, or yang, barrier designed to keep the negative exterior forces out and a yin barrier which we sometimes create to keep our own negative energies in – tall hedges and walls and drawn curtains. Wherever the ancient Chinese had a wall, there would be a window, or "Moon Gate", in it through which to see the world beyond and open up future possibilities.

◀ *"Moon Gates" were built into ancient walls in China to afford a glimpse of the world outside.*

▲ *This intricately decorated window can be found in a temple in China.*

▼ *Crystals are used to bring a sparkle to stuck energy. Suspend one in a window and the light will shine through it, creating a rainbow effect on a wall or ceiling.*

Crystals

Colour resonates with us on both a conscious and a subconscious level, and can affect our moods. The combination of crystal and light gives a lively dancing pattern which will enliven a dark room if the crystal is hung in a window. Where energy is stuck, crystals can help to move it on.

Crystals should be used with care. They have many facets which break light up into tiny segments and can do the same to other energies. If the energy of an area is not working, do not hang up a crystal to repair it – or the problem will be exacerbated. A small crystal is adequate for the average home, but larger ones would be needed for a large area.

► *Coloured glass panels in a window add life to a colourless room. They also provide privacy and so are ideal for a bathroom or for ground floor rooms.*

▼ *This lovely room has been transformed by the balanced pairs of stained glass windows. Little extra decoration is needed.*

Coloured Glass

Coloured glass makes a bolder statement than crystal and its effects can be stunning. Many urban houses have side doors which look out on to a wall and there is a temptation, if they are overlooked by a window from a neighbouring house, to keep a blind permanently down. Replacing the plain glass in a door or window with bold coloured glass which supports the elements of the area will bring a wonderful energy into a dark room and transform it. Stained glass is especially decorative and suitable for most rooms in the home.

Sight Enhancers

Natural light, Lamps,
Candles, Glass and crystal, Colour,
Still water, Moon Gates,
Reflective metals,
Windows, Mirrors

THE SENSES: SOUND

Each of the Five Elements governs a different musical quality and sound. We all connect to a particular sound and in Chinese medicine the tone of our voice is categorized according to the elements and used in diagnosis. We each have our own favourite sounds. Gentle background music, the rustle of leaves, bird songs – all have a therapeutic effect. Where noise is rhythmic – a dripping tap, music from a neighbour's party, even someone sneezing at regular intervals – it can grate on our nerves.

Pleasant sounds in the right place and at the right time can soothe and refresh. Bubbling water will create a peaceful ambience and slow us down. If we want to bring life to a place, honky-tonk music, drums and cymbals will fulfil the purpose. Background sounds are comforting and the sound of passing traffic or a ticking clock can be reassuring.

Wind Chimes

Wind chimes feature in Feng Shui as an enhancer and it is interesting to note how people respond differently to their

▼ *The vibrations from Tibetan bells will energize a room.*

various tones. Take care when using wind chimes near fences since your neighbours may not enjoy their sound as much as you do.

Wind chimes are used to slow energy down, for example, where a staircase faces the front door, but only if they are activated as the door opens. Chimes are also used in the kitchen where people stand at the sink or stove with their backs to the door, because it is comforting to know that the chimes will sound if anyone enters.

Chimes should be hollow to allow the chi in. They can be used to enhance the Metal area of a building, particularly if placed outside the door of a west-facing house, until 2003, when they should be removed. Do not use them in a Wood area (east or south-east) because in that position they are detrimental to the energy of the area.

▼ *The deep-toned, soothing ticking of a grandfather clock is a reassuring sound.*

▲ *Here wind chimes help to balance the negative effect of a sloping ceiling.*

Water

The sound of gently bubbling water can be relaxing and there are many delightful indoor water features available. Water should be placed in the north, the east, where it is particularly auspicious until 2003, and in the south-east. From 2004 until 2023, the south-west is auspicious. Fish tanks are recommended, but must be clean, and contain living plants and natural features. Neglected tanks and unhealthy fish will have a negative effect. The preferred number of fish is nine, one being black to absorb negative chi.

Sound Enhancers

Wind chimes, Moving water, Music, Clocks, Rustling leaves

THE SENSES: TOUCH

Too often disregarded, touch is as vital as the other senses and is linked to our primeval desire to be in contact with the Earth. No mother can forget her first contact with a new baby – skin on skin is the most basic yet the most magical feeling there is. The tactile sensations in our homes affect our feelings of comfort and security. A scratchy plant that brushes our ankles as we return home will colour our evening, and a cold or harsh feel underfoot as we step out of bed affects the start of our day.

People who have impaired vision develop their other senses and touch becomes much more important. Guide dogs provide physical contact as well as being their owner's eyes. Isolated elderly people are said to live longer if they have pets to stroke.

When we are depressed, physical contact such as a hug from a relative or partner plays an important part in the healing process. Those who are deprived of physical affection as children often have difficulty making relationships.

▲ *No mother ever forgets her first skin-to-skin contact with her new baby.*

The materials with which we surround ourselves in our homes make a considerable impact on us. Few people can resist the urge to stroke a beautiful wooden bowl, although they might pass by a steel sculpture without touching it. Visitors to stately homes are asked to refrain from stroking fabrics and priceless furniture, but it is an irresistible urge, especially if the furnishings are particularly sumptuous. If we clothe ourselves and cover our furniture in fabrics which feel soft and luxurious, it will positively affect the way we feel. The yin-yang balance in our homes is revealed in the sense of touch. Yang rooms like the kitchen and study are full of yang metal objects which are utilitarian, we would never dream of connecting with these except on a working basis. In yin rooms (bedrooms and other rooms for relaxation) we put on warm and comfortable clothing and snuggle into soft beds and sofas.

▲ *Velvet furnishings and accessories feel wonderfully luxurious.*

◀ *Different textures provide sensual appeal and give a room character.*

TOUCH ENHANCERS

Plants, Wooden objects, Fabrics, Pets, People, Fruit, Smooth objects

THE SENSES: TASTE

This is not as easy as the other senses to describe in terms of Feng Shui yet it forms as great a part of our well-being as any sense. The Chinese see the tastes affiliated to the Five Elements as an integral part of life. If we are to change our perceptions and lifestyles, part of the process includes how we treat our bodies. If the chi is to flow unblocked, then we need to live in a holistic way in every aspect of our lives.

"We are what we eat" expresses the view that our diet directly affects our health. The frantic lifestyles that many of us lead mean that we often grab what we can to eat without taking balance into account. Modern medicine may come up with the cures, but if we eat healthy balanced diets then we are less likely to become ill in the first place.

▲ *Spend time preparing home-cooked meals rather than resorting to store-bought foods.*

Using yin and yang and the Five Elements in the kitchen is a science in itself. Chinese herbal medicine balances the constitution using the same techniques as Feng Shui does to balance an environment. (Chaucer's red-faced, lecherous Summoner in *The Canterbury Tales*, a lover of onions and leeks, is a classic case of an excess of the Fire element.) Being aware of the balance of elements in our food, and of the nutritional value of the man-made fast food products which we now consume, enables us to take charge of all aspects of our lives. The benefits and disadvantages of genetically engineered food products are currently being debated, but we do not need scientific reports to tell us that we should make time in our lives to use natural ingredients and not rely on packaged food when we do not know the effects of the chemicals they contain.

◀ *Using fresh natural ingredients keeps us healthy – and tastes wonderful.*

Supportive Foods

Once we have consulted the "Chinese Animals" Table and discovered which element governs our sign, we can see below which food types support us. Using "The Relationships of the Five Elements" table, we will then be able to see which of the elements are beneficial to us and which are not, and adjust our eating habits accordingly.

Wood	sour
Fire	bitter
Earth	sweet
Metal	pungent
Water	salt

THE SENSES: SMELL

Large stores know only too well the power of the sense of smell. Who can fail to be tempted by the aroma of freshly baked bread at the supermarket entrance, pumped through grills to lure us into the store where the bakery is almost always in the farthest corner?

Animals excrete pheromones to attract their mates and to mark their territory. Our homes also have a unique smell and most of us, if blindfolded, could tell which of our friends' homes we were entering. First impressions make an impact and if our homes smell less than fresh, this can affect how comfortable we and our visitors feel there.

▲ *The smell of freshly-baked bread and natural foods heighten our senses.*

▲ *A herb path by the back door will smell wonderful and give us pleasure.*

▼ *Scented oils give pleasant aromas and can make a colour statement too.*

There is something very different about the subtle smell of lavender as we brush past it in the garden on a warm evening after rain and the artificial lavender-scented air-fresheners sold commercially. Natural smells affect us in a way that manufactured scents never can, with the added advantage of not causing us respiratory problems or polluting the atmosphere. There is nothing to beat the flower-perfumed fresh air which wafts through an open window from a garden, balcony or window box. Many cultures use incense to sweeten the air, and we are now beginning to rediscover the long-lost knowledge of the benefits to health of certain aromatic oils.

Smell Enhancers

Fresh air, Aromatic oils, Plants, Fresh potpourri, Fruit

COLOUR

The Tao teaches that out of the interplay of yin and yang all things come. Yin is the blackness which absorbs all colours and yang the whiteness which reflects them. They give rise to the Five Elements and their associated colour representations, from which arise the whole spectrum of colours. Colour is vibration and we each respond to it on many levels, consciously and unconsciously. Colour affects how comfortable we are in different environments and can affect our moods. Our use of colour also affects how others perceive us. Colour is used to cure physical ailments and can be used symbolically to enhance spaces or evoke emotions.

▲ *This room works wonderfully well. All the elements are there but not contrived.*

When we use colour we are also working with light since light contains all colours, each with its own frequency. Every situation is different – each home and each room within it. The light quality depends on the aspect, the size of the windows and how they are decorated, artificial light sources and the size of the rooms. The materials we use on floors and in decorations and furnishings have the ability to reflect and transmit light or to absorb it. We can use colour to create illusions – of size (dark colours absorb more light than lighter ones); of depth (natural pigments draw light in or reflect it according to the time of day and the season); and of movement (spots of colour around a room create movement and energy there).

Light quality varies around the world. In Africa, pigments, fabrics and skins in browns, beiges and terracottas are used where the sun beats down under a bright blue sky. In Britain, where the climate suggests an indoor life and the light is much less vibrant, the same colours signify closing in and, used to excess, can lead to withdrawal and depression. Similarly, the intense colours of Indian silks and the warm colours of the Mediterranean palette have to be used with care when introduced in countries where light quality differs. However, they can play a useful role in moving the energy and, with thought, can be effective.

▼ *African colours – browns, beiges and terracottas – predominate here.*

▼ *Mediterranean colours make us think of sunshine and holidays.*

Beware Peach

Using the colour peach in your bedroom is asking for trouble if you are married. "Peach-Blossom Luck" is a well-known concept in China, meaning a husband or wife with a roving eye. A married person may be drawn into adultery. A single person, however, will have an active social life but will probably be unable to find a life partner.

◀ *In this conservatory, the Metal and Wood elements are in conflict.*

▶ *The colours green (Wood), red (Fire) and yellow (Earth) balance the Five Elements.*

The Five Elements

The five colours associated with the elements evoke the quality of the energy of each one. We use them to highlight areas of our lives we wish to concentrate on, and the Bagua diagram gives us the associated colours for each direction. In Feng Shui balance and harmony are essential. We should decorate our homes according to our tastes or we will never be comfortable there. We should remember the purpose of the room and the element associated with the direction it is in. Then we can achieve true balance and harmony. It would be treating the subject superficially to ensure that a room has, say, a cushion in each of the Five Elemental colours, but a single green-stemmed red artificial tulip in a glass vase in the south of an all-white room would bring in the Wood element in the green stem, and the Fire element in the red flower. The Metal element is represented by the white room, the Water element by the light moving through the glass vase and the Earth element in the sand used to make the glass and as the medium which gave rise to the flower.

The Colours

White represents a fresh canvas and black symbolizes a clean slate upon which we can create a picture with the colours below, as well as the many shades and hues which evolve from them.

Red: Red is stimulating and dominant, it reduces the size of rooms and increases the size of objects. It is useful as an accent colour. It is not suitable for dining rooms, children's bedrooms, kitchens or workshops. It is associated with warmth, prosperity and stimulation, but also anger, shame and hatred.

Yellow: Yellow is associated with enlightenment and intellect, it stimulates the brain and aids digestion. Its positive qualities are optimism, reason and decisiveness, while its negative are craftiness, exaggeration and rigidity. Suitable for hallways and kitchens, but not for meditation rooms or bathrooms.

Green: Green symbolizes growth, fertility and harmony; it is restful and refreshing. Its positive associations are optimism, freedom and balance, and its negatives envy and deceit. Good in therapy rooms, conservatories and bathrooms but not in family rooms, playrooms or studies.

Blue: Blue is peaceful and soothing and is linked with spirituality, contemplation, mystery and patience. Its positive associations are trust, faithfulness and stability. Negatives are suspicion and melancholia. Blue can be used in meditation rooms, bedrooms, therapy rooms and as a means of enlarging spaces, but not in family rooms, dining rooms and studies.

Purple: Encouraging vitality, purple is impressive, dignified and spiritual. Positive associations are excitement, passion and motivation, negatives are mournfulness and force. Use in bedrooms and meditation rooms but not bathrooms or kitchens.

Pink: Pink is linked with purity of thought and has the positive association of happiness and romance with no negatives. Suitable for bedrooms but not kitchens or bathrooms.

Orange: A powerful and cheerful colour, orange encourages communication. Its positive qualities are happiness, concentration and intellect, and its negative is rebelliousness. Use in living or dining rooms and hallways, but not in small rooms or bedrooms.

Brown: Brown suggests stability and weight. Its positives are safety and elegance, while its negatives are dinginess, depression and aging. Good for studies but not for bedrooms.

White: White symbolizes new beginnings, purity and innocence. its positive qualities are cleanliness and freshness, its negatives cold, lifelessness, starkness. Use for bathrooms and kitchens, not suitable for children's rooms and dining rooms.

Black: Black is mysterious and independent. Its positive qualities are intrigue, strength and allure, while its negatives are death, darkness and evil. Often used in teenagers' rooms and in bedrooms, it should not be used in young children's rooms, therapy rooms, studies or living rooms.

CLUTTER

Clutter is a state of mind. It can be the things we haven't done which prey on our minds, like unreturned telephone calls and appointments not made, or the ideas and perceptions we hoard which prevent us from doing the things we really want to do. Everything we do not use or wear, or which we are keeping in case it comes in handy one day, constitutes clutter. Inherited objects, and those given to us as presents which we do not like but feel guilty about parting with, are also clutter.

For one reason or another, perhaps due to our upbringing or past experiences, or because we doubt our own abilities, we hang on to situations and ideas which do not let us move on. We may stay in a job thinking we are indispensable or we are doing it out of a sense of loyalty, but often it is because we are afraid to take the leap and change direction. We may stay in a relationship through fear of emotional upheaval, or not accept a job away from a familiar area through fear of the unknown. All these attitudes clutter our thought processes but by clearing out our physical clutter we see the benefits of "letting go", which will help us to clear out the mental clutter restricting our development.

▲ *This low-beamed cottage room looks oppressive with fussy decoration and too many ornaments.*

▼ *A similar room but less cluttered gives a lighter, more airy feel.*

▲ *Any extraneous objects would look out of place in this cool, clutter-free bedroom, a perfect place to unwind.*

Clearing Out

"Things" constitute a major problem in most homes. Useless kitchen gadgets, empty gift boxes to recycle, presents we hate or have outgrown, inherited objects which fear of embarrassment or guilt will not let us part with, and an endless list of other items. We do not need these things in our lives if we are to open up and let new experiences in. Give them to charity shops or sell them at car-boot sales and buy something you really want.

Most of us hold on to clothes "in case" we might need them, grow back into them or our children might like them one day. It is far better to live for today and create space for something new which we will enjoy wearing now.

Books are difficult to get rid of as many people believe it is a sacrilege to throw them out. If books sit and gather dust for years on end, unread and not referred to, they too constitute clutter and stuck energy and we should move them on. The world is changing fast and information becomes out of date almost before it is in print. Should we require a

▲ *If these overladen shelves are thinned out, there will be room for new books.*

fact in ten years' time, the information will always be available elsewhere. Magazines and newspapers also constitute clutter. We are unlikely to read last week's, or even yesterday's, paper and we can always extract any information we require from magazines provided we file it immediately in a place where we are likely to find it again.

Clutter represents stagnant energy and the list is endless – blown light bulbs we keep forgetting to replace, dead wasps and dropped leaves on the window ledge, scum marks round the bath, the unfilled vinegar shaker, the squeaking door. Each of these requires only one minute's attention, but their accumulated effect can make years of difference to the pace and quality of our lives.

Do not attempt to rid the whole house of clutter in one go. Start in a small way with a drawer, and complete the whole task of clearing out, tidying and getting rid of unwanted items before moving on to the next.

▲ *There is no clutter here but enough objects and colours to make the space interesting.*

Energizing our Homes

When we move into a new house, or have had an unpleasant experience in our home, the energy there can become stuck and feel heavy. We can lighten it to some extent by clearing out all the clutter and by cleaning everywhere thoroughly.

Vibrations are important and we resonate at a level which is in harmony with the natural vibrations of the Earth. The senses also work at a vibrational level and if we can improve their quality in our homes we will feel the benefit. Often the vibrations which have caused the previous owner to behave in a certain way or adopt a certain way of life will have the same effect on us and we should take note of any problems which have befallen them before moving to a new home.

There are various methods we can use to improve the vibrations in our homes. Having cleaned and rid the house of clutter, open the windows and make a noise in every room (check first that the neighbours are out). Bells, gongs and clapping are all useful in raising the vibrational level. Take particular care to go into the corners, where energy is likely to have become stuck. Natural light should be present in the form of sunlight and candles, placed in the four corners of the room and in the centre. Smell can be introduced in the form of incense or aromatic oils. Spring water, charged by the vibrations of the moon, can be sprayed around to introduce negative ions back into the air.

▼ *Candles represent Fire. Use with care in the South and to support the West.*

▲ *Burning aromatic oils or incense raises the energy in a room.*

▼ *Candles in the corners and centre of a room will help move any stuck energy.*

USING THE SYMBOLIC BAGUA

We all wish at certain times in our lives that some aspect was working better. By focusing on a particular aspect of our lives, we can often stimulate the energy to make things work well for us. Used as a template that we can place on the plans of our home, the Symbolic Bagua gives us a tool for focus with its division into eight life sections. The eight life sections of the Bagua are: Career, Relationships, Family, Wealth, Helpful People, Children, Knowledge and Fame and each area has its own enhancers. By using some of the methods described on the following pages we can hopefully harness some of the "magic" of Feng Shui for ourselves.

The enhancements used in Feng Shui are designed to focus the mind. For example, we can create the belief that it is possible to stabilize something in our lives by using heavy objects such as stones or pictures of mountains. We can move on a "stuck" situation by creating or alluding to movement, for instance, using water or wind-blown items. Whatever image we use must have meaning for us in that we can see it physically and relate to its symbolism. Thus we should use images from our own cultures and experiences. Whatever we use, it should not clash with the element of the direction but if possible should strengthen it.

CAREER

This concerns itself with where we are going in life, either in our jobs or in our journeys through life. It can also mark the beginning of a project. ENHANCERS INCLUDE: moving images, a photograph of an aspiration such as a university, or a company brochure if applying for a job.

RELATIONSHIPS

These play an important part in our lives. Getting on well with people and having the support of partners, family or friends play a major role in a happy life.

▲ *A perfect arrangement for a table in the Relationships area of a room.*

ENHANCERS INCLUDE: double images for romance, two vases or candlesticks, a photograph of yourself with your partner or group images of friends, a poster or photograph, or a collection of something. Plants are useful to improve the chi, and ribbons or wind-activated objects will energize it as they move, provided there is a breeze. Do not use them if there is no breeze.

FAMILY

Our families, past as well as present, will have coloured who we are, how we relate to the world around us and will have

▼ *Framed photographs can be placed in the Family area of a room.*

contributed to our health and well-being. ENHANCERS INCLUDE: Family photographs and documents, and heirlooms.

WEALTH

This is often taken to be monetary wealth, but it also covers the richness of our lives, fulfilment and the accumulation of beneficial energies around us. ENHANCERS INCLUDE: coins, plants, empty bowls and movement, for example, an indoor water feature.

▲ *Chinese coins for the Wealth area – the circle symbolizes Heaven, the square Earth.*

HELPFUL PEOPLE

Interaction with others is an essential part of life, and this area is a very important one. "What goes round, comes round" and "You reap what you sow" are Eastern and Western ways of saying the same thing. If you are willing to help others and need some help in return, this is the area to focus on. ENHANCERS INCLUDE: telephones and telephone directories, and business cards.

CHILDREN

Not quite the same as family, since children are the future rather than part of the past. This area also covers personal projects – the tasks and jobs you nurture from their conception to their conclusion. ENHANCERS INCLUDE: photographs of children, project details, and your artistic and other achievements.

▲ *Family photographs of children are placed in the Children area.*

Knowledge

This is the area for wisdom and education, not of the enforced variety, but that which is sought after and which can enrich our lives. ENHANCERS INCLUDE: books, framed words of wisdom and pictures of mentors.

Fame

This does not mean notoriety for its own sake, but recognition of an undertaking well done and a sense of fulfilment. ENHANCERS INCLUDE: certificates, newspaper cuttings, products of achievement.

Feng Shui cannot help you to win the lottery but if you have worked hard and followed an honest and ethical path towards self-fulfilment, then the magic may work for you. If this happens, you will probably not want to win the lottery anyway and other, more rewarding bounty may come your way.

The Power of Feng Shui

Feng Shui works in mysterious ways and the results of any action taken may not be quite as expected. Our actions trigger the energy required to achieve the outcomes we seek. This may not correspond to what we think we need or offer a quick fix. A consultant will offer solutions having ensured that everything is balanced. If we decide to undertake some of the recommendations and not others there will be no balance. Proceed carefully. Instigate one change at a time and give it several days before introducing the next.

The following case study illustrates the unpredictable nature of Feng Shui. Richard and Anne had lived in their house for ten years and had never settled. Through lethargy they had let it run down and now could not sell it. The electric lights blew regularly and there was evidence of a water leak outside the house. The only decorating they had done was to paint the living room walls a deep pink which, together with the red carpet laid throughout the house, resulted in an overload of Fire energy.

Richard and Anne did not want to spend money on a new carpet, so they were advised to paint the walls white to drain the Fire. They had already installed a large fish tank in the Wealth area since they wanted their money to move. They put several recommendations into practice, but not the major one – the walls. The result was that the energies took over. Within a week, the washing machine flooded the ground floor, ruining the carpet and forcing out the Fire energy, the overloaded electrical system finally blew and the fish in the tank died. The Chinese use fish as a sacrifice to human bad luck, believing they soak it up on behalf of the people.

Thus Feng Shui achieved its objectives and moved the energy on. Richard and Anne were left with no choice but to fix the electrics and change the carpet, and this time they chose wisely. The changes made the house sellable and they were able to move. Never underestimate the power of Feng Shui, be prepared for the unexpected.

Home Enhancer

An enhancer for any space that will nurture the supportive energy in any home is a feature which represents all five elements. Fill a glass or crystal bowl (Earth) with blue glass nuggets (Earth and Water), top up with water and a floating candle (Fire) and some flowers or petals (Wood). Add coins (Metal) to complete the cycle.

The Centre of the Bagua

The centre is a special place. In a house it is where the occupants meet and where the energies accumulate and flow on. It should be treated well, be bright and welcoming, and not be cluttered. Do not introduce a light fitting with five bulbs here; glass and crystal light fittings will stimulate the area far better. A round rug often works well.

The Right Time

Most of us will have heard or read of people who have used Feng Shui and received rewards – a job, a long-awaited child, or a partner We may be tempted to take Feng Shui on board and tweak every area of our homes in order to achieve perfection. Life is not perfect, however, and it is constantly changing. Essentially, the energies of the various directions change over time. Thus if we activate a particular area when the energies are good, things will be fine. If we leave whatever we have done when the energies are inauspicious, then we will create problems.

The adage, "If it ain't broke, don't fix it" applies. Remember when using these symbolic measures that the compass directions and their related elements are still important.

INVESTIGATING YOUR HOME

The following Feng Shui case study can only offer a glimpse into the kind of analysis which takes place when investigating a home.

William and Julia and their son Steven moved into their apartment a year ago. Julia feels comfortable there but William and Steven do not, and Steven has gradually become very run down and cannot concentrate on his schoolwork. William does some freelance work at home to supplement his income, but has not been getting many clients lately. There is tension and the couple's relationship is suffering. A Feng Shui consultant investigates the birthday of each person, their animal, the corresponding element and the compatibility of the animals.

William is a Fire – Rooster, Julia is a Metal + Rat and Steven a Water – Pig. This indicates that while William and Julia have a workable relationship with Steven, William and Julia's relationship can be difficult. According to the Five Elements relationships, Fire (William) is weakened by Metal (Julia), who in turn is weakened by Water (Steven). Being a Metal Rat with yang characteristics, Julia is quite strong and domineering so can hold her own. As a Fire Rooster, William can be inflexible and is not easily swayed by others' emotions so may not be sympathetic to Steven. Fortunately, as a Water Pig, Steven accepts that things are difficult and is perceptive enough to steer clear when necessary.

▼ *This bed is well balanced by the matching tables and lamps on either side.*

▲ *The position of the bed is crucial. It should be protected behind and face an auspicious direction for the occupants.*

Next, the consultant looked at the magic numbers, the corresponding east and west directions, each person's favourable and unfavourable directions, and the compass direction of the house.

William is a 7 and belongs to the west group. Julia, a 4, belongs to the east group and Steven, an 8, belongs to the west group. The house faces south-east, an east group direction, and is therefore most supportive of Julia. William's best direction is north-west, which is missing from the house. His office falls between the south and south-west sectors. The south-west is his second-best direction and the south his sixth. Steven's room has geopathic stress by the head of his bed. His best direction is south-west and his second is north-west. Julia's best direction is north and the second south. The consultant then looked at the shape of the house, Steven's room, William's desk position and William and Julia's bed. He made recommendations listed below.

KEY TO DIAGRAM

1. A mirror here symbolically completes the house shape and seemingly draws in the energy of the missing section. A metal frame is used which represents the element of the area.

2. The head of the bed was re-positioned to face south-west, Steven's best direction, and to remove him from the stressed area.

3. Steven's desk now faces north-west, his second-best direction. This also enables him to see the door and protects him from the fast-moving chi along the long passage. The bookcase, aided by the plant on top, also protects him from the chi in the passage.

4. Semi-circular tables with silk flowers slow the chi further. The passage was too dark for live plants.

5. William's desk now faces north-west, his best position. A plant behind him prevents stagnant energy from building up in the corner. A plant on the desk deflects fast-moving chi through the door and hides the point which would symbolically stab him as he enters.

6. The "mouth of chi" to the stove, the point of entry of the energy source and symbolic of wealth, comes from the south, Julia's second-best position.

7. In this room the bed is best in Julia's best position, north. A mirror should not reflect the bed, so a small mirror has been used here (see 1).

8. Two square tables, signifying containment, are placed on either side of the bed.

9. A picture of a couple is placed here to symbolize togetherness in the symbolic Relationships area.

10. In the compass Relationships area, which is Earth, stones have been placed on the bathroom and toilet windowsills.

11. A plant is placed on the windowsill here to support William's personal Fire element.

▼ *A floor plan of William and Julia's room after the changes were made. The numbers correspond with **the** captions in the box, left.*

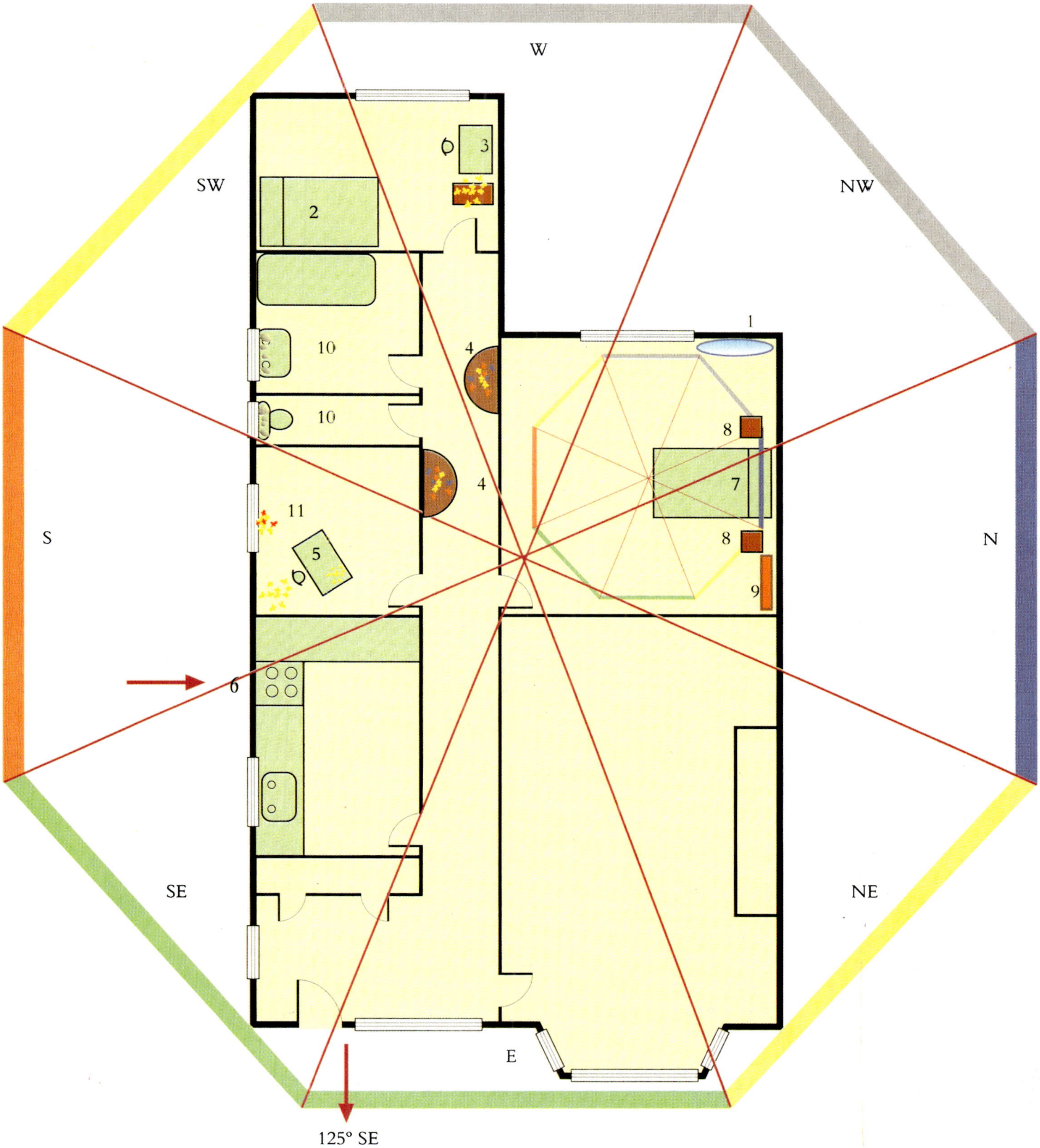

PUTTING THE PRINCIPLES INTO PRACTICE

Now that we are familiar with the basic principles of Feng Shui, it is time to look at our homes room by room and see if we can arrange them differently to create spaces that will nourish us. When we move energy about there may be unexpected consequences, so it is important to proceed slowly and discover what will work for us. Allow children to create spaces that are meaningful for them at each stage of their development.

HALLS, LOBBIES AND STAIRCASES

When we step though the front door, the first impression we have of a house is the hall. If it is light and spacious with a pleasant, fresh smell, and is clean and tidy, then our spirits will rise. A long dark corridor, the smell of last night's cooking and a stack of newspapers in the corner will set the tone for the whole house. If the energy channels of the house are restricted or blocked, this can have a knock-on effect. Those who live with narrow, dark hallways may suffer restriction mentally or as a blockage in one of their body channels. Psychologically such a place is depressing. It is possible to deal with this by using bright colours and mirrors. Coat hooks at levels to accommodate even the smallest family members and shoe cupboards or racks can all make our homecoming easier. The last thing we need to see on returning is a mess; we will not look forward to returning home.

◀ *A brightly lit and well-kept hallway is very welcoming when we return home.*

▼ *Plenty of coat hooks and storage space prevent the hall from becoming cluttered.*

THE VIEW FROM THE DOOR

If a door opens immediately on to a wall, people will feel overwhelmed and they will feel life is a struggle. A landscape picture which attracts the eye will give the illusion of drawing us on into the main part of the home. An entrance opposite the back door or window will funnel chi straight out and it will not have the opportunity to circulate. Keep doors closed, place plants on windowsills or install coloured glass into the back door window to reflect chi back into the room. If the first room seen from the door is the kitchen, it will be the first port of call on returning home. Food will be on our minds before we do anything else. Children will tumble in on returning from school with outdoor clothes and school bags to raid the fridge. An office opposite the door will encourage us to rush in to check the answerphone. Work will be on our minds and we will not be able to relax. Toilet doors should be kept closed at all times, according to Chinese wisdom, so that we do not watch our wealth being flushed away, and a closed lid is an extra precaution.

▼ *In this spacious hall, natural finishes, and a variety of shapes, colours and textures create an energetic space.*

HALL CLUTTER

Coats, Shoes, Bags, Junk mail, Free papers, Laundry, Items to take upstairs

Communal Lobbies

In buildings which were once large houses but are now small flats, or in badly managed apartment blocks, the communal entrance lobby is often a problem. There are two ways of approaching a dirty, messy, badly decorated lobby: negatively, by blaming others, or by taking positive action. Stuck personal chi is often a contributory factor to stuck energy in a house so it is in the interests of all the occupants to move it.

▼ *Plants either side of the entrance welcome the residents of this apartment block.*

CASE STUDY

Nancy lived in a house that had been converted into four flats, with a communal hallway and staircase. The turnover of residents was high and the communal areas were a mess. Approaches to the landlord and other tenants failed, so Nancy painted the hall herself and put up a shelf with a box for each flat into which she sorted the mail and free papers. A bright poster and a plant completed the project. Almost immediately, the neighbours became more friendly and began to stop for a chat. The turnover of tenants slowed down and within two years Nancy and her neighbours bought the freehold of the property and set about renovating it. As a result the house was transformed and has become a very desirable place to live.

▲ *The front door of this house opens directly on to the stairs. There is no barrier against the chi, which enters through the door and rushes through the house too quickly.*

Staircases

Often the front door of a house or apartment opens straight on to the staircase. Again the chi will be funnelled without having the chance to circulate so it is a good idea to block the view of the stairs by using a plant, a bookcase or other piece of furniture. If this is not possible, a round rug or a crystal chandelier will gather the chi in the hall. A wind chime which sounds as the door opens will also help to slow down the chi.

Some attention should be paid to how staircases and hallways are lit and decorated. Low ceilings can feel restricting and make the moving of furniture difficult, and a steep stairwell causes problems when decorating, but overcoming these difficulties and making the best of your hall and staircase will pay off.

The staircase should be in proportion to the dimensions of the rest of the house. Steep stairs conduct chi too quickly. Modern conversions often have spiral staircases leading to the bedroom area. These are considered inauspicious in Feng Shui because they resemble a corkscrew through the home. Wrap some ivy or green silk around the staircase and make sure a light shines from top to bottom. Stairs with open treads allow the chi to escape. Place plants, real or symbolic, representing Wood energy underneath.

▲ *A large plant placed in this position makes all the difference. It masks the corner of the stairs from view of the front door and slows down the chi.*

Chi Flow Improvement in a Hallway

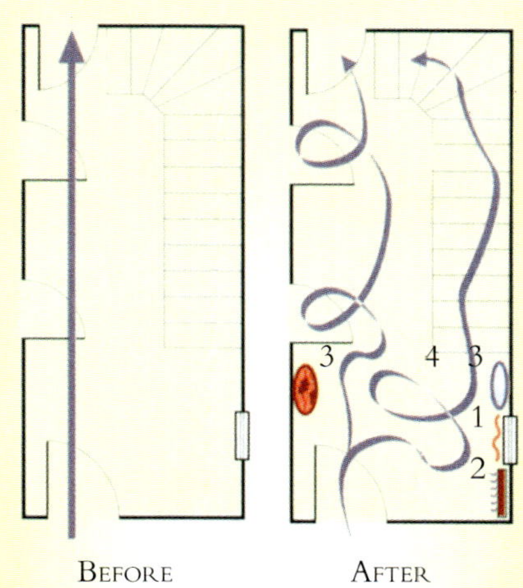

1. Muslin curtains create a pause between the outside and the house.
2. Children and guests leave coats, shoes and umbrellas neatly on hooks and racks. These also block the view of the stairs from the door and hide outer garments from the inside.
3. At the foot of the stairs a mirror reflects a plaster plate with a painted landscape, which has the effect of drawing visitors deeper into the house.
4. The children can go up to their rooms at this point and may not even enter the kitchen until suppertime. If the chi flow upstairs works, they may even have washed their hands first!

LIVING ROOMS

A living room is used for a number of activities – for relaxation, as a family room where games are played, and an entertainment room for watching television and playing music. In some homes, particularly in apartments, the living room may have a dining area attached, or part of it may be used as a study or office space. The arrangement of the room is therefore important if these diverse functions are to be supported successfully.

▼ *Natural materials, lots of colour and a pleasant view give this living room an energetic feeling.*

Living areas should be welcoming, and the colour scheme can help this. Proportion is also important. In barn or warehouse conversions with large open-plan spaces and high ceilings, it is preferable to create small groupings of furniture rather than attempt to create a single room within the space. In small rooms, try to keep bookcases and built-in wall units low, otherwise the room will feel top-heavy and appear to close in. It is especially important to be able to screen off study or office areas so that work is not constantly preying on the mind when we are trying to relax.

SEATING

Living rooms are yin spaces full of comfortable, fabric-covered seats which are also yin. Chairs and sofas with high backs and arms are protective and represent the Tortoise, Dragon, Tiger formation offering support to those who sit in them. A footstool nearby marks the Phoenix position.

Those sitting in the room should, where possible, not sit with their backs to the door. Guests should feel welcome when they come, so offer them the prime positions facing the door. In rooms where chairs and sofas are not backed by

▶ *All these chairs are supportive to the occupants, adding to the peaceful energy of this elegant room.*

a wall, create stability behind the seating by placing a table or bookcase there. Furniture is always best if it has rounded edges. If the bedroom leads off the main living area, make sure that the furniture is not sending a "poison arrow" into the room from a corner. Keep doors from the living room closed.

Backs to the Door

If you have a visitor who does more than their fair share of the talking, position them with their back to the door to reduce their dominance in the group. In addition, uninvited guests who you would like to leave as soon as possible should be also be placed outside the main group.

▲ *The Earth colour on the walls and lamps is welcoming, but the blue Water energy drains it.*

▼ *Plenty of Earth colours on the walls and in the furnishing fabrics make this a nurturing and cosy room.*

Seating Arrangements

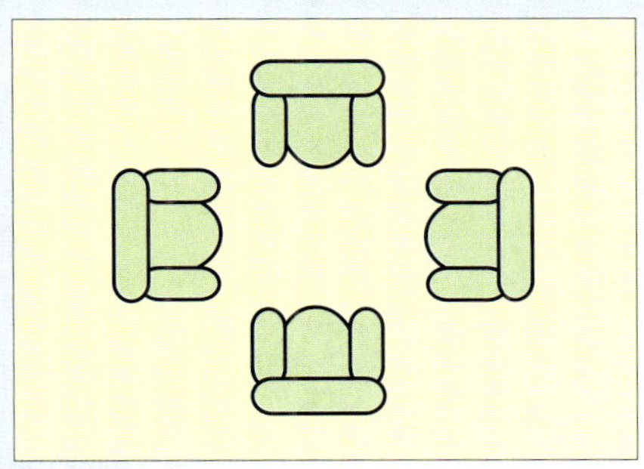

▲ This seating arrangement is suitable for a harmonious family or social gathering. The "circle" is used in all cultures for community gatherings.

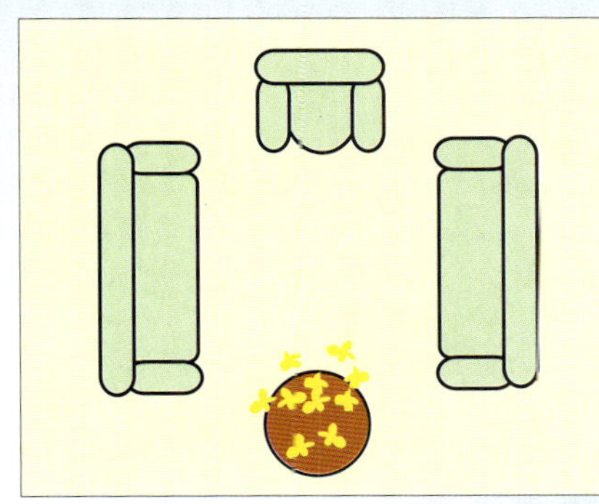

▲ This arrangement is useful for a meeting as it focuses people on whatever is taking place, but also has space to allow the energy in.

▶ In this arrangement the table is sending a "poison arrow" into the bedroom. Re-position the furniture to prevent this.

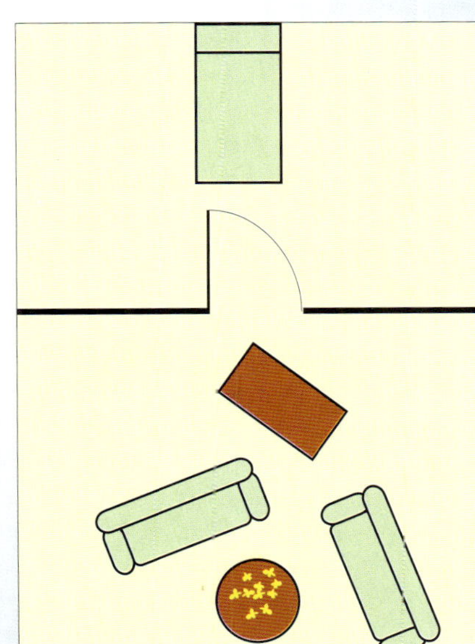

▼ The television arrangement spells death to social chat and family unity.

Fireplaces

In previous centuries fires were used for cooking, warmth and protection, and were carefully tended. The communal fire was the focal point of family life. These days a real fire is less common, and when it is present it is often a secondary heat source, lit only at festival times or at weekends, rather than a vital source of life. A coal or wood fire, however, always makes a room feel welcoming and draws family and friends toward it.

Since a fireplace is an opening into the room, a mirror above it is beneficial to symbolically prevent the chi from escaping. A fireguard will be necessary, especially where there are children. Plants positioned on either side of the fireplace represent Wood energy, which will symbolically feed the fire and enhance its gathering qualities.

The chimney wall often juts into the living room, creating alcoves on either side. Be aware of this when placing chairs as people sitting in them may be the recipients of harmful chi from the corners. Soften any jutting angles on the mantelpiece with hanging plants.

▲ *A cosy living area has been created in the middle of this vast space.*

Lighting

A variety of lighting is necessary, particularly if the room is used for a number of purposes. Bright lighting is required for family activities and for children playing, and also in north-facing rooms which get little natural light. In addition, there should be softer lights; uplighters in the corners or wall lights, and task lighting if there is a desk in the room.

▼ *A larger sofa would give more support in this well-proportioned room.*

Screens

Ideally, kitchens and dining rooms should be separate from the main living room. Where they are attached or adjoining, screen them off in some way or food will become too important and grazing habits will be encouraged.

A Balance of Light

▲ Here the blue (Water) energy is overpowering the green (Wood) energy and the red (Fire) energy.

▲ The red lamp makes an enormous difference, restoring the balance of the various energies in the room.

▲ *The additional colours and the mixture of whites turn this into a warm room.*

Televisions and Stereos

Always arrange the seating so that it does not allow the television to be the main focus of the room. Where the TV is the focal point, instead of a warm, gathering fire, the family will sit in rows and communication will be negligible. (However, this is better than each child having a television in their bedroom, which can result in a total breakdown of the social aspects of family life.) Position stereos as far away from seating as possible to avoid electromagnetic radiation.

Furnishings

If the living room is painted in a single colour, small areas of stimulation are necessary to keep the energy moving. Too much fabric can harbour dust and fade, creating stagnant energy, but in a room where people gather curtains help to create a cosy feeling. Undressed windows and ones with blinds can be harsh and, being rectangular, add to the Earth energy of the room. In rooms that have many rectangular features and are also decorated in Earth colours – magnolia, brown, mustard – the energy will feel sluggish and can make the occupants feel depressed. Keep family rooms well-ventilated and allow in as much natural light as possible.

◀ *A small television set is far better than a large set that will dominate the room.*

▶ *Natural materials and fresh colour give this room a good feel.*

Paintings and Objects

We should always be aware of the effect of the images with which we surround ourselves, since they reflect our inner selves. Gruesome images and spiky objects can reflect inner turmoil, whereas bells, rainbows and pictures of the seasons will reflect inner peace. If we live alone our living rooms will reflect our desire for a peaceful haven or our need for companionship and we can use the space to create positive atmospheres.

Images and artwork displayed in family spaces should be cheerful and reflect pleasant and harmonious themes. Ideally, photographs of the family should be displayed in this room. If one child is more artistically talented than the others, in the interests of family harmony, his/her achievements should not be spread all round the room or the other children will feel that they are failures by comparison. Guns, swords and other weapons have no place in the living room.

It is important that the contents of the home, especially the communal areas, should be balanced and reflect the lives of all the occupants. If our working lives are hectic, our living rooms will reflect our desire for a peaceful haven. Lonely people should, however, use this room to reflect their need for companionship and remove all single images – such as pictures of lone figures; ornaments should

▲ *This is a room designed for sitting and chatting. The round table ensures the conversation will not get too serious.*

▼ *This oval urn prevents stagnation in an otherwise gloomy corner.*

▼ *We should surround ourselves with positive images. The clean lines of this carved wooden bird make the energy soar.*

Living Room Clutter

Newspapers and magazines
Full ashtrays
Used cups
Children's toys after bedtime
Fallen plant leaves
Unpaid bills and unanswered letters on the mantelpiece

be grouped in pairs, and the room should be used to create a positive energy.

Where we share our homes with friends, with a partner, or as part of a family, we need to create personal spaces within which we feel comfortable and where we can express ourselves. Relationships with those whose horoscopes or numbers conflict with our own are common and we will be familiar with the phrase "opposites attract". Formulae may suggest, however, that one partner should live in an east group house and the other a west group house. We have to be practical. Where the energies of a house favour one occupant more than the other, it is important to take this into account and enable the other to express themselves within the house and to position themselves in favourable directions in bed and when working and relaxing.

► *We should position ourselves in favourable directions surrounded by supportive images.*

CASE STUDY

When David and Sarah retired to the coast from their family house in the country, they left behind a large garden which Sarah had lovingly tended for 20 years. David, a keen angler, purchased a share in a boat and joined the local fishing club, and soon had a full and active social life. Photographs of his activities, pictures of boats and his prize catch preserved in a glass case along with accompanying trophies appeared around the house. Having decorated the house and finished arranging the tiny garden, Sarah became bored and felt unfulfilled in her new life, but since David was so happy she kept to herself the fact that she preferred life in the country.

As David had an office and a workshop, it was agreed that Sarah should have part of the house designated as her own space and the living room was chosen as her personal area.

1. Sarah, a Water Rooster, was being overwhelmed by too much water in her new environment. A large plant in the North symbolically drained some of the Water energy.

2. Born in 1934, Sarah's magic number is 3, making her best direction south, so the seating was arranged accordingly.

3. David's fishing trophies and photographs were placed in his study and, since she did not want to hurt his feelings but did not like having dead animals in the house, Sarah compromised and suggested that the prize fish could go into the bathroom and not be banished to the workshop. Sarah framed some watercolours she had painted at their former home and hung them on the wall instead.

4. To dispel the idea that this lifestyle was to be Sarah's lot for the rest of her retirement, and particularly since the windows faced west and the setting sun, the rising growth energy of the east was stimulated with a picture of the rising sun.

5. A mirror placed in the south-east, also representing Wood, reflected the garden and drew it into the house to support Sarah's love of the countryside.

6. After reading a Feng Shui book, Sarah decided to try to activate the Relationships area to see if she could find new friends. Using the Symbolic Bagua, she put up a poster of a group of people chatting, which was also reflected in the mirror, thus doubling the effect.

When the changes had been made, a neighbour visited and admired Sarah's watercolours and suggested she should display them at the local garden show. Someone admired and purchased them, and with the money Sarah bought a greenhouse where she now grows exotic plants which she paints portraits of and sells. Interestingly, the picture of the rising sun is, according to the Symbolic Bagua, in Sarah's Offspring or Projects area. She is now an active member of a gardening group, where she has made lots of friends and is busy all the time.

DINING ROOMS

The dining room is a social area where family and friends can meet, talk and enjoy good food together. As snacking and "grazing" typify modern eating habits, the dining room has diminished in importance. For the Chinese it is a centre of wealth, where a full table, often mirrored to apparently double the quantity, is indicative of the financial standing of the family.

Dining room colours should be bright and stimulating to whet the appetite. Dull, lifeless colours should be avoided as they suppress the appetite. Lighting should be chosen with care to complement the food and not cast shadows over the table. Candles can be romantic, but may get in the way when people are serving themselves or become irritating if they are too tall or flicker. Beware of pictures and ornaments that conjure up inappropriate images – hunting scenes or

► *If there is a window behind the dining table, it is important that the chairs have backs to them for support.*

▲ *This wonderful dining room has a lovely view of the garden. Small shelves would protect diners from the axe-like glass overhead.*

▲ *A lovely setting for a meal. The candles are low enough not to get in the way or prevent people seeing each other properly.*

▼ *An excellent dining room – the chairs are backed by a wall and the mirror reflects the table, doubling its apparent size.*

▲ *Kitchen diners make a good setting for an informal meal, and round tables are ideal as they encourage lively conversation.*

▶ *Low candles such as these pretty shell candles are safer than tall ones at the table.*

a china pig collection are not suitable if you have vegetarian friends. The best images to display are ones of fruit, the fresh, clean outdoors, or of friends dining. If mirrors are used, position them so that diners will not feel uncomfortable.

High-backed solid chairs, preferably with arms, represent the supportive Tortoise, Tiger, Dragon formation. Sitting positions are considered to be very important. The prime positions in the room should have a solid wall behind them and a view of the door. The most vulnerable positions are those with a door behind them, followed by seats with their backs to a window.

Table shapes are also important and can affect the quality of the meal. Round tables tend to make your guests leave early because the chi spins round them, while square tables allow more stability. Rectangular tables are difficult as those at either end tend to feel left out. The best shaped tables are octagonal, which not only enable guests to interact with everyone else on the table, but also represent the Cosmos as reflected in the Bagua.

Balanced Eating

Much has been made of balanced eating recently but this is not a new concept. Since ancient times, diet has formed part of the same philosophy as Feng Shui. Meals are planned to create a yin-yang balance and with the nature of the Five Elements in mind. Some foods are regarded as having yin qualities and some yang, and different tastes are associated with the Five Elements.

We should learn to recognize the signals that our bodies and our state of mind give out and recognize whether we are becoming yin (feeling tired and slowing down) or yang (unable to relax and stressed). We can balance our diets by ensuring we eat the same proportion of yin foods – such as alcohol, chocolate, citrus fruits, coffee and sugar – and yang foods – such as cheese, eggs, meat, pulses and salt.

▲ *Conservatory dining rooms are becoming popular and can create light, spacious areas for eating in all the year round.*

◀ *In such a large area as this your guests might feel slightly ill-at-ease. High-backed chairs would help dispel any nervousness. A round table is a good shape for this room.*

Yin and yang attributes are attached to each of the Five Elements, and in Chinese medicine herbs and other remedies, including food, are recommended in order to maintain a healthy and balanced body. In northern countries (yin) there is a tendency and need to consume more cooked foods (yang) while in southerly areas (yang) more raw foods are consumed. Eating native products in season is highly recommended.

Tastes and the Elements

Wood	Fire	Earth	Metal	Water
spring	summer	late summer	autumn	winter
sour	bitter	sweet	pungent	salt
yin	yang	yin	yin	yang

THE BAGUA AND FAMILY SEATING

We have seen that each sector of the Bagua can represent several things. The sectors are associated with particular manifestations of the energy of one of the Five Elements – in its yin or yang form. Each also represents a certain type of energy reflecting a direction, season or time period. The Symbolic Bagua suggests the journey of life, with each sector representing a particular aspect – career, wealth, relationships and so on.

Here we look at the energies of each sector in terms of the family. In the past the Bagua may have been used to allocate rooms in a house, but great fun can be had using the Bagua in seating plans at the dining table. The diagram (right) shows the arrangement of family members around the Bagua. Each represents the energy of the direction they fall within, and this can add further insight into the qualities of the energy in that location. Bear in mind that we are looking at centuries-old imagery; house-husbands and executive mothers should appreciate that this is an energetic quality, not stereotyping.

FATHER: Representative of solidity, the leader and the head of the household. Sometimes called the Creative energy.

MOTHER: Complements the Father. A nurturing, supporting energy. Also known as Receptive energy.

ELDEST SON: Also known as the energy of Thunder and the Dragon, whose energy erupts from below and soars upwards.

ELDEST DAUGHTER: Called the Gentle energy, this energy is perceptive and supportive and represents growth.

MIDDLE SON: Sometimes called the Abysmal energy, which suggests hard work without much reward.

MIDDLE DAUGHTER: A Clinging energy, representing a fire, bright and impenetrable outside but burning-out and weakness within.

YOUNGEST SON: Also called the Mountain energy, suggesting a firm stillness and waiting.

YOUNGEST DAUGHTER: Also known as the Joyful, or the Lake, which suggests a deep inward energy or stubbornness and a weak, excitable exterior.

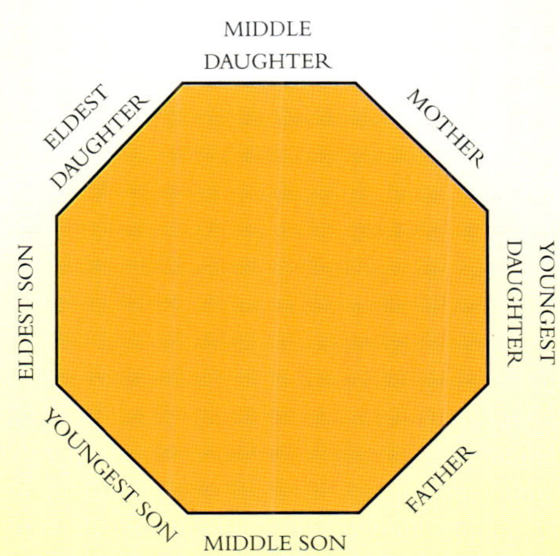

THE DINNER PARTY

The Bagua can be used for all sorts of social occasions. Imagine that an executive is retiring from your company and you and a rival are in the running for the job. You arrange a dinner party and invite your boss, your rival and a young employee who reminds you of yourself when younger and whom you have taken under your wing. You can use the Bagua to seat your colleagues and their partners to ensure that you will get the job.

Out of respect, the boss and his/her partner are in the prime positions. When the boss is not giving any attention to the vivacious spouse of your protégé (with his back thus turned to your rival) and is concentrating on eating, the first people he/she will see when he/she looks up are you and your partner, and also your protégé. Your rival, seated in the worst position, representing hard toil for no reward, and his partner are too far apart to be able to support each other. The attention of the boss's spouse is taken up by the bubbly person chatting to the boss, and your partner opposite. After several attempts at conversation, with no support, your rival's spouse gives up. The result is that you get the job, and your protégé moves into your shoes.

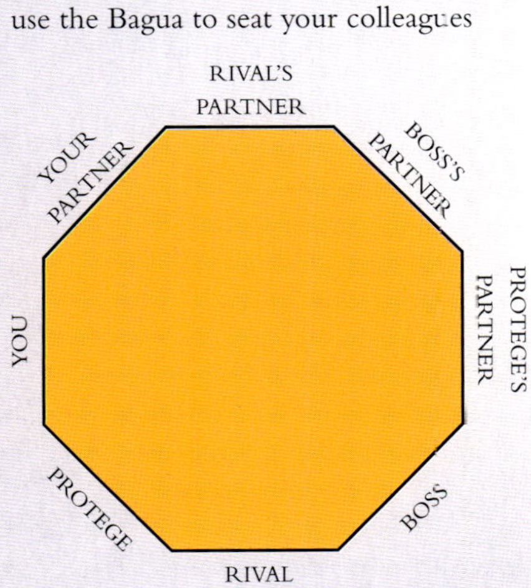

◀ *Manipulate situations by using ancient interpretations of the energies of the Bagua.*

▶ *Whatever the occasion or intention a decorated table with well-presented, nourishing food will be supportive.*

KITCHENS

The kitchen is probably the most important room in the house and, being multi-functional, often the most difficult room to deal with. Apart from its primary purpose for storing, preparing and consuming food, it is a meeting place for family and friends, a children's play area and occasionally even an office. More than any other room, the kitchen holds clues to a person's lifestyle. It is the health centre of our lives and it is important that it functions well and supports us.

The direction a kitchen faces has a powerful effect on its function. In ancient China, kitchens were open to the south-east to catch the breezes that would help ignite the cooking stove. This practical application of Feng Shui reflects the principle of living in harmony with nature. When we have discovered in which direction our kitchen lies, we can use "The Relationships of the Five Elements" table to help us create balance.

A red kitchen facing south will be overloaded with yang Fire energy which needs to be drained. "The Relationships of the Five Elements" table shows that Earth drains Fire, so incorporating a stone floor or some stone pots would be appropriate. As the Fire element is far too dominant, representation of the Water element in the form of a picture of water or a blue blind or tablecloth would also considerably lessen the effect. Plants would not be advisable here since they belong to the Wood element, which feeds Fire and makes it stronger. In the case of all kitchens, the Fire element, represented by the cooker and electrical cooking appliances, is in conflict with Water, represented by actual water and the fridge. A delicate balance has to be maintained.

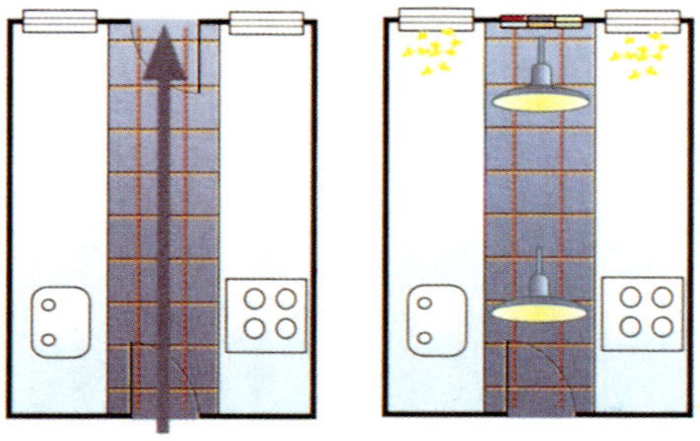

▲ *Left: Chi rushes through this kitchen, creating a feeling of discomfort.*
Right: Ceiling lights and plants by the window slow down the chi and contain it.

▲ *Task lighting is ideal in kitchens. Here it gives focus in a high-ceilinged room, where other lights would cast shadows.*

Some modern kitchens are so streamlined that nothing is on display. Since the major features consist of only one or two colours or materials, the kitchen can appear lifeless. Sometimes a dash of red, or a green plant can bring a room to life. Ideally, kitchens should contain something from each of the elements.

The Stove

The stove is considered to be of great importance. Where possible, the energy source which flows into it, the electric socket or the gas pipe, should be in your most auspicious location. It is important not to feel vulnerable while standing at the stove. The reasoning behind this is that, since food is the prime source of nourishment and health for the family, it is important that the cook should not feel jumpy or the food will be spoiled through lack of concentration.

A reflective surface positioned behind the cooker, or a chrome cake tin or toaster nearby, will enable the cook to be aware of anyone entering the room. A wind chime or other sound device activated by the door opening will also serve the same purpose.

▲ *The kitchen stove is the heart of the home and should face in an auspicious direction.*

▲ *If you cook with your back to the door, shiny objects can reflect the space behind you.*

▲ *Keep your cooking area as clutter-free as possible.*

CHI FLOW IN THE KITCHEN

As elsewhere in the house, chi should be able to circulate freely round the kitchen. It cannot do this if the kitchen door is in direct line with the outside doors and windows since it is channelled straight through. If this is the case, you should aim to slow it down by physical or psychological barriers. The simplest method is to keep the door closed. Barriers could include furniture, vegetable trolleys or large plants. More subtle methods such as mobiles, lampshades and colour can be used to create visual and psychological barriers. Barriers can be detrimental, however, and a tall fridge or cupboard by the door will block the natural flow of chi into the room.

Fast-moving chi is not the only problem. Stagnant chi is particularly harmful in a kitchen. It can occur in a room with

▲ *Smooth, rounded lines allow the chi to move gently around this lovely kitchen.*

◄ *In a kitchen where the chi flows straight out of the window, place some red glass, plants or another barrier on the windowsill to slow it down.*

▼ *Eye-level cupboards over the cooking area are oppressive; open shelves would be better.*

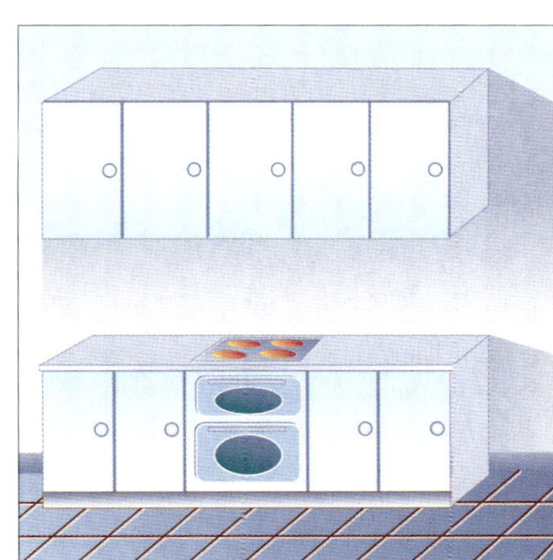

CASE STUDY

This typical modern kitchen has both good and bad points.

1 The cooker, sink and fridge are in an excellent triangle formation.

2 The corner of this work surface has been rounded off so there are no "poison arrows" which otherwise would have pointed at the chairs.

3 The energy is not moving in this corner. A plant or mirror here will help to move the chi along.

4 The chairs have their backs to the door and are vulnerable. A large plant or vegetable basket would act as a barrier. Alternatively, the table and chairs could move out of the corner so the door is visible from each chair.

no window and poor circulation, or in a room with dark inaccessible corners. One cause of this is simply having too much furniture in the room, which impedes movement. If we catch our hip on the corner of a table each time we need to get to the fridge our body chi will not flow as it should because we are forever twisting to avoid it. At the end of a long day, a ready-made meal may seem an easier option than dodging the furniture to obtain fresh ingredients from the fridge. Rather than put things away, we may be tempted to leave out milk bottles and food, which can have health risks as well as cluttering up the kitchen.

Kitchen Clutter

Rotting fruit and vegetables
Out-of-date packets and jars
Unlabelled boxes in the freezer
Unused gadgets
Rarely used electrical appliances
Over-full waste bins
Odd pieces of crockery
Plastic bags
Bits of string
Laundry
Crumbs
Fallen plant leaves
Things which "might come in handy"

Piles of newspapers, overflowing rubbish bins, crumbs and stains on work surfaces all represent stagnant chi. Another undesirable feature of many apartment kitchens is the cat-litter tray. Bathrooms and toilets are not desirable near a kitchen because of the antipathy of the Water element to the Fire element of the kitchen, as well as for more obvious reasons. If we take trouble with the location of our own toilets and bathrooms, we should also give serious thought to those of our pets.

Pointed corners are a feature of most kitchens – the edges of appliances, the corners of work surfaces, knives, shelf edges and the edges of slatted blinds all send out chi that makes us feel uncomfortable. Knives should be kept out of sight in a drawer and work surfaces should have rounded edges, if possible. Among the worst sources of this inauspicious chi, known as "poison arrows", are wall cupboards. Most of us have banged our heads on an open door, but even when shut the cupboards can be oppressive. There is a tendency to store far too much in the kitchen – out-of-date jars, gadgets we never use, a dinner service we only bring out on special occasions or when the person who gave it to us visits. If we examine the contents of the kitchen, we will probably be able to throw away or relocate many items to give us more space and enable the chi to flow. There are many useful storage systems available which will enable us to make optimum use of the space.

▼ *Efficient storage systems reduce kitchen clutter; review the contents regularly.*

▲ *Waist-high cupboards by a work surface are preferable to overhead ones, which can be oppressive, especially in a small kitchen. Keep any frequently used equipment to hand and store cooking equipment, rather than crockery or food, inside cupboards that are adjacent to an oven.*

The Healthy Kitchen

Kitchens appeal to all our senses. Magazine pictures tantalizingly portray them as rooms featuring bowls of fresh fruit and views over lawns and flower beds. Healthy, freshly prepared meals can be seen on tables where friends and family gather to socialize. Delicious smells, tastes, merry sounds, abundance and happiness radiate from these pages but the reality is often different. Modern kitchens, far from supporting and stimulating us, can unbalance and affect us negatively. The noise from kitchen gadgets, the contamination of food by substances used in packaging, dangers posed by the cleaning agents we use on our work surfaces, the chemicals used in food production, all serve to assault our senses and diminish our well-being.

▲ *There is plenty of Wood in this country-style kitchen, which provides excellent levels of energy.*

CASE STUDY

Mary's kitchen was dark and oppressive. The small area in front was a particular problem because the staircase formed a deep slope, and the space on the left was too narrow for conventional units. The main area felt claustrophobic, with work surfaces and wall cupboards sending out chi in the form of "poison arrows". The cooker could not be moved to face Mary's best direction but this was considered secondary to getting the chi flow right.

1. Red, yellow and green opaque glass was used in the south-facing door and window overlooking a brick wall to stimulate the south Fire element. The light coming through the glass sent a rainbow effect into the room which stimulated the chi there.

2. The plants on the windowsill were placed to stimulate the Wood element of the East.

3. The work triangle is in place. Care was taken not to place the fridge opposite the cooker, so there is no conflict between the Fire and Water elements.

4. Pale yellow cupboards and a terracotta container in the north-east introduced the Earth element.

5. Stainless steel pans hung in the north-west stimulate the Metal area.

6. These oddly sized and shaped walls were made into cupboards to make the shape regular. The one on the right was built over and around the washing machine and drier. Glass doors were put in front of the window to enable the coloured light to shine in. Mary placed her china collection on glass shelves here.

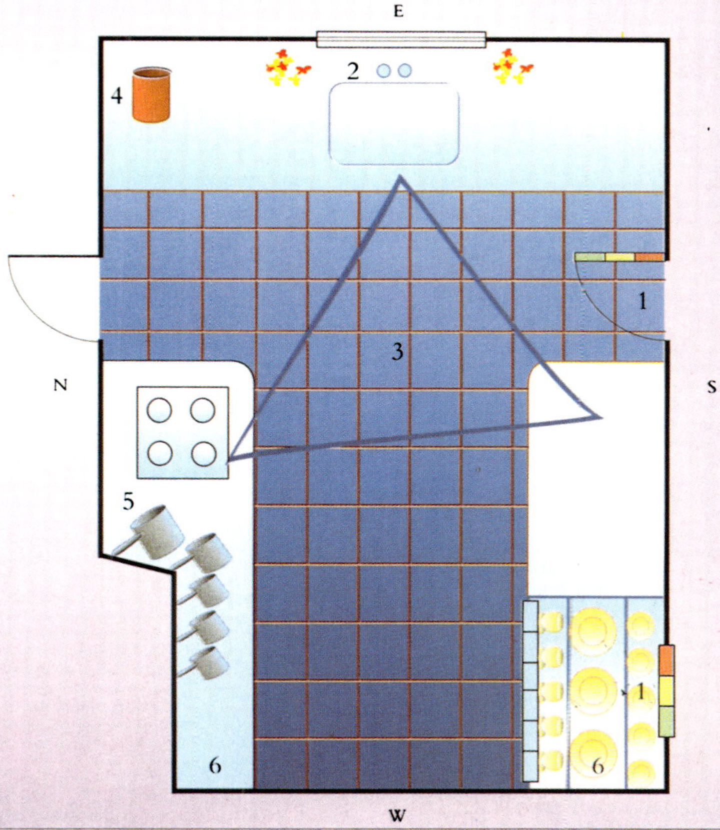

BEDROOMS

The bedroom is considered to be one of the most important rooms of the house in Feng Shui. Adults spend a third of their lives in bed, while children and teenagers often spend even more than this. We must therefore be certain that these rooms are suitable for relaxing and regenerating us, as well as for encouraging romance in our lives.

Beds

A bed should face in one of our auspicious directions, which means that the top of our heads should point that way when we are lying down. Where partners have different auspicious directions, there has to be a compromise; for example, if the house is a West group house and favours one partner, then the bed direction should favour the other.

The best bed position is diagonally opposite the door. The element of surprise is never recommended in the bedroom. If the occupants of the bed do not have a reasonable view of the door, a mirror should be placed to reflect anyone entering. Having the foot of the bed in direct line with the door is known as the "mortuary position" in China because coffins are placed in that position when awaiting collection.

Doors and windows situated opposite each other are not considered auspicious. If a line of chi between two windows – or a door and window – crosses the bed, this is thought to cause illness.

▲ *Four-poster beds can be claustrophobic if they have heavy wood and elaborate fabric canopies, but this elegant bamboo bed without any excess curtaining gives a very light effect.*

▼ *The symmetry of the tables and lamps at each side of this bed is perfect. Each side of the bed should have identical furnishings.*

▼ *Here the view of the garden is auspicious, but less spiky ornaments behind the bed would be better for relaxation.*

▼ *This soft, dreamy room is very restful. Do not have too many books in the bedroom as they are mentally stimulating.*

FURNISHINGS

Images in the bedroom should be in pairs, particularly in the Relationships corner of the room. Images of a solitary figure in a single person's bedroom indicate loneliness, as does a single bed. It is possible to feel isolated and insecure within a marriage. If this is the case, hang a picture of a couple on the wall and display pairs of objects. Photographs of parents, children or friends have no place in a couple's bedroom.

Mirrors in the bedroom should not face the bed. The Chinese believe that the soul leaves the body as we sleep and will be disconcerted to come across itself in the mirror. A modern interpretation

Ideally, beds should be raised off the floor with enough space for air to circulate underneath. Storage drawers full of old clothes and crates of old magazines and other items stored beneath them create a stagnant chi which is not desirable.

Beds should be made of natural materials which can breathe. Wood is the usual choice although bamboo is also used. People belonging to the Metal element often favour metal beds. Since metal conducts heat and electricity, be very careful to keep electrical equipment and heaters away from the bed. Water beds are not recommended because they cause conflict between Fire, the electrical heating source, and Water, as well as creating instability while we sleep.

Headboards offer support but should always be tightly secured. They represent the Tortoise position, and as such, should be higher than the Phoenix, or the footboard. Beds should be backed by a wall, not a window, which feels insecure and can let in draughts.

Where a double bed is in a confined space and one occupant has to climb over the other to get in or out, harmony will not prevail. The best position for a bed is with a wall behind and enough room on either side for a small table or cupboard. These should always be balanced at either side; one will not do.

▲ *Headboards offer support and this magnificent carved wooden headboard is a particularly fine example.*

▼ *This is an attractive bedroom but the mirror should not reflect the bed. En suite bathrooms are not recommended either.*

CASE STUDY

Although Joe and Amy had a comfortable house, lovely children and were blessed in all aspects of their lives, they revealed separately that they felt lonely and isolated. A look at the bedroom revealed all. On a shelf opposite the bed sat a TV, video and stereo system. Joe enjoyed watching videos in bed and waking up to his favourite rock bands. Amy disliked Joe's choice of videos and her collection of self-improvement books on relationships and stress sat on the next shelf. On the top shelf were photographs of the children, and a box of toys to keep them amused when they came in early in the morning was on the bottom shelf. On the walls to either side of Joe and Amy's bed an image of a solitary man and woman gazed wistfully at each other across the room.

Following the Feng Shui consultation, the toys were removed to the children's rooms, where they were encouraged to play on waking. The two pictures were placed side by side, where the wistful gaze could turn into a lustful glance, and the TV, video and stereo were relocated. Joe is no longer worried that Amy is miserable and unfulfilled as she no longer has need of her books.

▲ *A dressing room is ideal as it frees the bedroom for rest and romance.*

might be that most of us are not at our best in the mornings and would not want our tousled image to be the first thing we see on waking. It would be much better to see a picture of the sun rising or a fresh green landscape. Street lights outside the room can also create reflective images in a mirror, which may disturb us when we are half-asleep. In contrast, strategically placed mirrors facing a wonderful view will draw it into the room.

The bedroom should not become a storage area or an office, nor serve any function other than romance and sleep. If you have space in your house, dressing rooms are ideal since they remove most extraneous things from the bedroom. Most bedrooms, however, contain wardrobes and drawer space. Keeping these clear of clutter means we can close them easily and make sure we have plenty of room to hang up our clothes. Garments strewn over chairs for days on end constitute clutter and worry us psychologically since we know we will have to deal with them eventually. The worst form of storage is the overhead cupboard linking wardrobes on either side of the bed. This acts in the same way as a beam and can leave those sleeping under it feeling vulnerable. The same applies to anything else hanging over the bed.

Electrical Equipment

Electrical equipment in the bedroom is not desirable for two reasons. First, it detracts from the main functions of the

▼ *The beam over this double bed symbolically divides the couple occupying the bed.*

Clutter in the Bedroom

Pill bottles
Cosmetics
Used tissues
Piles of clothes
Old unworn clothes and shoes
Full waste bins
Piles of unread books
Notebooks and work
Mobile phones
TVs and music systems

room. Secondly, the harmful electromagnetic waves that are generated can have an adverse effect on those sleeping there. Ionizers positioned close to a bed present the most serious threat, but even clock radios send out waves over a considerable distance.

Electric blankets are a real problem because they encase the bed in an electromagnetic field. They should be unplugged from the wall before anyone gets into bed.

All electrical items should be on the opposite side of the room from the bed, and this includes electrical clocks. One advantage of this is that it makes the snooze button redundant. People find more time to eat a proper breakfast in the morning and are more punctual for work when they have to get out of bed to turn off the alarm.

It is surprising how many people have telephones sitting on bed-side tables. They have no place in a bedroom as they prevent relaxation, especially if late night social calls are common. The best place for mobile phones outside office hours is in a briefcase, switched off; everyone is entitled to some time for themselves.

▼ *Cramped spaces under slanting walls are not recommended in Feng Shui as they restrict the flow of chi.*

▶ *A harp has been placed in the Wealth corner of this room to lift the energy of the sloping wall.*

Bed Positions

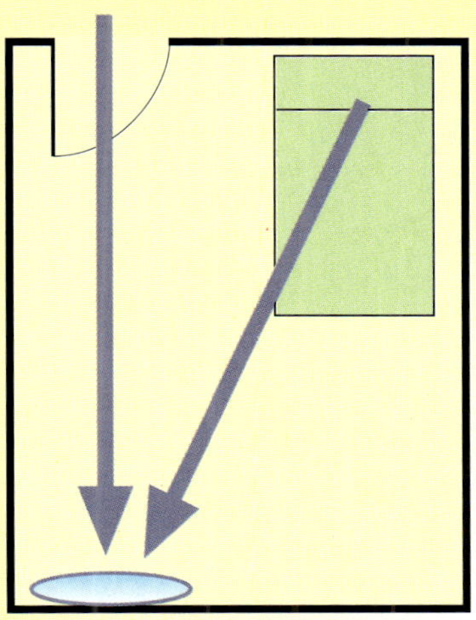

1. If the bed is positioned so that the occupant cannot see who is entering, place a mirror opposite the door.

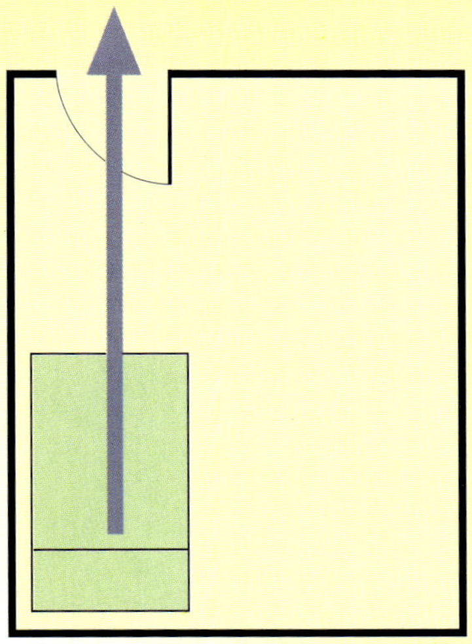

2. When the foot of the bed is in direct line with the door this is known in China as the "mortuary position".

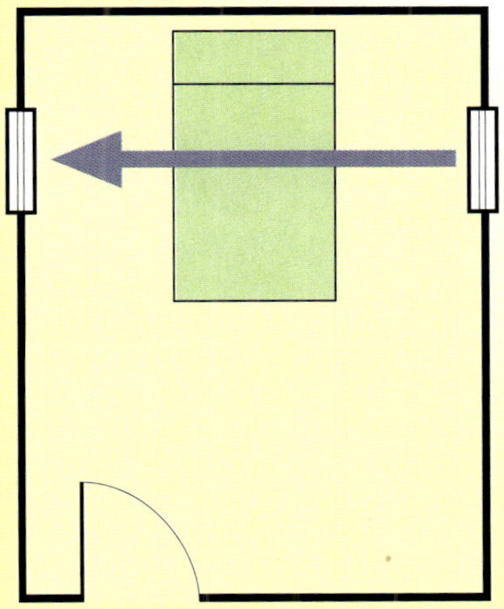

3. A line of harmful chi crosses this bed from two facing windows.

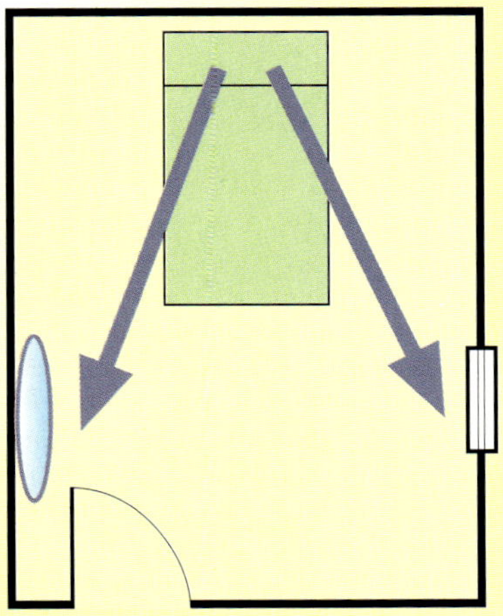

4. A mirror opposite a window can draw in wonderful views.

THE NURSERY

Medical research has shown that pollutants in decorating materials and furniture may be responsible for breathing difficulties and cot deaths in susceptible babies. Decorate the room for a new baby as long as possible before it is due and air the room thoroughly. If this cannot be done, put the baby in the parents' room until the smell of fresh paint has disappeared. Decorating materials should be manufactured from natural products and cot bedding preferably made from natural untreated fibres.

Stimulating the Senses

We can help small children to distinguish colours and shapes by providing them with suitable stimulation. A mobile hung above the foot of a baby's cot will keep it fascinated for a long time and provide comfort before it falls asleep. Do not place one directly over the head of the baby as this can be threatening.

Very small children could be suffocated if furry toy animals fall on their faces so keep these out of the cot but place

► *This is a bright, cheerful room with plenty of stimulation for a baby.*

▼ *Bright colours and shapes give lots of visual appeal during the day.*

▼ *A chalkboard gives a child scope for freedom of expression.*

▼ *This large chest will take many toys and keep the room free from clutter.*

▲ *This first bed for a young child has a canopy to keep it cosy.*

them where the baby can see them, perhaps on a nearby shelf. A bright wall frieze can also occupy a baby's attention, as can a large colourful poster.

Sound can be introduced in a number of ways. Fractious babies who do not sleep well may be soothed by taped music, and the sound of voices from a radio may help the insecure to fall asleep. Musical mobiles can be useful in lulling a baby to sleep, but they might be disturbed if you have to keep rewinding the mobile. Babies soon learn to do things themselves and the look of wonder on its face as a child discovers it can make something happen is magical. By tying bells and rattles to the bars of the cot we help the child on its way to independence, but these are best not left in the cot at night or they will disturb its sleep.

The sense of touch is stimulated by numerous textures – furry, soft, hard and smooth. Allow your child access to a variety of experiences but secure playthings to the cot or you will be forever picking them up from the floor. Do not be tempted to introduce manufactured smells to small children as they are too strong. The familiar smell of a mother or well-loved teddy is far better. At teething time, ensure that all materials which can be put into the mouth conform to safety standards and that cot paint is lead-free.

Possible Hazards

Pets can be a problem if they snuggle up to the baby for warmth or become jealous of the attention it receives. Suitable safety precautions should be taken inside the home. As children begin to crawl, and later to walk and climb, ensure that all fires and electrical sockets are securely covered, that windows are secure and stairs have barriers at the top and bottom.

▲ *Brightly decorated furnishings in this bedroom lift the energy in a dark corner.*

▼ *Wood energy, symbolized by the frieze of trees, suits the growing child, who needs to be allowed freedom of expression.*

CHILDREN'S ROOMS

Children's rooms can be a challenge as they often need to fulfil two opposing functions – sleep and play. Although parents aim to ensure that sleep takes place at night and play during the day, a look at some children's rooms indicates why they do not always get it the right way round as there is no division between the two. Children's rooms should also support them and their needs as they grow. Where a room is shared, each child should have a private space within it that they feel is their own.

The energy of the east with the rising sun in the morning is ideal for children. The west with the setting sun at night is good for hyperactive children who cannot settle, although this direction is normally better for elderly people to sleep in.

The heads of beds should face their supportive directions, although this is not always possible when there is more than one child in the room. It is more important that they should feel safe, and a view of the door is essential for children. Rooms with dark corners which house strange shapes and cast shadows on the walls can prove disturbing for young children with vivid imaginations.

Beds

Wooden beds are preferable because they do not pick up electromagnetic radiation. Bunk beds are not considered suitable since they depress the chi, both of the child on top who is close to the ceiling and the one underneath who has a body above, often a fidgety one. Canopies over the bed have the same effect and can also harbour dust. Cupboards and beams can also have a debilitating effect. Children's beds should have a headboard and should not back on to a window or a door.

▲ *A stark, but restful child's room. The bed would be better backed by the wall.*

▼ *Plenty of storage space means that toys can be neatly stacked away.*

Decoration

As children grow, mentally as well as physically, part of the learning process is to be able to make choices. Children instinctively know the type of energy

Clutter in Children's Rooms

Broken, irreparable toys
Outgrown toys
Books they never look at
Outgrown clothes
Dry felt-tip pens
Games and jigsaw puzzles with pieces missing

▲ *A reassuring first bed for a young child, as the canopy offers protection.*

they require to support them and should be allowed to design their own bedrooms and have a major say in the decoration and colours, even if it is not to the parents' taste. We can always shut the door and we should respect it when it is shut. Children need their privacy as we do and if we set an example by knocking and asking permission to enter, then we can expect the same in return.

If there is a family room or playroom elsewhere, then excessive stimulation in the form of toys should not be a problem in the bedroom. Where the room serves a dual purpose, create a separate sleeping area and provide storage for toys to be put away out of sight at night.

Furnishings

If the floor is hard, a soft rug by the bed is welcoming in the morning and will give a gentle start to the day. Furniture with curved corners helps to prevent minor accidents. If your child has chosen the colours, you can select shades and hues to suit the child's personality – cooler ones to balance an active child and brighter ones to stimulate a more reticent personality.

It is disturbing how many very small children have their own television sets in their rooms as this must inevitably isolate them from their families and hamper their social interaction outside. Apart from this consideration, the electromagnetic radiation from TVs and computers in children's bedrooms is a cause for concern, particularly as these rooms are often small and confine the electro-pollution. Where possible, remove all electrical items from children's rooms and relocate them in other areas of the house.

▼ *Low windows can create a fear of falling, the puppet theatre here acts as a screen.*

▼ *A child's room should give her or him the space and facility to read and be creative.*

TEENAGERS' ROOMS

Teenagers' rooms are evolving places where children who are growing into adults can express themselves – their happiness, their loves, their hurts and their anger. The latter may be directed against us if we attempt to curb their individuality and try to impose our personalities and values on the private space that will nurture them through to adulthood. The needs and the tastes of a thirteen-year-old are very different from those of a seventeen- or eighteen-year-old, and the room may be changed on almost an annual basis. Some principles will remain constant, however. We can encourage our child to place their beds in an auspicious position and introduce them to Feng Shui, which they may come to regard as a help when they encounter some of the usual trials of growing up.

▲ *The high, sloping ceilings do not impinge on this modern room.*

▼ *This is a pretty room for a young teenage girl beginning to move away from childhood.*

Older teenagers' rooms are multi-functional and usually act as bedroom, study, sitting room and entertainment area for their friends. It is no wonder that their occupants sometimes become

Teenage Clutter

Sweet wrappings and crisp packets
Unwashed clothes
Over-flowing wastebins
Do not touch anything else
in a teenager's private space

▲ *Black and white – a bold colour choice – is popular with teenagers.*

confused. Teenagers need our support when they ask for it, even though they do not welcome unsolicited advice. They require their own space, physically and intellectually, but they also need positive affirmation from adults. Hold out against a television in the bedroom and encourage the use of family rooms. A computer in the study will draw teenagers out of their bedrooms and preserve this space for sleep and relaxation.

▼ *The bright decor and pretty feel of this room might not suit an older teenager.*

CASE STUDY

Marie, aged sixteen, was going through an "awkward" phase. Her mother, Ella, was at her wits' end trying to get her out of bed in the mornings to catch the one bus guaranteed to get her to school on time. Every morning was a battle, and the resentment festered throughout the day and affected family harmony in the evening. Homework was left undone and Marie's studies were suffering.

A Metal Ox, Marie could be stubborn and, although a girl of few words, she occasionally exploded. Her arrogant manner irritated her father, a Fire Ox, who didn't take kindly to being opposed or to Marie's surliness. He became impatient with his wife, an Earth Goat, who knew Marie needed support and was torn between them in arguments.

Ella decided to take action and offered to redecorate Marie's bedroom and let her choose the decor. Out to shock, Marie chose purple for her room and was surprised when her mother, who knew purple to be stimulating for the mind and good for raising self-esteem, acquiesced.

1. Ella took Marie to a fashionable store and invited her to choose something for her room. As she had hoped, Marie chose a multi-coloured bead curtain for the window.

2. Ella suggested that Marie should turn her bed around so that she could see the curtain.

3. Ella removed the old square bedside table, since the square shape symbolizes containment, and ordered a round one.

4. The alarm clock was placed on Marie's desk so she no longer had access to the snooze button and had to get up to turn it off.

5. To go on the new round table Ella gave Marie a framed photograph showing the family boarding a plane to go on holiday; this energized the "Family" area of the Bagua.

6. Taking a chance, Ella purchased two huge silk sunflowers and suggested they would look lovely in the top right-hand corner of the room – the Earth "Relationships" area of the Bagua represented by the magic number 2.

Now when Ella calls Marie in the morning, she opens the window slightly so the bead curtain moves and tinkles, stimulating the chi. When the alarm rings later Marie has to get out of bed to turn it off, but she is already awake. Family harmony has been restored and they meet on friendly terms more often. Feng Shui is a mixture of common sense and psychology as well as harnessing unseen forces of the universe.

BATHROOMS

The position of the bathroom is considered to be important in Feng Shui because water is synonymous with wealth, and thus the disposal of waste water symbolizes the dispersal of the family fortune. Changing climatic conditions have highlighted how precious a commodity water is, and that measures should be taken not to waste it. Conservationists recommend saving water from baths and sinks to water gardens. Dripping taps are symbolic of wealth running away. When we consider that a dripping tap, leaking at a rate of one drip per second, wastes 1,000 litres (264 gallons) per year, we can see the sense in applying ancient rules to modern problems. Baths and sinks which are clogged, apart from being a constant source of irritation, can also be a health risk so it is important that we fix them as soon as possible.

▲ *This spacious and opulent bathroom provides room to relax in.*

▼ *No need for morning queues in this large and airy bathroom.*

Position

Bathrooms should be positioned well away from the front door as this is not an image we want visitors to our homes to subconsciously take away. It is most important not to have bathrooms close to kitchens for health reasons, but they should also be away from dining and sitting areas so that guests won't be embarrassed to use them.

Toilets

It is not desirable to see the toilet on entering the bathroom and, if possible, it should be situated where it is hidden from view. Screens can be utilized or the toilet positioned behind the door. Toilet doors should be closed and the seat cover closed at all times.

Bathrooms are considered to be linked to the body's plumbing system so a large bathroom using too much water can lead to health problems concerned with evacuation, while cramped bathrooms are connected with restriction in bodily functions. Large bathrooms are also associated with vanity and an excessive

obsession with cleanliness, whereas small bathrooms are restricting and can cause accidents as people manoeuvre round.

Mirrors and Cabinets

The use of mirrors can give the illusion of more space. Generally, mirrors opposite each other are not considered to be auspicious in Feng Shui because they conjure up an image of constant movement away from the self, with no grounding influences. However, unless

▼ *Use plants and coloured towels to balance the Water element in a bathroom.*

▲ *Screens can be used to hide the bathroom from an entrance or en suite bedroom.*

► *The reflective materials in this bathroom help to counteract its heavy ceiling. A large plant or dash of colour would also help.*

▼ *Curvy, watery lines and Metal shapes work well in this unusual bathroom.*

we spend a vast amount of time in front of the bathroom mirror, this is acceptable if it improves the suggestion of space. Mirror tiles are not recommended, or those which in any way cut the image. Fixed mirrors are preferred to those which jut out from walls and normal mirrors are preferred to magnifying mirrors that distort the image.

Bathroom cabinets are places where stagnant chi can easily accumulate. Most cosmetics have a limited shelf life and many cabinets contain items dating back years. There is a limit to the number of eye baths, tweezers and combs which are required in a lifetime.

En Suite Bathrooms

The growing trend to have en suite bathrooms is not in accordance with Feng Shui rules. Where possible, create a separate room for the toilet or else make sure the bathroom area in the bedroom has a well-maintained ventilation system. En suite bathrooms that have been built into the bedroom often create an L-shape with a corner jutting into the room, so action needs to be taken to ensure that this does not point at the bed.

Clutter in the Bathroom

Full waste bins
Empty bottles and toothpaste tubes
Unnecessary soap dishes
Unpolished mirrors
Out-of-date medication
Untried cosmetic samples
Bath oils and perfumes which are never used

▲ *A good balance of colours, elements, plants and natural materials raises the energy in this bathroom.*

► *Keep any clutter in the bathroom down to its absolute minimum and keep any soap dishes or holders clean and unclogged.*

Relaxation

Very few of us find the time to relax sufficiently and this often affects our health, both physical and mental. The bathroom is one of the few places where we can escape from the world and be alone. Bathrooms should be decorated so as to enable us to wind down at the end of a busy day, or allow us some peaceful moments in the morning.

▲ *An ideal bathroom – it would be difficult to resist rushing home to relax in this at the end of a hard day.*

▶ *The huge mirror doubles the space in this elegant bathroom. A frame to the top and bottom would contain the chi.*

The colours we use to decorate the bathroom affect how we feel there. Blue is a soothing colour, associated with serenity and contemplation. Colour therapists believe that it lowers the blood pressure, promotes deeper exhalation and induces sleep. Green, on the other hand, rests the eyes and calms the nerves. Whatever colours we choose, we can create a space to relax and soothe ourselves by playing gentle music and by adding a few drops of essential oils to the bathwater. Bergamot, lavender and geranium alleviate stress and anxiety, while camomile, rose, lemon balm and ylang ylang are used to alleviate irritability and to create a peaceful mood. The bath is an ideal place for self-massage while taking a bath or having just had one. Try stroking one of these oils towards the heart to stimulate the circulation.

Taoists consider that the nutrition we receive from the air when we breathe is more valuable to us than food and water. As we inhale we draw in energy, which provides energy; when we exhale, we cleanse and detoxify our bodies. The art of breathing properly has been part of the Chinese health regime for centuries, and is based on balancing yin and yang and creating the correct chi flow around the body. It is thought that illness occurs when the correct chi flow is not maintained. Use your time in the bathroom to practise controlled breathing.

Meditation is another relaxation technique. The Chinese call it "sitting still and doing nothing", which is a deceptively simple description of an art that can take years to perfect. Whether our aim is to reflect on the day or to let our minds wander freely and wind down, the bathroom is the ideal place.

CONSERVATORIES

Conservatories are a popular way of extending our homes and they act as a mediating space between the garden and the house. Ancient Chinese architects designed homes and gardens to interconnect and regarded each as being essential to balance the other. Glimpses through windows and latticed grilles gave views over lakes and vistas, and gardens were planted right up to the house.

Some conservatories are used for plants or as garden rooms, and are places to sit in to relax. Others have become an integral part of the home, taking on the role of dining room, sitting room and in some cases kitchen. Depending on its purpose and aspect, the conservatory can be decorated in various ways.

▲ *A conservatory is a glorious place to relax in all weathers.*

The Conservatory Kitchen

The conservatory kitchen can become very warm in the summer and adequate ventilation will be necessary. It is not considered auspicious to have a glass roof in the kitchen because the symbolic wealth, the food, will evaporate away. Practically speaking, it is not comfortable to work with the sun, or with the rain, beating down above, and a blind or fabric should be put up to block the sky. Choose fabrics that are easy to clean and ensure that they do not hang too low and are not highly flammable. The same conditions apply to conservatory kitchens as to conventional ones. If working with the door behind you, place a sheet of metal or a large shiny object so that you can see anyone entering the room.

▼ *This conservatory opens into the kitchen, enabling the cook to join in the conversation.*

▶ *An indoor garden which opens into a family kitchen, the conservatory provides an ideal outlook when eating or preparing meals.*

The Conservatory Dining Room

The conservatory dining room should be treated in the same way as a conventional diner, but there are difficulties. The conservatory room often opens directly into the kitchen and occasionally also into the main living area. There will be doors to the garden and two or three of the walls will be glass. This makes it very difficult to sit with support from behind, so it is important that chairs have high backs, and preferably arms, to provide this.

Depending on the aspect, the evening sun may cause glare so protective measures, such as blinds, should be available. Conservatories can be very warm until quite late in the evening and fans can help to move the air around.

◄ *What a healthy way to dine – absorbing energy from the landscape as much as the food and company.*

Any water features in the conservatory are not conducive to good digestion and should be turned off during meals.

The Conservatory Living Room

Whether it is used as a living room or simply for enjoying an apéritif at the end of a long day, the conservatory will be a tranquil spot so long as adequate shade and ventilation are provided.

A water feature will cool the air and be soothing, providing it is placed in an auspicious spot according to the Five Elements. North is auspicious as it is the Water position. If the conservatory sits in the east or south-west, then this is the spot for a water feature, which will symbolize present and future prosperity.

▲ *A wide variety of different foliage plants adds interest to this small conservatory area.*

▼ *Curtains are not really necessary when you have a wonderful view like this.*

BALCONIES AND WINDOW-BOXES

Many apartments have balconies which are purely cosmetic and act as barriers between neighbouring apartments when the doors are opened. Others are larger but do not really enable outdoor living as such, having no room for tables and seating. Some apartments have neither but may have an external windowsill on which to put plants or window-boxes. All these small spaces bring the natural world inside our homes.

The outlook in many urban apartments is bleak. The most auspicious sites overlook a park or a river, but most overlook a busy road or even a brick wall.

► *Flowers in a window-box are guaranteed to lift the spirits.*

▼ *Even in a small space there is usually room for a windowsill display.*

CASE STUDY

A flower-lover who lived on the seventh floor was so troubled by pigeons nibbling his plants that he decided to give up trying to grow them. Yet his balcony still looked wonderful from below. He had purchased lots of green silk plants and ivy strands, and a collection of flowers to represent the seasons. Set in oasis and weighted with gravel, these saw him through several years and few people could tell the difference.

► *Silk plants are very effective in awkward sites and don't need watering.*

Windowsills

A kitchen windowsill, inside or outside, is a useful place to have a herb collection and bring not only the sight of the natural world into your home but also the smell and the taste.

The window box on the far left contains nasturtiums, pansies and marigolds, all of which are edible and can be used for flavour and garnishes. The window box in the picture on the near left contains chervil, coriander, fennel, garlic, purple sage, French tarragon, savory, oregano and basil – an entire herb garden in a box.

Many apartments overlook the windows of other apartments and we can be overlooked by dozens of eyes as we wash up or stand on our balconies. The Four Animals formation suggests that we need to define our space. By placing a window-box on our windowsill we not only define the Phoenix position, we also fill our homes with the Wood energy of growing plants. Recent studies have shown that hospital patients who overlook a garden recover more quickly than patients who do not have such a view. A healthy display of green plants to greet us in the morning will spur us on for the day ahead and welcome us home in the evening.

Growing plants on a balcony can be problematic. Compost (soil mix) is heavy and can be difficult to transport to the apartment and also to dispose of later. Cosmetic balconies may not be able to cope with heavy weights and we must be mindful of this when choosing containers and plants. Bulbs can be a useful solution since they require a comparatively small amount of compost. A succession of bulbs throughout the year will connect us to the seasons, which is auspicious in Feng Shui. Providing we keep them watered until the foliage has died down, we can lift the bulbs and store them for the following year. Depending on the direction in which the balcony faces, the colours of the bulbs may be chosen to correspond to the direction or to focus on a life aspiration, using the Bagua. Of course this is not essential; other plants may be used. It is preferable to plant shrubs and miniature trees and to use annual plants as spots of colour, rather than attempting to uproot plants and dispose of them several times a year.

▲ *This green oasis in a bustling city is shaded by an awning which, with the well-maintained plants, creates a protected space.*

◀ *Even a small outdoor space such as this will provide plenty of energy.*

SWIMMING POOLS

Large volumes of water exude powerful energies and great care should be taken in siting pools with regard to the effect they will have on the area and the house, and on the elemental cycle of the location.

Large areas of still water are yin and in theory accumulate chi to balance the yang energy of the home. Where they are situated too close to the house, they can deplete the yang energy and cause problems. Auspicious shapes are those with rounded edges and kidney-shaped pools which appear to hug the house.

▲ *This swimming pool is the correct size for the house and the points are hidden by the large bushy plants.*

Pool Shapes

This kidney-shaped pool has no harmful points. It appears to hug the house and its shape is auspicious.

The corners of this L-shaped pool are sending "poison arrows" at the house and the swimmers.

Without the planting to obscure part of its view from the house, the energy of this pool would be overwhelming.

▲ *The flowing, natural lines of this swimming pool are in harmony with the surrounding garden.*

▲ *Here large rocks add stability to this lovely pool, while the vegetation brings life and vitality.*

▼ *Flowing curves and gentle planting make this swimming pool very inviting. The entrance to the house is well-balanced.*

Where straight-sided pools are at an angle to the house, the edges of the pool can send "poison arrows" of chi to the detriment of the inhabitants.

Although a body of water in theory accumulates chi, there are other factors to be taken into consideration. The surrounding landscape, symbolically the Dragon, may have been excavated to create the pool and will probably have been damaged, or the appearance and energy of the place may have been damaged.

Another factor is the direction of the swimming pool. A large body of water in the south will destroy the Fire energy there. The east and south-east are good locations since the water will feed growth and at the same time its energy will be kept under control by the Wood.

The colour of the pool tiles is important and care should be taken to retain a balance of the elements in and around the pool. Pale blue is a favourite colour, but again will not suit all locations. Refer back to "The Relationships of the Five Elements" table to ensure a balance has been maintained.

The size of the pool must be in proportion to the house and the surrounding landscape. An enormous pool in a small back garden can symbolically "drown" the occupants. Consider also the direction of the sun at various times of the day when you are choosing a site.

Indoor Pools

These are not recommended in Feng Shui and need to be well secured if they are part of the house. If you already have one, it should be kept separate from the house by closed doors. Pools in basements are considered a destabilizing influence, and rooftop pools are thought to symbolically "drown" residents and weigh them down.

THE HOME OFFICE

Home offices differ from studies in that they are more yang because they have more contact with the outside world. For this reason, they are better placed close to the entrance so that work does not impinge on the whole house and visitors do not have to walk through the living accommodation. Home offices can be difficult places, particularly when situated in the main body of the house. There is always a temptation to take time out to do household tasks, or for the family to drop in. Although home working allows flexibility, it demands a high level of self-discipline in order to work for long enough but not too long, to allow time for social activities. A balance has to be maintained. Ideally, home offices should be placed where visitors have access via a separate door and apart from the main house, in a wing or even in a separate building in the garden.

▼ *A garden studio or office, removed from the main house, is an excellent idea.*

▲ *This luxurious office space is obviously designed for meetings with clients.*

▶ *If the chair and desk positions in this study were to be reversed it would open up a view of the outside world.*

Office Position

The ideal position for the office is in your best direction or in one of the other three favoured positions. The south-west is not favoured for office locations since the energy levels are falling there. Wherever it is situated, some care in the north will be advantageous.

Any "poison arrows" should be deflected or hidden, using mirrors or screens. Metal supports Water so hollow metal wind chimes or a metal object would be helpful. Water is also auspicious here but do not use the area to display plants as they will drain the energy.

Desk Positions

Desk locations are the same as those for the study but if there is a secretary or another person working in the home office the desks should not face each other. The secretary should sit nearer to the door to protect the employer from having to deal with mundane matters. Both desks should have the support of a wall behind and both should have suitably supportive chairs which follow the favourable Four Animals formation. If a desk is close to a door, a plant on the edge will protect the occupant from unfavourable chi.

When visiting clients are received in the office, the owner's chair should always be backed by the wall facing the door and the clients should be seated in the

The Bagua and Desks

Use the Bagua to arrange your desk according to Feng Shui principles.

1. This represents Career or the start of the day and should be clear to open up possibilities for the day ahead.

2. The Relationships area is suitable for brochures and details of people with whom you will come into contact in the course of your present project.

3. A plant here in the Elders area will help to freshen the air and symbolize longevity and stability.

4. Accounts and paying-in books should be placed here in the Wealth area, but not cheque books, which represent money going out.

5. Use this central area for the task in hand and then clear it away. Do not leave things to pile up here.

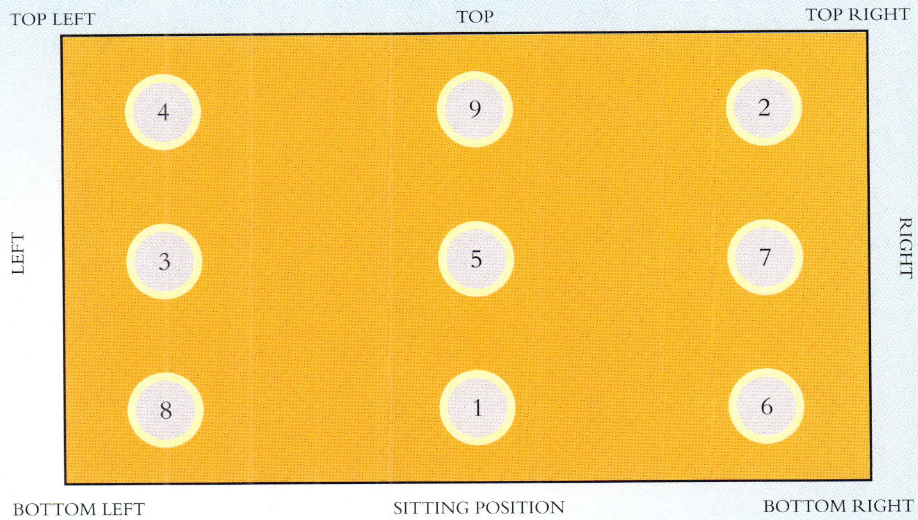

6. The Helpful People area is the place for the telephone and address book.

7. The Children or Projects position is ideal for putting the current project files.

8. Knowledge and Wisdom – the place to store reference books.

9. The Fame area and the Phoenix position. A crystal paperweight here will denote the boundary of your desk, and of the current project. An uplifting image or landscape hung on the wall in front will represent future possibilities.

▲ *This studio's view would be improved if the foliage outside wasn't so dense.*

subordinate position in a smaller chair, with their backs to the door.

Having sorted out the best location for the furniture, focus on the contents of the desk, either using compass directions or symbolically. Take care that any measures taken are not in conflict with the element of the area. Task lighting should always be diagonally opposite the writing hand to prevent shadows.

The Office Environment

Be aware of the approach to the office from outside and check for dustbins and other obstacles, overhanging branches and anything which will detract from your entrance. Inside the house, the same attention is necessary. Clients who come to visit you will not want to clamber over toys or other paraphernalia, which present an unprofessional approach.

It is important, particularly when the office is a section of a room that is used at other times for another purpose, to mark the boundaries – by a screen, piece of furniture or even a rug. Inside the space, aspirational images, landscapes, good lighting and bright colours all make a psychological contribution to success.

A clutter-free office environment is essential and work spaces should be clear of everything but the task in hand. Do not have stacked filing trays which, symbolically and literally, allow the work to mount up. Deal with letters and telephone calls the same day and note conversations and dates meticulously. Discard catalogues as new ones arrive as well as all out-of-date paperwork.

▼ *This uncluttered desk is arranged following Feng Shui principles.*

Financial Tip

Tie three Chinese coins together with red thread or ribbon and place them in the back of your accounts book for good luck.

HOME STUDY OR STUDIO

The home study may be used by one or more members of the family to study for school or college examinations, for continuing education later in life or for pursuing a hobby or interest. It should be situated in a quiet part of the home, if possible. If study areas form part of another room – the bedroom, sitting room or even the kitchen – care should be taken to ensure that the activities of the two areas are kept quite separate, for example, by screening. It is not a good idea to use a bedroom as a home study, because it will no longer be a place to relax in.

► *Screens can be used to conceal work equipment in bedrooms and living rooms.*

Desk Locations

The three desk positions below have the support of a wall. You can also see the door and anyone entering. The desk on the right is directly opposite the door. The three desks below right are vulnerable from behind and anyone working in these positions would feel nervous.

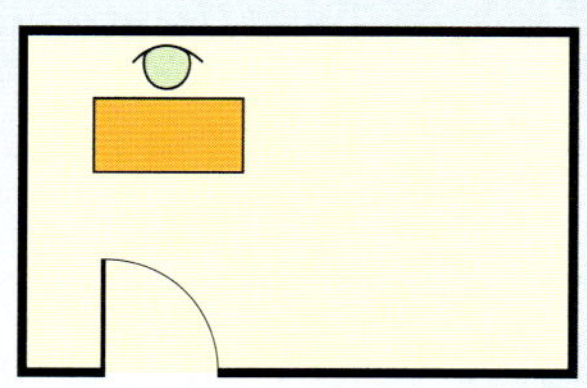

Good: facing the door

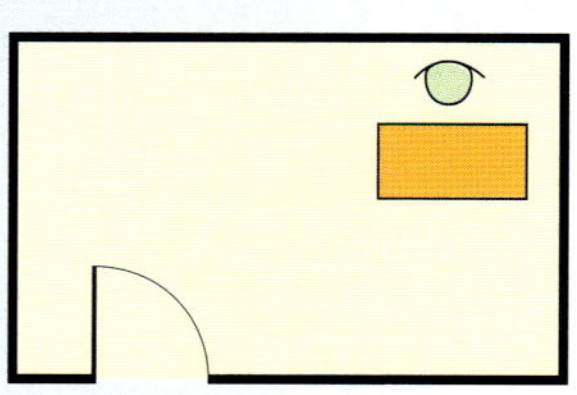

Good: diagonally opposite the door

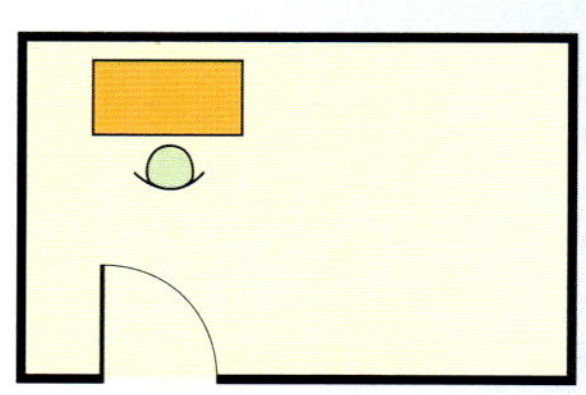

Bad: back to the door

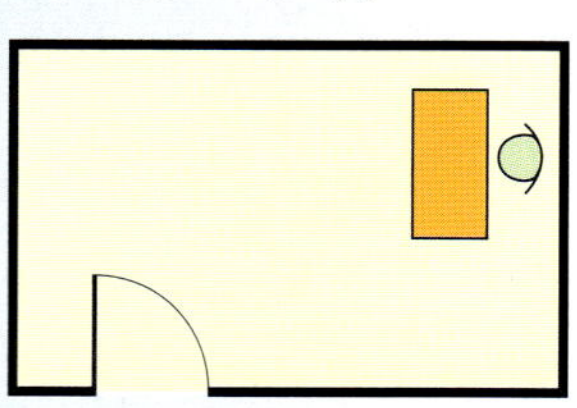

Good: with a view of the door

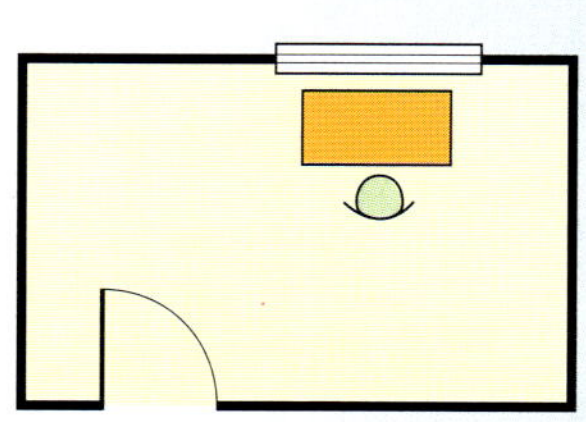

Bad: facing a window

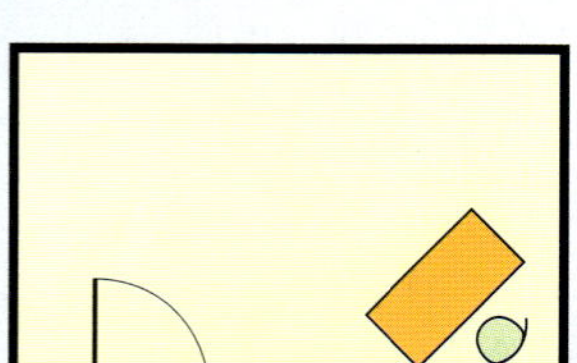

Good: here you can see who is entering

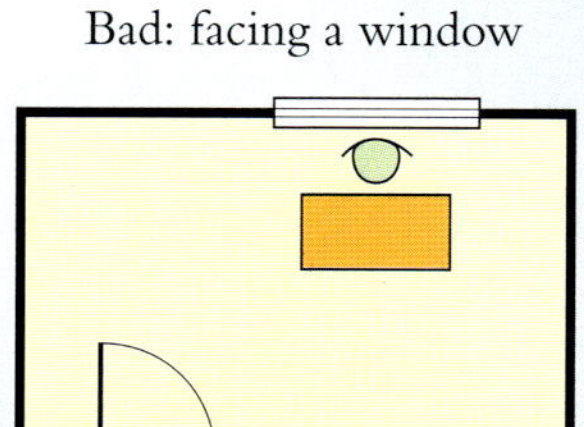

Bad: back to a window

Desk Positions

The position of the desk is crucial if maximum benefits are to be gained from studying and it should be placed to avoid any areas of damaging chi.

The view from a study window should be pleasant but not detract from work. A view of the neighbours' swimming pool and barbecue area will not be conducive to work. Sitting opposite the windows of a neighbouring house is not recommended since it can cause discomfort, as can facing telephone wires or having roof points aimed at the office. If

▼ *An ideal solution – the folding doors allow light and air in during the day, and you can close down the office at night.*

there are distractions outside, the window should be covered by muslin, or something similar, to admit light but keep distractions out. Plants placed on the windowsill might serve the same purpose. Studies should have a good supply of fresh air in order to prevent tiredness.

When a considerable amount of time is spent in one position, the furniture should be ergonomically correct. Chairs should fit comfortably under desks and the seat should be at the correct height for writing and using a keyboard. If a conventional computer is used, it should be placed as far away as possible from the chair to reduce the radiation from the screen. Where possible, use a laptop computer. Trailing wires are dangerous and cause irritation, so tie them together

▲ *It would be difficult to work in this room. The stacked bookshelves are also reflected in the mirror and are overwhelming.*

◀ *A Mayan chime ball hung in the window deflects the "poison arrow" created by the roof of one of the buildings outside.*

Clutter in the Study

Piles of used paper
Piles of unread journals
Out-of-date books
Cluttered hard drive
Noticeboards with out-of-date information
More than two adhesive notes
Broken equipment
Run-down batteries

and tape them out of the way. Printers should be positioned to ensure the paper can eject easily. Plants in the study help to improve the air quality and also add some yin balance to the yang machines.

Order in the Study

The study should be as streamlined as possible and there should be a place for everything. Cupboards, shelves and bookcases will keep books and equipment off the desk surface. Coloured files and filing boxes store information and prevent paper mountains appearing on the desk and floor. Coloured adhesive bookmarkers avoid piles of open books and journals stacking up on the desk, but the marked items should be read in a day or two otherwise the stickers will be a constant reminder of things left undone.

Journals can pile up. You should try to read them immediately and discard them if they contain nothing of interest. If it is necessary to keep them, a small card index in subject order with the journal title, date, article title and page number will help you to quickly locate the items you want.

Once a piece of work has been completed and recognition received for it, it is unlikely that it will ever be referred to again. Consider whether a paper copy is really necessary. If not, store all completed work on floppy disks, which take up considerably less space. Remove past work from the computer hard drive to free up space and improve performance.

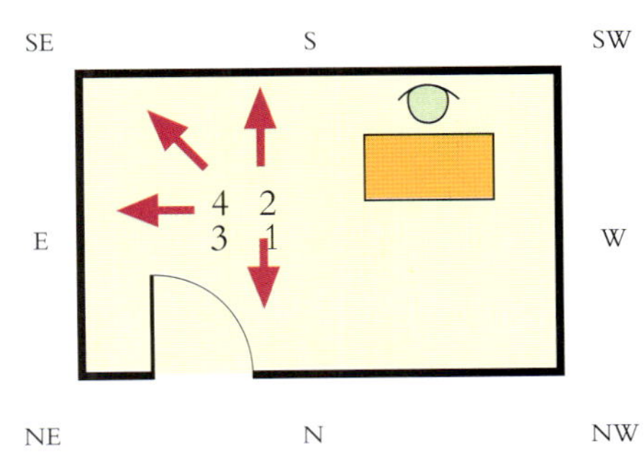

▲ *Ensure you face your best direction (or one of your other three favoured directions).*

FENG SHUI AND YOUR CAR

▲ *Our cars, just like ourselves, need to be kept healthy and in good condition.*

Many people spend hours at a time in their cars which become like mini-homes. Like our homes, they become a reflection and extension of ourselves. Negative chi in cars has the power to create lasting damage and destruction to their owners and to others. Cars are extensions of ourselves. With the right treatment they serve us well. Some people talk to their cars, others give them names and personalize them. In some parts of the world they are blessed. Negative energy breeds negative response, so we should aim to build up a caring relationship with our cars.

Generally, cars follow the classic Four Animals formation, being taller at the back than the front, and having support on either side. Car seats should also follow this formation. Cars which slope away to the back and those which open at the back can leave us feeling insecure, as anyone who has driven off as a rear door or boot (trunk) lid has flown open can testify. Small pick-up trucks are vulnerable from behind since their cargoes can fall off or may be stolen.

▼ *Yellow, an Earth colour, representing stability, is auspicious.*

The rear lights act as our Tortoise, warning those behind to brake. It is therefore essential to ensure they are clean and in working order, and that spent bulbs are replaced immediately. Cars with reclining seats, such as expensive sports models, also suggest vulnerability behind since the Tortoise position is weak. Their "laid-back" effect is often reflected in the driving habits of the owners of such cars.

Car Ornaments

Stickers on the rear window can strengthen the Tortoise position, particularly those which say "Please Keep Your Distance" or "Baby on Board" and other, polite, warning signs. Jokes and stickers which are difficult to read have the opposite effect in that they encourage the car behind to come closer. Stickers should not obstruct the window.

Any ornaments that act as a distraction behind should be avoided. The windscreen can act as the Phoenix and moving objects, like hanging ornaments, can create instability and affect concentration. Do not allow loose items to collect in the back of the car as sudden braking will send them cannoning around.

▲ *The white Metal energy drains the flamboyant red on this quirky car.*

Even people who would not admit to being superstitious carry talismen when they travel. In the West, a small St Christopher symbol is believed to be protective because he was the patron saint of travellers. Other cultures have their own protection symbols. Attitudes to numbers on registration plates also indicate cultural differences. The Chinese avoid 4 because it resembles the word for death, while Westerners prefer not to use 13 and treble 6 for superstitious reasons.

▼ *Our cars reflect our personalities. An untidy car is as revealing as an untidy home. Secure anything that rattles.*

The Car and the Senses

Fresh air is necessary in cars, in order to link the occupants with the world outside and to cleanse the air within the confined space. If the air is not fresh, the driver can become tired and lose concentration. To freshen the air we can introduce natural oils, which also affect our moods. Rosemary, neroli and lemon oils are helpful for calming anger and promoting clear thinking.

Vision is important in the car and a clean screen and headlights enable us to see and be seen clearly on a foggy day and at night.

If we regard the car engine in the same way that we do our bodies, then we can appreciate that for the car to be healthy and function well its tubes have to be unblocked and its components well maintained. Regular servicing is therefore important.

Element	Helped by	Harmed by	Weakened by	Weakens
Wood	Water	Metal	Fire	Earth
Fire	Wood	Water	Earth	Metal
Earth	Fire	Wood	Metal	Water
Metal	Earth	Fire	Water	Wood
Water	Metal	Earth	Wood	Fire

Personality and the Car

Our cars reflect our personalities in the same way as our homes do. A neat, clean car generates a different impression of its owner to a dirty one. The colours we choose also affect our attitude to a car and the perception other drivers have of us. How many of us give red cars driven by very young men a wide berth? When choosing cars we would do well to bear the Five Elements relationships in mind.

▲ *Red sports cars show too much yang. Black accessories will reduce the impact.*

Choosing the Colours

We should ensure the colours of our cars do not conflict with the colour of the element associated with our Chinese animal. For example, a young and rather macho male, particularly a Fire Horse, should not choose red because this colour will intensify the fire. A dark blue or black to cool the Fire, and Metal – white or grey – to weaken it is preferable, and safer. On the other hand, a driver who cannot concentrate and who is a Water Pig will need some Wood (green) to draw them on and some Metal, white or silver, as support.

▼ *Young male energy is excessively yang. Black, a yin Water energy, will drain it.*

Car Clutter

Rattles left unfixed
A worn spare tyre
Spent lamps
Confectionery wrappers
Fast-food cartons
Car park tickets
Rubbish in the boot (trunk)

Car Numbers

Number associations vary between different cultures. In China, they often depend on sound. The number 4 sounds like the Chinese word for 'death' and is therefore considered unlucky. The number 8 on the other hand sounds like the Chinese word for "happiness" and is well-regarded. 88 is therefore doubly auspicious, meaning "double happiness". Car number plates containing the number 888 are very sought-after and command high prices.

PETS

Feng Shui is about environments and people and originally pets would not have played any part in the design of homes at all. Animals were domesticated as long as 8000 years ago but until quite recent times they were mainly used to work for their owners, and regarded as property rather than as best friends to human beings. Today, pets play a very important role in the lives of their owners and their presence has to be taken into account when applying Feng Shui principles to the home.

▲▼ *Today pets – in particular cats and dogs – are an important part of a family unit and need to be considered in Feng Shui.*

Dogs and Cats

Whether we or our pets choose their sleeping places it is possible to ensure that the colour and pattern of their beds and bedding are in harmony with the elemental energy of the position. The table opposite shows the colours associated with each direction. Should a cat choose to sleep somewhere other than its basket, then there may be some geopathic stress which they are attracted to, or they may just enjoy snuggling up.

Frogs and Wealth

A china frog, carrying a coin in its mouth and placed inside the front door (particularly if it is the west or north-west, the Metal areas which signify money), supposedly attracts wealth to the house.

Colour of Bedding

Direction	Colour
East	Green
South-east	Green
South	Red
South-west	Yellow, brown
West	Grey
North-west	Grey
North	Blue/Black
North-east	Yellow, brown

Pets and Health

Although we get pleasure from our pets and studies have shown that stroking animals can actually relieve signs of stress, we should not be blind to the fact that they can cause health risks in the home. More than once clients have wondered why people do not stay long when they visit and the answer is so obvious. A litter tray in full view in the kitchen is the greatest turn-off for a guest, particularly when they have come to eat. Likewise, caged animals in children's bedrooms can create an unhealthy energy unless the cage is well maintained, and they are best located elsewhere. It might also be prudent to consider the health of the animals and we need to provide conditions which mirror their natural habitats and lifestyles as far as possible if our pets are to remain healthy. Just as human beings enjoy better health with good food and exercise, so pets will remain healthier if they are not imprisoned in confined spaces and fed on poor diets for the duration of their lives. The mental health of our animals is also important and problems often occur where pets are locked in a house or flat alone all day and often through the evening as well.

▲ *Fish are considered to be very auspicious in China where they are kept to attract wealth to the household.*

▼ *An alert, intelligent dog such as this collie makes an ideal family pet.*

Fish

Fish symbolize success and wealth in China and an aquarium by the entrance or in the sitting room is thought to encourage this. Eight gold fish and one black one in a tank are believed to be an auspicious combination. When fish die it is not regarded as a sad occasion since it is thought that they are absorbing the bad luck of the family and the fish are replaced immediately. In the West, where animal welfare issues are considered, unless the tank can be large enough to provide a reasonable environment for the fish, a picture or image may be more acceptable. An indoor water feature in the south-east will serve as well. Outdoor pools, provided they are large enough and well maintained, provide a more natural environment. When in a front garden place them to the left of the front door, never to the right.

Animals and Symbology

The use of animals as luck symbols is widespread in China and their symbolism lies deep within the culture of the country and does not necessarily translate into other cultures with their own symbols. Where a symbolic quality is desired, an ornament or picture will suffice to invoke the desired energy to an area.

Symbolic Chinese Animals

Bat	luck
Bear	protection
Crane	health and longevity
Deer	luck and wealth
Elephant	wisdom
Fish	success
Horse	recognition
Leopard	protection
Lion	authority and protection
Stork	longevity
Tortoise	longevity

▼ *Animals need healthy diets as well as humans and our pets will be happier if they are fed regular, balanced meals.*

犬

雞

鼠

龍

猴

THE FENG SHUI GARDEN

THE ORIGINS OF FENG SHUI LIE IN AN ANCIENT CIVILIZATION WHICH GREW THEIR CROPS BY TAPPING INTO THE BENEFICIAL ENERGIES AROUND THEM. GARDENS OFFER US THE SAME OPPORTUNITY TO CONNECT TO THE NATURAL WORLD AND THE UNIVERSE BEYOND. IN THE GARDEN WE ARE IN PARTNERSHIP WITH OTHER LIVING THINGS. IF WE WORK WITH THEM, BALANCE AND HARMONY WILL FOLLOW.

豬

INTRODUCTION

When we purchase a house or move into an apartment our first concerns are likely to be the number of bedrooms, the size of the kitchen and the condition of the roof. Rarely do we choose a home on the basis of its garden, even though it can play an important role in correcting the imbalance created by the frantic pace of modern living. We are driven in pursuit of work and its rewards, bombarded with stimulating experiences via the media, and we can even shop 24 hours a day if we want to. These yang activities take their toll on our mental and physical health. An excellent way to redress the balance is to create quiet havens for ourselves in our gardens.

When we recall the books we read as children, many of our favourite stories were set in the countryside. There can be few of us who have not, at some point in our lives, peered into a hole in search of Brer Rabbit or walked by a river hoping to see Ratty and Mole or Mr Toad sweeping by in his magnificent car. The magic of raindrops on a spider's web, the first ladybird to land on a small pudgy finger, a beautiful mahogany-coloured chestnut and the swish of autumn leaves as we wade through in shiny boots, these are all early experiences which link us to the natural world.

▲ *However small, a garden can offer us a retreat from the hurly-burly of modern life.*

► *Studying details such as a spider's web enables us to make links with nature.*

▼ *Green spaces in the inner city give the inhabitants a relief from stress.*

Until quite recently, gardens for contemplation were the preserve of the rich. Poorer people cultivated the soil for their survival, but their hard work did keep them in touch with the land. There are many children now who have never seen fruit or vegetables growing or experienced the magic of watching a tiny seed develop into a plant. Our gardens are furnished like our homes with everything bought off-the-peg from garden centres. But the mood is changing. In big cities like London and New York there are moves to create community gardens on derelict sites between inner-city buildings and skyscrapers. More and more schools are creating gardens to teach children about the natural world. The demand for food uncontaminated by chemicals is growing as we begin to realize the folly of some of the current trends in industrial food production. It seems that there is a latent longing to reconnect with the natural world.

In the Feng Shui garden the design principles of the ancient Chinese landscapers are used to create, not Chinese gardens, but indigenous ones which relate to our own psyche as well as to the spirit of the place where we live. By using local plants and natural methods to grow them we can make a garden in which we can distance ourselves from the hurly-burly of modern living and gain repose. Even if we live in an apartment block, we can take the initiative by tending the ill-kept communal spaces which provide our window to the outside world. We need to have restful yet energizing green spaces when we return to the nurturing space of our home.

The following pages reveal how the ancient principles of Feng Shui can be employed in our gardens today to create supportive and nurturing environments. We will see how centuries-old formulae can be translated into modern-day garden design techniques and discover how yin and yang and the Five Elements can be interpreted outside.

Feng Shui is the art of directing the energy of an environment to move in ways with which we feel comfortable. The plants, furnishings and other objects we surround ourselves with have an impact on how we feel about the garden and how we use it. The ever-present unseen energies of the earth and the universe can be exploited to our advantage.

▲ *Choose plants to suit the soil and situation for a healthy, harmonious garden.*

▼ *With some pots, seeds and imagination, we can create tranquil and beautiful spaces.*

FENG SHUI PRINCIPLES IN THE GARDEN

Taoist principles lie at the heart of Chinese garden design and can be seen in the ancient gardens in the province of Suzhou today. Many of the principles are echoed in what is considered to be good garden design around the world. Other principles stem from the culture and mythology of China and are not included here, since every culture has its own beliefs and practices which are part of its heritage and should be preserved. Feng Shui allows for these differences. Hopefully, with an adaptation of the principles we will be able to develop our own gardens in a way which will enhance our lives.

CHINESE GARDENS

Chinese gardens originated in the centres of power, the homes of the wealthy and around religious sites, and they represent an attempt to recreate the perfection of nature and the unity of human beings, Heaven and Earth. In China, garden design conforms to the same philosophical principles as the other arts. It grew out of the fusion of the Confucian concept of art, as something created by human beings but modelled on nature, and the Taoist belief in the superiority of the natural world as an art form. It produced some of the most dramatic yet tranquil places in the world.

In China, the garden and home are considered to be a single entity. The garden is drawn into the house through windows and latticed panels, while the walls serve as backdrops to carefully chosen plants. Chinese gardens are designed to accommodate human beings and their activities so buildings are a major feature, whether for recreation, as viewing platforms, or as observatories. In the same way that European landscape architects like "Capability" Brown and Humphrey Repton used the natural scenery as a backdrop to their gardens, ancient Chinese designers incorporated mountains, natural water features and trees into theirs. If such natural features were absent they created them, building hills and importing large rocks to emulate mountains. It was said that the Sung Dynasty fell because the Emperor became obsessed with transporting huge rocks for his garden from a remote province and bankrupted the state.

Chinese domestic architecture determined a key concept of garden design. Houses were built around three sides of a central courtyard, and the empty centre is an important feature of Feng Shui. Whereas Western designers might fill the

▲ *Large gnarled rocks are used in Chinese gardens to symbolize mountains, and are often subjects of meditation.*

▼ *Mountains and water – shan shui – are essential features of the gardens of China.*

▼ *This garden in England shows natural planting typical of Chinese-style gardens.*

▲ *Open, enclosed and covered spaces all feature in the design of the Chinese garden.*

► *Openings in walls and windows offer inviting glimpses of pleasures to come.*

centres of enclosed spaces with geometrically aligned beds, the Taoist view of a space lies in its potential. It is not a lifeless void, but an energetic area brimming with possibilities. Walls are given meaning by inserting windows which look to the world beyond; rocks are brought to life by the hollows and crevices which give them character.

According to the Tao, human activity should never dictate the shape of the natural world, since all things should be allowed to develop naturally. Thus the clipped trees and hedges which can be seen in Western gardens do not occur in a Chinese garden where the natural forms of trees are allowed to develop. Whatever alterations are carried out in a Chinese garden, the result must look natural. Ponds, lakes and hills all resemble their natural counterparts.

The aesthetic principles behind all Chinese art forms, as well as the moral and ethical principles on which society is built, are all based on observations and interpretations of the natural world. Human characteristics are compared with natural phenomena, such as stone, bamboo and blossoms. Mountains and water, which play an integral part in the study of Feng Shui, feature largely in Chinese gardens and paintings.

Plants and Their Meanings

Aspidistra: Fortitude
Chrysanthemum: Resolution
Cypress: Nobility
Gardenia: Strength
Hydrangea: Achievement
Kerria: Individualism
Orchid: Endurance
Peony: Wealth
Pine: Longevity
Pomegranate: Fertility
Rhododendron: Delicacy
Virginia Creeper: Tenacity

▲ *According to Taoist principles, the interest of these stones lies in their holes, since it is they that bring the stones to life.*

► *The design of this garden is based on natural plant forms, rocks and water.*

THE FENG SHUI GARDEN

▲ *Observations of the natural world and an understanding of the laws of nature led to the creation of the formulae on which Feng Shui is based.*

The "Magic Square" on which Feng Shui is based represents a picture of the universe. Its arrangement lies at the heart of Feng Shui and represents the dynamic interaction of all natural phenomena and life forms. Much of the art of applying Feng Shui lies in interpreting the natural imagery associated with each section of the Magic Square.

We can interpret these natural phenomena at their face value or can read into them ancient concepts describing the workings of the universe. For example, scientists investigating the beginnings of life on Earth believe that huge storms were a catalyst which sparked life into action in the waters. This can be read into the interaction of the opposites Thunder and Lake on the diagram. In the same vein, the interaction of Sun and Water brings about photosynthesis in plants which enable the planet to breathe and on which all living things depend. The Wind, the Sun's rays and rain from the skies (Heaven) bring this about, while the Earth and Mountain create a stable and nourishing environment in which life forms can thrive.

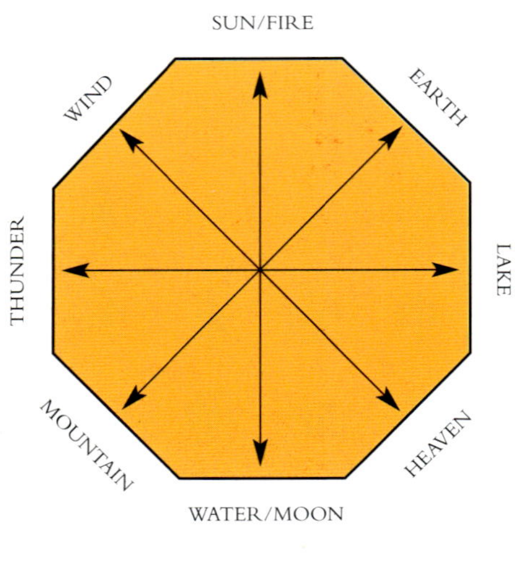

◀ *This arrangement shows how the dynamic forces of the universe interact to create life.*

▶ *Rice terraces in China follow the contours of the mountains, showing how human beings can work in harmony with Nature.*

In ancient China, garden designers were inspired by the wonderful mountain formations and the water-filled valleys. Poets wrote about mountains, seen from near and far, from above and below, and rocks were placed in gardens so that they could be seen from different vantage points. Scenes were designed to change with the seasons and the weather, and garden buildings and walkways were designed to take in these different views. Rocks and buildings were placed high on hills or mounds where they could be seen from a distance, or low in valleys, by lakes and pools. All the garden features were contained in large open spaces, within which smaller vistas opened up.

▲ *Zigzag walkways are designed to offer different views of the garden as they twist and turn through it.*

◀ *The Moon Gate invites us to move beyond our immediate space, symbolically opening up our vision.*

The Four Animals

The classic Four Animal formation governs the placement of each building and each vista in a garden. The backdrop, in the Tortoise position, is something solid, like a clump of pine trees or a rock, with trees and shrubs or more rocks to the east in the Dragon position. To the west, the area should be lower and flatter to keep the unpredictable energy of the Tiger under control, and in front, in the Phoenix position, should be a small clump of trees or a small rock to mark the boundary of the garden space.

YIN AND YANG

Nowhere is the duality of the two opposing yet complementary forces of yin and yang more pronounced than in the garden. The strong, solid mountains, or the rocks which represent them, contrast with the still, deep waters in the lakes and ponds. The image portrayed by each would not be so effective if they were not set in contrast to each other. The beauty of a single flower is more pronounced when set against a dark, rocky surface, as are the twisted branches of an ancient tree when seen against the sky.

There is a feeling of serenity in a Chinese garden, but not because it is lifeless and still. There is movement and also sound – the rustle of the wind through the trees and the call of birds and animals. Movement is suggested by the shapes of the rocks, which may be given evocative names like Crouching Tiger and Flying Dragon, as well as in the patterns within the weathered rock faces. The bent trunks and twisted stems of carefully positioned

▲ *An example of yin and yang – solidity and emptiness. The path tempts us forward.*

◀ *Solid rocks set off delicate plants and a tiny spray of water that wets the pebbles.*

▼ *The twisted stems of* Corylus avellana *'Contorta' would be lost against foliage but stand out against a white wall.*

Yin Plants	Yang Plants
Apricot	Bamboo (below)
Jasmine	Cherry
Magnolia	Chrysanthemum
Pear	Orchid
Rhododendron	Peony
Rose (below)	Willow

trees and shrubs contrast with pale walls or the sky. Ancient Chinese gardens provided the backdrop for social life in wealthy circles. Operas, dancing and music filled the gardens with sound. They were lit by lanterns which created their own tableaux.

Everything in a Chinese garden is strategically placed to highlight its beauty and impact and is seen in relation to everything else around it. An English cottage garden, filled with a rich variety of flowers, is lovely in a completely different way to one in which a beautiful stone or a single bloom is all that is needed to create a powerful visual impact. Every plant is endowed with yin or yang depending on its qualities or the symbolism of the character which represents it in the Chinese language.

▼ *A wooden arch acts as a Moon Gate to beckon us to a different part of the garden.*

▲ *A small rock and a pool can take on the characteristics of a mountain and a lake.*

Yang	Yin
People	Nature
Narrow	Broad
Hard	Soft
Dominant	Supportive
Straight	Curved
Solidity	Emptiness
Movement	Stillness
High	Low
Visible	Concealed
Exterior	Interior

Perspective is used in an interesting way in the Chinese garden. Vistas like those created by the great Western landscape designers are an integral part of Chinese design, but there is an additional emphasis. Sizes are seen to be relative. A vast mountain viewed from a distance can appear small, but a small stone close at hand can be given great importance. The notion of the "garden room", which has been part of Western design for a number of years, is also a traditional feature of Chinese gardens. Small gardens are created within larger spaces and larger vistas are opened up within quite small areas by using "windows" to give glimpses of the world beyond.

The Island of the Immortals

Ponds and lakes often contain an island in imitation of the sacred dwelling place of the Eight Immortals far off in the eastern seas. It is designed to lure them into the garden to reveal the secrets of eternal life. Trees are never planted on islands since this would symbolize isolation.

CHI – THE UNIVERSAL ENERGY

Chi is the life force present in all animate beings and is also the subtle energy expressed by seemingly inanimate objects. Gardens reflect the human quest for longevity, which in China means the maintenance of youth, rather than the Western concept of being long-lived. Every feature in a garden is placed there to achieve this aim; rocks and lakes represent permanence, and long-lived trees, shrubs and perennial plants are preferred to annuals or biennials. This makes the chi, the life force of the environment, strong and stable.

Rocks

Rocks are symbolic of the mountains which are the dominant features of many parts of China. Three types of rock were incorporated into the design of large classical gardens – huge rocks big enough to walk through, delicate upright rocks and those which had complex patterns or shapes. Rockeries were built in the north and west of gardens to provide shelter and to act as a contrast to pools, which were situated in the south and east to capture the beneficial energies believed to emanate from those directions.

Rocks may appear to be inanimate, but the Chinese perceive them to be powerful and to speak volumes in the veining on their surfaces and the symbolic expressions suggested by their shapes. Small stones, known as dreamstones, are set into the backs of chairs and hung on walls in garden pavilions. As objects for contemplation, they can lead us, via the energy channels in their markings, to pursue the Tao in our quest to be at one with the universe.

Water

Water brings energy to a garden. A still pond reflects the ever-changing heavens, and brings in the energy of the universe and the sun, the moon, the stars and the clouds that are reflected on the surface. Moving water brings sound and movement as it tumbles over pebbles and creates small whirlpools and eddies. Fountains did not feature in ancient Chinese gardens, but modern technology enables us to bring the energy of water into even the tiniest space.

Water symbolizes wealth and is believed to be a good collector and conductor of chi. Gently flowing water, entering a healthy pool from the east, is very auspicious, particularly when it meanders slowly away and cannot be seen leaving. Gold and silver coloured fish symbolize money and are therefore found in abundance in China. Although pools may be square, the planting should create a kidney-shaped arrangement which appears to hug a building protectively. Symmetrical arrangements do not exist in large Chinese gardens but are acceptable in smaller ones.

▲ *Water is an integral part of a Chinese garden, with a variety of paths and walkways to provide different vistas over it.*

▶ *Bridges with semi-circular arches are common in China. Reflected in the water, the arch creates a circle symbolizing Heaven.*

Paths and Bridges

Paths meander through Chinese gardens in the open or under covered walkways, gently curving from the east to bring in the auspicious rising energy, or more curved if coming from the west, to slow down the falling, depleted energy associated with that direction. Arched bridges span waterways, creating perfect circles with their reflections in the water, symbolizing Heaven. Others zigzag, an odd number of twists being yang and offering a soft yin vista of still water and plants. An even number of twists is yin, offering a yang view of rocks or buildings. Pagodas are often placed in the north-east and the south-west, sometimes referred to as "Doors of the Devil", to keep evil influences at bay, as these are the directions of the prevailing winds.

Trees and Plants

The planting in Chinese gardens is permanent so that the trees and plants build up an energetic relationship with their environment. We may find it strange that colour is not given special consideration, except when it reflects the passing of the seasons, but it is incidental to the main purpose of the Chinese garden.

▼ *The walkway at Jiangling Museum, China, links the building to its surroundings and offers different vistas as it zigzags*

▼ *An unobscured outside window such as this links the inner world of the house with the outer world beyond.*

▼ *The same window seen from the inside shows how the link is maintained and the garden beckons us outside.*

Buildings and Structures

Since people are an integral part of the garden, pavilions and decks are important features, encouraging them to congregate and pursue leisure interests. Bridges, paths and covered walkways give access to vistas and secluded places and enable people to enjoy gentle exercise. Walls and doorways link the inner world of the house with the outer world beyond.

Furniture and Other Objects

Seats and pots feature in the Chinese garden, but the main focus is on the rocks and the plants. In public gardens, amusing objects like huge colourful dragons appear at festival times. In parks, vivid beds of brightly coloured plants, often with swirling designs incorporated, reflect the public, or yang, space as opposed to the yin space of the private garden.

THE FIVE ELEMENTS

The Five Elements of Wood, Fire, Earth, Metal and Water are the agents of chi and they represent shapes, colours, and the senses. The aim in the Feng Shui garden is to create a space where no one element is dominant and in which there is a balance of yin and yang. The feel of a garden is very different when a balance exists, and we can achieve this in our planting schemes and by careful placement of garden buildings and ornaments. This is not to say that a garden must have something of every colour, or of every shape. There is an old Chinese saying, "Too many colours blind the eye", and we have all seen gardens that are full of brightly coloured plants, ornaments and features. They make an incredible visual show and grab the attention of passers-by, but are not conducive to relaxation or harmony.

The Feng Shui garden follows the example of the natural world in striving for a balance between shape and colour. It gives us the scope to experiment and introduce our favourite exotic plants or outlandish sculptures as well as intriguing garden buildings or brightly coloured walls – provided the perspective, proportions and balance are right. See "The Relationships of the Five Elements" table for details of the balancing elements.

▼ *Any plant, regardless of its shape or size, represents the Wood element. Tall, upright trees symbolize the Wood element shape.*

▲ *These three examples of Fire shapes – the cordyline, the potted conifers and the clipped bay – each have a different energy.*

Wood

All plants represent the Wood element which obviously dominates the planting in any garden, yet the shapes and colours of the plants and the settings in which we place them can suggest other elements. To introduce the Wood element specifically, we can use columnar trees and trellis with upright wooden supports.

Fire

Fire is suggested in plants with pointed leaves and the introduction of even a single specimen can transform a lifeless bed.

▼ *The rounded domes on this hedge suggest Metal but the meandering shape is Water, which follows Metal in the elemental cycle.*

Five Element Features in the Garden

	Wood	Fire	Earth	Metal	Water
Colour	Green	Red Purple	Yellow Orange Brown	White Silver	Dark blue Black
Represen-tations	Columns Furniture Decking Planters Logs	Pyramids Obelisks Arrows Points Lights	Rectangles Flat tops Squares Troughs Rock and stone	Domes Balls Hummocks Bowls Lead	Meanders Drifts Gravel Water features Glass

Triangles and pyramid shapes are also representative of Fire and many supports for climbing plants are available in this shape. When siting them, be careful that they are not out of proportion to the structures and plants surrounding them. The Fire element is powerful. A splash of red which represents this element is enough to make a definite statement.

Earth

Earth is suggested in paving and pathway materials. The real thing – the garden soil – is not on show in the Feng Shui garden since it will be covered with plants. Flat-topped fences, trellises and walkways suggest the Earth element. Too much of this shape can depress the chi of a place and it can easily dominate a garden surrounded by walls and fences. Introduce different shapes in garden buildings and structures and attempt to alter the shape of the view.

▼ *The metal shapes of these trees appear to dance, bringing a lively energy to the garden.*

Metal

Round shapes and domes represent the Metal element. The yin and yang aspects of this in the garden can be very different. Tall, closely packed oval conifers can be menacing to walk through. On the other hand, a series of small coniferous balls spread around the garden introduce an element of fun. All-white gardens can have a lifeless feel about them but in a small conservatory they have a pleasantly cooling effect.

Water

Apart from the real thing, the Water element is suggested by meandering shapes, both in paths and in planting. Gravel and heather gardens are an example of Water-shaped planting and similar effects can be achieved by low planting or by introducing drifts of the same plant or colours.

▲ *Low, meandering planting suggests the Water element, as it resembles a stream.*

The Transformation of the Elements

Just as yin and yang each transform into the other when their energy reaches its peak, so can the Elements transform into their opposites. The best example of this in the garden is where the Wood element transforms into Earth. In a predominantly green garden, with Earth-shaped boundaries and brown, wooden, rectangular furniture, the Wood is transformed into the Earth element and the result is a low-energy garden. The remedy is to introduce other shapes and splashes of colour to bring the garden to life.

THE UNSEEN ENERGIES

There are many unseen energies at work in the garden. Some manifest themselves in physical conditions which we can observe. Others, if we are unaware of them, can create difficulties when we are sitting and working in the garden. Many, however, work for our benefit and we must take care to create a safe haven for them.

Underground Water

There may be some areas in the garden which are situated over underground water sources. We need to be aware of this in order to choose plants which will survive in such conditions – it is no use putting in plants which prefer dry conditions here. Such areas will have a bearing on how we design the garden and we should mark them on any plan we make.

Underground streams can create a disturbance in the earth which may affect plants growing above them and could have an adverse effect on us if we are sitting or working above them for any length of time. Dowsing is the best way to find these and it may be worth engaging a dowser to check an area before you build a garden office or workshop. Distressed plants – trees which lean for no apparent reason, shrubs which develop cankers or plants which look sickly and die for no obvious reason – reveal that something is amiss.

▲ *Underground water can create difficulties in gardens in terms of geopathic stress and waterlogged areas.*

► *Trees have a relationship with their environment and provide a home to thousands of different species of animals and plants.*

▼ *If you respect the garden's natural ecological system you will be rewarded with a garden full of healthy, beautiful plants.*

The Soil

Our greatest ally in the garden is healthy soil. Before we plant anything we need to ensure that the soil is right for the plants we want to grow. Nurseries sell soil-testing kits and gardening books provide advice on the suitability of plants for

▶ *Ancient peoples ran their lives by the movement of the stars and watched the skies for signs to plant and harvest crops.*

specific conditions. Acid-loving plants will never thrive in alkaline soil and vice versa. A Feng Shui garden should go with the flow. It is virtually impossible to alter the soil permanently in order to grow your favourite plants, so before buying a new house it is worth looking in neighbouring gardens to see which plants do well in the area.

The soil is a living entity teeming with millions of micro-organisms, each with its own role to play in the ecology of the garden. In the Feng Shui garden these microbes are valued and we should provide them with the conditions in which to thrive, in terms of sun, rain and air, as well as food made from composting our garden and kitchen waste. The folly of planting through plastic or microporous sheeting, which prevents weeds but also suffocates the micro-organisms and causes the soil to become stagnant and lifeless, is now understood.

Spirit of the Place

Some people believe that trees and plants are imbued with spirits. Others respect the relationship that long-lived trees have built up with the Earth and the support and nourishment that they provide for micro-organisms, other plants and animals, including human beings. Every garden has its support team of mammals, birds and insects, and even snails, which have a role. The slightest tinkering in terms of chemicals or soil disturbance can have an unsettling effect on the ecological chain. In the Feng Shui garden we respect our fellow workers.

Cosmic Energies

Ancient peoples around the world respected the part played by the sun, the moon and the weather in their lives and the growth of their crops, and many festivals reflect this. The cosmos affects who we are and determines our characters. This also applies in the plant world although plants cannot take charge and manipulate circumstances as we can. We must determine the best conditions for them. By planting according to the movements of the moon, we can greatly improve the conditions for our plants. Planting by the moon's phases is an ancient skill and requires only watching the sky or consulting a diary giving the dates of the new and full moons.

▶ *The numbered days correspond to the days of the moon's cycle. It is advisable not to plant close to the equinoxes and the solstices.*

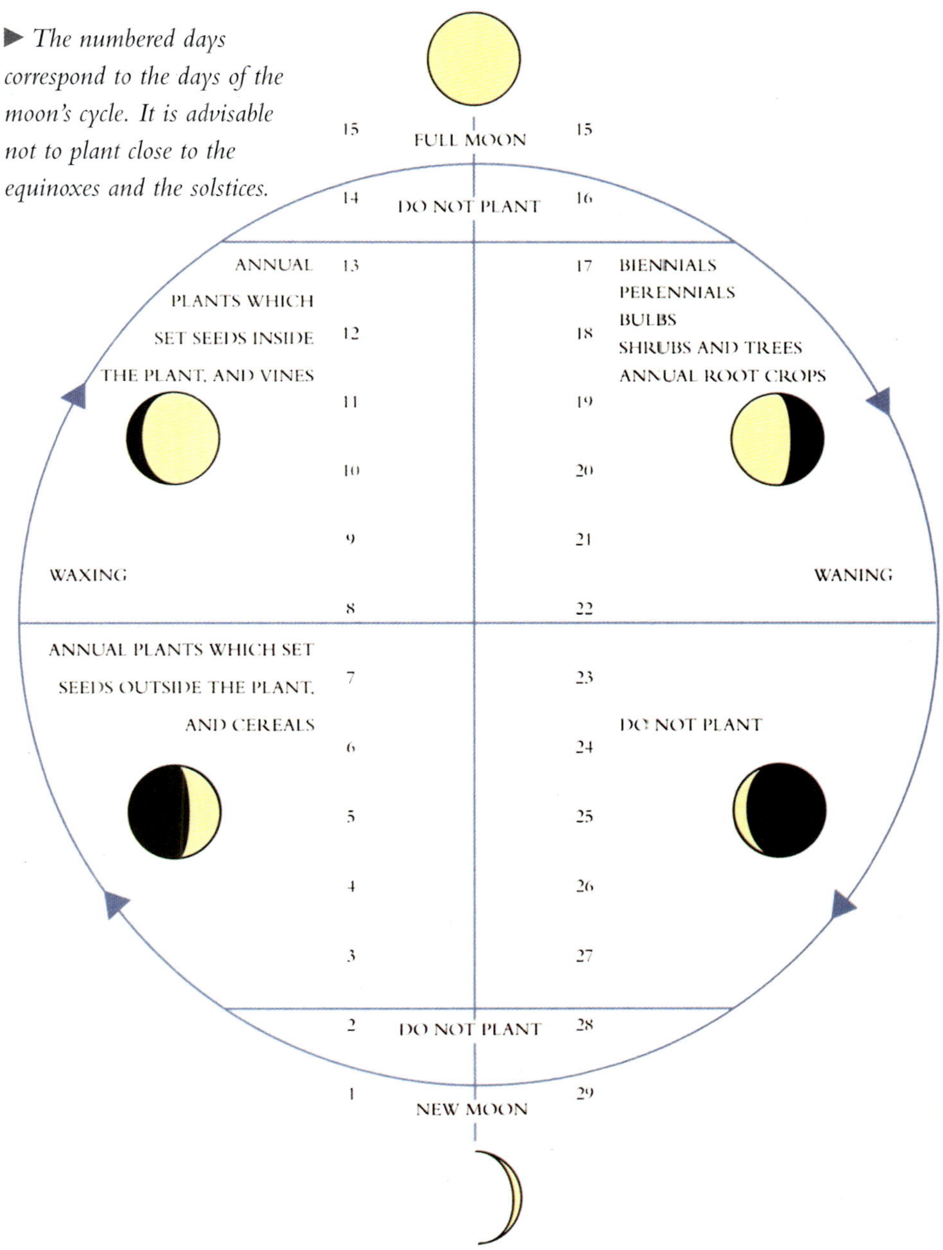

▼ *The new moon – time to plant annual flower seeds, leafy vegetables and cereals.*

THE SHAPE OF THE GARDEN

▲ *This picket fence defines the space and acts as a boundary without shutting out the world to a garden full of energy. The whole effect would be improved by taking out the dead tree on the right.*

The shape of the plot of land on which we build, or on which our existing home is sited, is important in Feng Shui. Regular shapes are best, so that there are no missing areas. We can use various means to make a plot appear more regular in shape than it already is. Fences and trellis can divide awkwardly-shaped plots into separate areas which are easier to deal with individually. The use of different materials as edging can create boundaries and, of course, plants can open up or conceal the most difficult spaces. Creative planting can create virtually any illusion we desire.

▼ *Trellis can be used to divide up gardens which have difficult shapes.*

▼ *This house sits well in its plot. The back gardens of houses built in Britain over the past century tend to be larger than the front but in most of Europe and in the United States, the reverse is true. Trees and shrubs protect the rear and sides and a fence shields the front, in line with the classic Four Animals formation.*

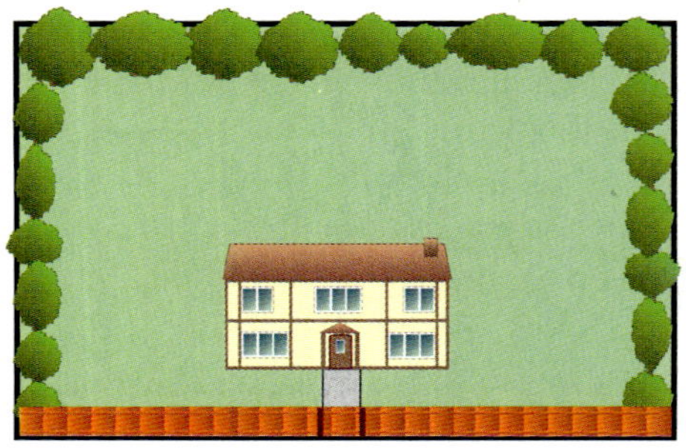

▼ *This house sits too far to the back of its plot. The tall trees here will be overwhelming to the occupants of the house and from a more practical point of view could even be dangerous in high winds. Local preservation orders should be checked before taking steps to reduce the height of the trees.*

▲ *By changing the shape of the plot within the garden and with careful planting, the harsh lines of a triangular plot are lessened.*

▲ *Trellis or other features, preferably rounded, will serve to reduce the effect of the triangle's points. Mirrors in the positions indicated (A and B) reflect interesting planting, not each other, and will give the illusion of pushing the boundaries out.*

The Rectangular Plot

A rectangular plot is regarded as the ideal shape. The house should be sited on the centre of the plot so that the garden is in proportion around the house.

The Triangular Plot

Triangular plots are not considered desirable in Feng Shui because the sharp points are felt to resemble knives. They are also difficult to deal with because they create three areas of stagnant energy. However, with careful planting and the erection of screens, it is possible to create the illusion of a regular shaped plot. An alternative is to plant heavily on the boundaries and use meandering paths within the garden.

Round and L-shaped Plots

Round plots are difficult. Although the chi is able to flow freely round, it is difficult to contain it and it is advisable to create other, more stable shapes within the circle for seating areas. L-shaped and other irregularly shaped plots are best divided into regular shaped sections to make them simpler to deal with.

The Bright Hall

The Bright Hall was originally a pool of water in front of a house. Its function was to gather energy and to preserve an open space there. It could take the form of a sunken garden or simply an open, gathering space. These days it is the space in front of the front door. It should be in proportion to the front of the house, and be well maintained and uncluttered.

▲ *The chi flows quickly around this circular plot. Contain it with a shrub hedge and create inner areas for seating.*

▲ *A trellis or fence positioned as shown will regularize this L-shaped plot.*

CASE STUDY

Care has to be taken when designing a Bright Hall, as Tom and Rhoda discovered. They created a wonderful Bright Hall in front of their house. Made of mellow stone and edged with red brick, which blended with the house, it was welcoming and greatly enhanced the front entrance. However, a Chinese Feng Shui consultant pronounced it inauspicious and suggested they have a straight step instead. They were flabbergasted but the reason was that on coming out of the house, the round edge turned into the lip of a jug, symbolically pouring money away down the sloping drive and into the road.

Some people have a greater level of perception than others but the skill can be acquired with practice. Before building or planting we should mark out our ideas and view them from all angles.

▲ *Viewed from the front this well-built Bright Hall appears to create a welcoming space in front of the house.*

▲ *However, seen from this angle, it resembles the lip of a jug, symbolically pouring money away.*

DRAWING THE PLAN

Before creating a Feng Shui garden it is first necessary to investigate the compass directions around the site to determine the direction of the prevailing winds and to site the plants according to their preferences. When we are sitting or working in the garden it is useful to place ourselves in auspicious directions. We also need to investigate the positions of the Five Elements of the site to create a balance between them and with the features which we place in the garden.

Draw a Plan

Using graph paper to a suitable scale, take measurements for the length and breadth of the garden and mark

- ◆ House and garage
- ◆ Walls and fences
- ◆ Large trees and shrubs
- ◆ Garden buildings
- ◆ Semi-permanent features such as ponds, rockeries and patios.
- ◆ Features in the surrounding environment such as trees, other buildings, lampposts and so on.

Take a Compass Reading

1. Remove watches, jewellery and metal objects and stand clear of cars and other metal fixtures.

2. Stand with your back parallel to the front door and note the exact compass reading in degrees.

3. Note the direction, e.g. 349° North, and mark it on to the plan of the garden as shown in the diagram. You are now ready to transfer the compass readings on to your Bagua drawing.

4. Place the protractor on the Bagua diagram so that 0° is at the bottom at the North position.

5. Find the compass reading for your home and check you have the corresponding direction – if not you may be reading the wrong ring.

6. Mark the position of your house.

7. Look at the "Directions" table on the opposite page to double check the compass direction.

Transfer the Directions to the Plan

1. To find the centre of the plan, match the main boundaries across the length of the plan and crease the paper lengthways.

2. Match the main boundaries across the width and crease the paper widthways.

3. Where the folds of the creases cross

You Will Need

- ◆ A scale plan of your home. If you own your home you will already have one. If not, it will be necessary to draw one, in which case you will also need a tape measure and graph paper
- ◆ A compass with the eight directions clearly marked
- ◆ A ruler
- ◆ A lead pencil and five coloured pencils – green, red, yellow, grey, dark blue
- ◆ A tracing of the Bagua with the suggested information marked on
- ◆ A protractor

▼ *The Bagua should be superimposed on the plan to line up the main entrance with its corresponding direction and element.*

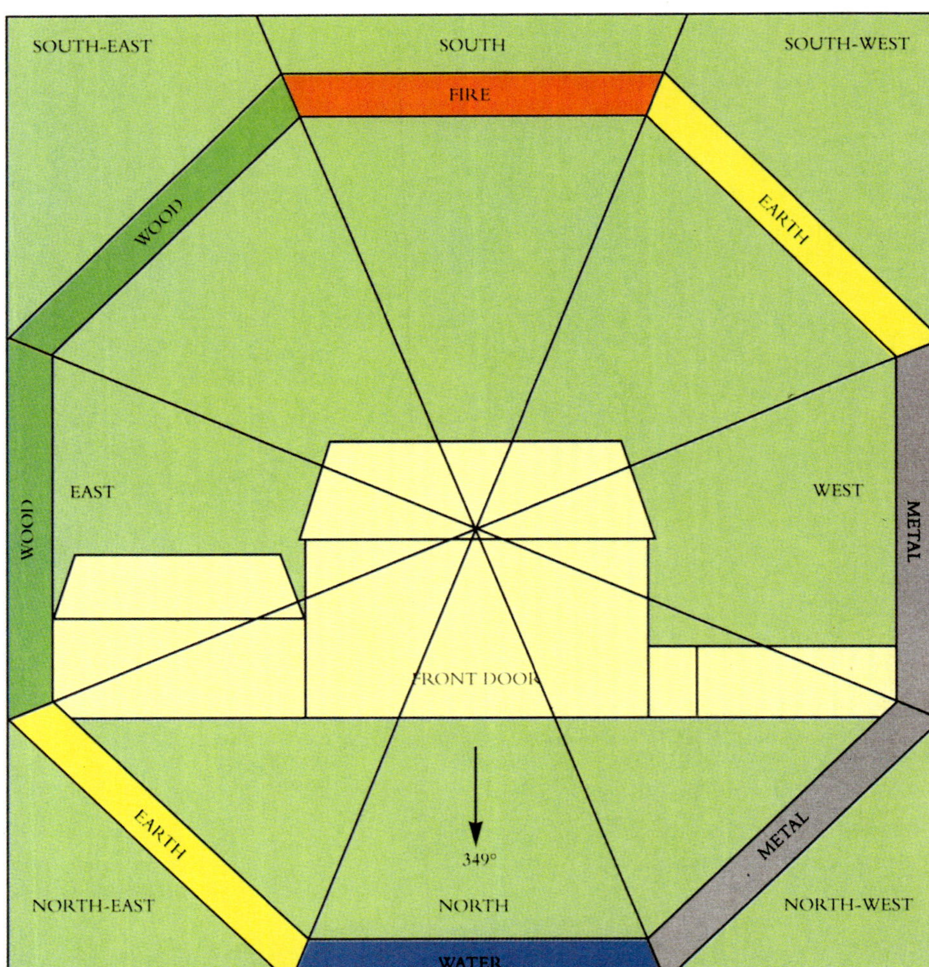

Directions	
North	337.5 – 22.5°
North-east	22.5 – 67.5°
East	67.5 – 112.5°
South-east	112.5 – 157.5°
South	157.5 – 202.5°
South-west	202.5 – 247.5°
West	247.5 – 292.5°
North-west	292.5 – 337.5°

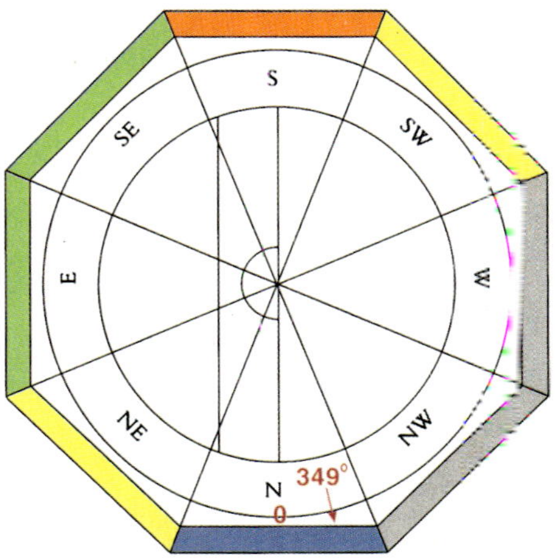

▲ *A circular protractor will help you line up the compass direction and the Bagua.*

▶ *Semi-permanent features like this pond, and all buildings and boundaries, should be marked on the plan.*

marks the centre of your garden.

4. If your garden is not a perfect square or rectangular shape, treat a protrusion less than 50% of the width as an extension to the direction.

5. If the protrusion is more than 50% of the width, treat the remainder as a missing part of the direction.

6. Place the centre of the Bagua on the centre point of the plan and line up the front door position.

7. Mark the eight directions on the plan and draw in the sectors.

8. Transfer the Bagua's colour markings on to the plan.

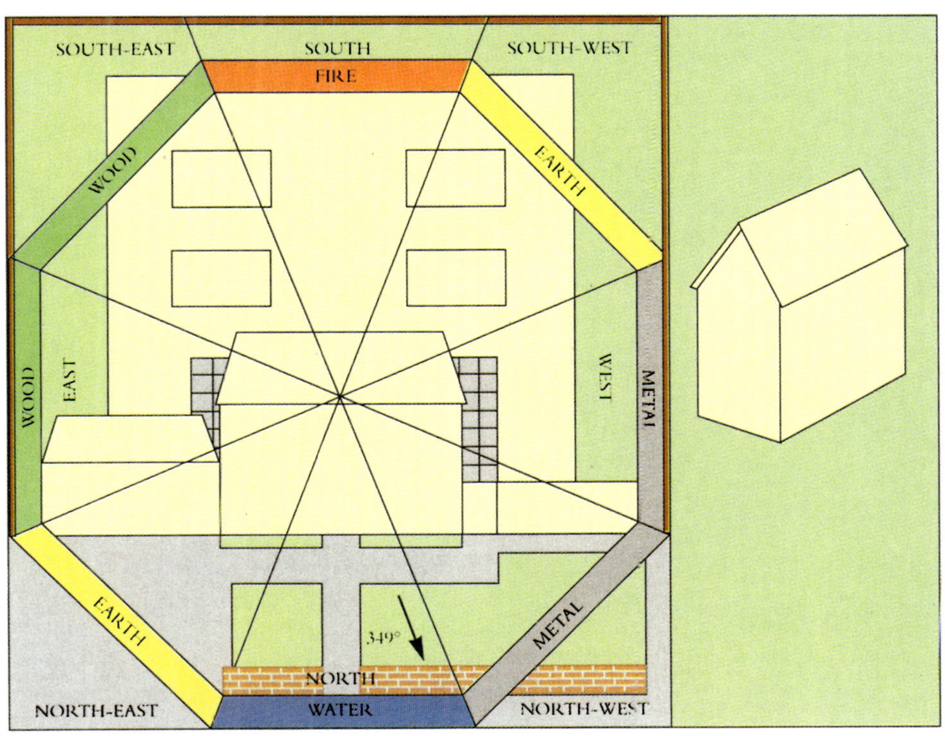

▶ *Once you have marked on the existing main features of your plot you will be ready to investigate the Feng Shui potential of your garden.*

CASE STUDY

Mike and Sarah wanted a more interesting garden which required as little maintenance as possible. The neighbours on their left complained that the four-year-old *Cupressocyparis leylandii* trees were blocking their light and those on the right that they were killing nearby plants. Mike came to realize that they were a high-maintenance feature as they grew so fast. With three sons under the age of 12, they required a large space for ball games. Sarah wanted to grow some fruit and a few summer salad vegetables.

▼ *Once you know your magic number you can determine which directions are beneficial and will support you. Whether you are relaxing in the garden or enjoying a meal with family or friends you can choose to place your chair to face your best direction.*

Where to Sit

1	SE or N
2	NE or SW
3	S or E
4	N or SE
5(m)	NE or SW
5(f)	SW or NE
6	W or NW
7	NW or W
8	E or S
9	E or S

▲ *While not exactly looking after themselves, interesting gardens like this require reasonably low maintenance.*

▼ *Water features come in many shapes and sizes and, placed in auspicious positions, can bring good luck and focus thought.*

▼ *We can bring water into the garden even in the smallest space, as illustrated by this Japanese-style water feature.*

The family wanted a low-maintenance pond to attract wildlife. Sarah also wanted a water feature on the patio.

Much to everyone's relief, the *leylandii* were removed and the soil was improved with organic matter and compost.

1. The four "cornerstones" were addressed first. In the south-west, an ivy-covered trellis was erected to filter the wind. A solid hedge would have set up wind turbulence.

2. A blossom tree was placed on the lawn to filter the north-east wind and to encourage the vibrant energy of the east on to the site.

3. A closed-back arbour was placed in the south-east to hide the compost bins, ideally placed in the Wealth area to provide sustenance for the garden, and to stabilize the area. The Fire-shaped roof moves the energy forward.

4. In the north-west a rounded metal plate was positioned showing the number of the house.

5. A light is placed in the north-east.

6. A rockery is sited in the Phoenix position in the front garden.

7. The path meanders to a spacious step, and pots with round-shaped plants as guardians sit on either side of the door.

8. A shrub is grown on the wall between the garage and house to help reduce the impact of a north-east wind.

9. A shrub here balances the one on the other side.

10. A yellow-berried pyracantha is placed here to stimulate the Metal energy and to give some prickly protection against unwelcome intruders.

11. A meandering stepping-stone path leads from the garage and the side gate, giving a balanced formality to the garden but affording different vistas as it curves.

12. The large back lawn area is surrounded by trees and shrubs – staggered, like fielders, to catch the children's stray balls and also to provide a pleasant walk around the garden.

13. The pond is backed by evergreen plants and shrubs to prevent leaves from falling into it. Situated in the south-west it signifies future prosperity and should be kept healthy with oxygenating plants.

14. On a square wooden table stands a round metal sundial with an arrow pointing upwards. Every one of the Five Elements is used here to stimulate the Fame and Future Possibilities area of the symbolic Bagua.

15. Sarah places perennial plants and bulbs in an urn in front of the arbour – silver and gold to represent money in the summer months and red berries in the winter months to stimulate the Wealth area of the Symbolic Bagua.

16. A medium-height evergreen tree is planted here which will eventually block the point of the roof of a neighbouring house. Meanwhile, a concave mirror is placed on the side of the house to symbolically absorb the "poison arrow".

17. Trellis is erected around the edge of a paved area to protect the house from any thrown balls and to enable Sarah to grow espalier-trained fruit. Herbs are grown in the flower beds as companion plants and salad vegetables are grown in the gaps.

18. A small water feature in the east stimulates the area of current prosperity.

19. Sarah's small greenhouse enables her to overwinter her perennial pot plants.

20. The patio chairs are positioned so that Sarah and Mike are backed by the garage wall, facing favourable positions. The protective Four Animal arrangement corresponds to the back, front and side aspects of the house and not to actual compass directions.

USING THE BAGUA IN THE GARDEN

The symbolic Bagua is generally discussed in terms of the house, yet we can use its magic in the garden too. If there is a certain aspect of our lives on which we need to focus, the symbolic Bagua gives us a tool to stimulate the energy associated with it, particularly when we look out on the area through the kitchen or sitting room windows. As in the house, we can divide the garden into rooms when applying the Bagua since it is not usual to be able to see the whole garden from one vantage point.

The enhancements used are designed to focus the mind and to create a stabilizing effect by using or alluding to heavy objects such as stones or mountains, or to shift something in our lives by creating or alluding to movement, water, or wind-blown items. Empty pots and

▲ *A garden full of energy – different shapes, colours and levels, and a variety of materials, add to the interest.*

▲ *A herb garden directly outside a window is a good area to apply the Bagua.*

◀ *Use pots of plants in a group as a focus point in the garden.*

SUGGESTIONS FOR ENHANCEMENTS:

- ◆ Rocks, stones and large pots for added stability
- ◆ Wind objects to stir up the energy and create movement
- ◆ Fountains and water features for abundance
- ◆ Empty urns and dishes to accept the gifts of the universe
- ◆ Lights to illuminate paths or particular features in the garden
- ◆ Collections and art works for achievement
- ◆ Pot plants for focus

CASE STUDY

Paul and Claire both work from home. Paul is a writer who has had two novels published. He would like a more settled life, with a regular contract with a publisher, and would like to branch out and write for TV. Claire runs an aromatherapy practice and is planning to develop an idea and sell products by mail order. They both adore gardening and, when they are not in their respective study or workrooms, they spend much of their leisure time there. They have enhanced the appropriate areas of the Bagua in their home and would like to do the same in the garden.

1. Paul placed a bird table in the Helpful People area of the small side garden outside his office window in order to encourage the calls from publishers and TV companies to roll in. As organic gardeners, Paul and Claire do not like spraying insect pests, so small birds are very welcome in the garden. Paul greased the pole of the table to keep the birds safe from cats and prevent squirrels from taking the food. He takes care to observe which plants the birds are attracted to naturally and uses seeds from those plants to feed them, since he feels that bread and commercially produced bird food may harm them. He also places a dish of clean water there every day.

2. In the Fame area, Paul placed a large terracotta sun which smiles at him when he looks up from his work and will hopefully help him to fulfil his ambitions.

3. In the small garden outside Claire's therapy room, she placed a dish containing her rock plant collection in the Offspring area in order to focus on her business plans.

4. On the trellis separating Claire's garden from the main garden, the couple planted a *Trachelospermum jasminoides* – an evergreen climbing plant with fragrant white flowers which will last for most of the summer. This is in the Offspring area of the main garden.

5. Opposite the climber, Paul and Claire created a pond with a fountain, in the Family area of the main garden, having first checked that the water was not in an inauspicious position with regard to the Five Elements.

urns can suggest an empty space waiting for something to happen – this is particularly helpful in the Wealth area, for example. Whatever image we use must have meaning for us in that we can see it physically and relate to its illusion and symbolism. Thus we should use images from our own culture and experience. Whatever we use should not clash with the element of the direction, but if possible should strengthen it. A pot of plants suggesting the colour of the element can always be used, or an enhancement suggested on the facing page.

Since the enhancements are meant to trigger an emotion or action, we should place them where we can see them. If we have a large front garden, gardens to the side and at the back of the house, the chances are that there will be areas which we rarely look at. Those areas which are more useful to us in placing the Bagua are those which we constantly look at. For example, if we have a herb garden outside the kitchen window, or if our study faces the side garden, then these are the areas to concentrate on.

GARDEN FEATURES

For the most part we cannot determine the natural phenomena in our gardens or in the wider environment. We are, however, responsible for the plants and features we install there. With an understanding of the principles which govern Feng Shui, we can choose furniture, buildings, plants and colours which work in harmony with each other and the surrounding area and which create a balanced and supportive environment for us. We can also deliberately introduce features which clash in order to create a more vibrant energy in the garden.

PATHS

Paths carry chi through the garden and their size, shape and the materials they are made of can affect the movement of the energy. This will affect the way we feel about and perceive the space.

FRONT GARDENS

Generally speaking, paths lead to entrances, doors or gates. When they are straight, they channel energy quickly so we tend not to notice the garden and instead simply move between our homes and the outside world. In the Feng Shui garden, the aim is to use the front garden as a space between home and the outside world where we can gather energy in the morning and slow down at the end of a hard day.

To enable us to slow down, paths should gently curve or meander, presenting us with different angles and views as we move along them. If we have no control over the shape of the path, then placing pots along them or planting so that the lines of a straight path are broken up by overhanging plants are possible alternatives. Another option is to make breaks every so often, either with beds containing plants or some kind of ornamental feature, or by creating a visual barrier using different materials.

▼ *There are points of interest all along this gently curving path.*

▲ *Winding paths slow us down and allow us to observe the garden. Note how the spiky potted plants bring this garden to life.*

BACK GARDENS

Paths should also meander around the back garden so that we constantly happen upon different views. Ideally, we

▲ *This straight path channels chi to and from the door far too quickly.*

▲ *This curving path slows down the chi and offers us different views.*

▲ *Pots spaced along a straight path will help to slow down the chi.*

▲ *Straight paths broken up in this way help to slow the energy down.*

▲ *The use of different materials also helps to slow down the energy.*

▲ *This meandering path gives the right impression but is a little too narrow.*

should not be able to take in the whole area in one glance. Where gardens are large, paths can tantalizingly draw us through gaps in trees, walls and trellises into other garden rooms beyond. Offices and sheds are places to which we often need to get in a hurry. A straight path is acceptable here, but in the case of the home office, an alternative, meandering route would be ideal.

MATERIALS FOR PATHS

Stone blocks (below), Brick, Gravel, Cobbles, Tiles, Bark, Wood, Concrete slabs, Grass

MATERIALS

Paths need to be stable and suited to their purpose. In a large garden they may need to carry heavy barrows, and therefore deep gravel would not be suitable. Cobble stones are not suitable path materials in the homes of elderly or disabled people since stability is especially important. Materials can vary in suitability between different areas – for instance in a wooded area bark paths with log edgings are fine, but grass paths and smooth surfaces are not a good idea in such damp places as they become slippery.

The materials we use will depend on local architectural style and we should aim to harmonize with it. Coloured concrete might blend into a modern urban garden but would look out of place in a rural garden, as would mellow weathered stone in an urban basement. Although the materials chosen must blend with the surroundings, we can make our paths individual by blending different materials into the design. Brick edging for concrete paths or the use of two different coloured bricks are just two of many ideas we can use.

Crazy paving is rarely used in the Feng Shui garden since its broken appearance symbolizes instability. However, it does feature in ancient Chinese gardens. Where crazy paving is well-laid, on a stable concrete foundation, the joints do not crack and the paving does not lift, it can be safely used.

▲ *Although straight, this wide pathway is practical in the herb and vegetable garden – and the plants hang over to slow down the flow of energy.*

▼ *Hidden pathways in different materials – which one should we take?*

BOUNDARIES

We all need boundaries in order to feel protected and safe. As children, our boundaries are formed by the family unit and, as we get older, they expand to include school, our work and the organizations we join. When we become adults we continue to live within the boundaries of our social, recreational and professional groups. Our most important space is our home where we go to be ourselves and for support and rest. Boundaries are important in our relationships with our neighbours and with the world at large, as demarcation lines which give us a sense of security.

▲ *A front garden divides the home from the outside world but maintains a connection.*

Front Gardens

In China, the ideal is to have an open view in front of a building, with a small barrier to mark the boundary and, of course, to be facing south. In the West, the reverse is often the case and in temperate climates most people prefer a south-facing back garden. In Feng Shui it is recommended that a front barrier should never exceed the height of the downstairs windowsill, or waist height. To maintain a balance in life, it is important to be able to connect, not only with the immediate outside world but also with the universe, and we should all have a view of the sky and the changing seasons. People who shut themselves off from the world will be at best disenchanted or, at worst, suffer from a depressive illness. Privacy is important but we should not become disconnected from the world or the people in it.

▼ *Boundaries protect us and our homes, but should not cut us off from the world outside.*

Back Gardens

The boundaries we choose for our garden perimeters can act as a backdrop for our plants as well as providing protection. In order for us to feel secure they should be well maintained. Good maintenance helps our relationships with our neighbours, as quarrels over boundaries frequently feature in neighbourly disputes. Thoughtless planting of unsuitable hedging plants, like the fast-growing *Cupressocyparis leylandii*, has been known to result in neighbours ending up in court. Whether we build walls, erect fences or use trees and hedges as our boundaries we need to keep a sense of proportion and plant things which will not outgrow their space or interfere with buildings, other plants or the well-being of our neighbours. If there are insecure areas in the garden perimeter we need to create barriers which will repel intruders. Plants such as holly and pyracantha serve this purpose admirably, but do not place prickly plants where you might brush up against them accidentally.

Smaller boundaries within the garden divide it up into different areas. These can take the form of hedges, fences or trellis, or even a change from grass to flower bed or from path to lawn. We can use a single shrub or a pot to create the illusion of a barrier. Like the Moon Gates in ancient Chinese gardens, gaps in

▼ *A gate such as this gives protection without isolating the home from outside.*

▲ *Cupressocyparis leylandii is a good hedge but needs to be kept under control.*

▶ *A pyracantha hedge makes an effective, prickly, barrier.*

hedges, doors in walls and paths through trellis and arbours allow us a glimpse of an area beyond our immediate space. In small gardens the same effect can be achieved by using mirrors and *trompe-l'oeil* designs on walls to draw the eye.

Materials

Boundaries can be created from a variety of materials, or grown, using suitable plants. In either case, skill is required to

Materials for Boundaries

Brick, Pre-cast blocks, Close board wooden panels, Woven wooden panels, Chain link, Post and rail, Wattle hurdles, Split bamboo, Trellis, Chestnut

Hedging Plants for the Side Garden

(1.5–3m/5–10ft)

Cotoneaster simonsii, Berberis stenophylla, Escallonia macrantha, Aucuba japonica

create a visually pleasing and lasting effect. If a plot curves, then placing a straight wall along the boundary will spoil the look. If a hedge is built using mixed planting, incorrect weaving and supports will create a problem for the future. When positioning fences and hedges it is important to remember that windy conditions can affect plants as well as people sitting on the other side of a solid structure. In such places a permeable structure is often preferable. Fencing materials and the finials used on the posts can suggest the shapes of the Five Elements and this needs to be taken into consideration when balancing the elements.

▼ *Old brick walls are a perfect garden backdrop. Complementing materials should be chosen with care, as in this garden.*

Boundaries and the Five Elements

Fencing materials and shapes can introduce the elements in to your garden. Make sure you balance them with care.

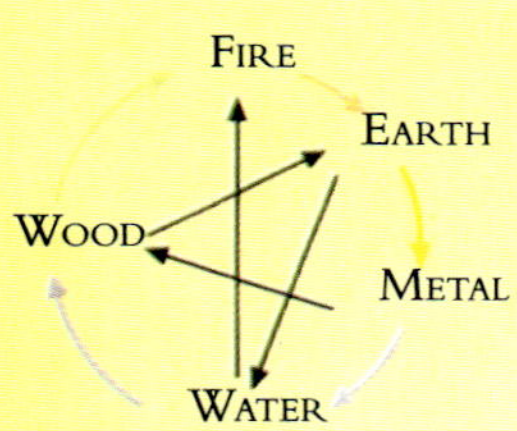

▲ *This is the Destructive Cycle.*

▲ *The first illustration shows the harmful cycle of Wood and Earth. In the second, Fire has been added for balance.*

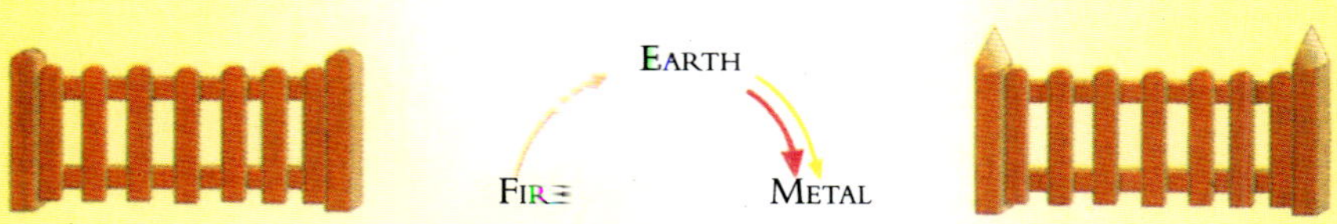

▲ *The first illustration shows the weakening cycle of the elements. In the second Fire has been added as a balance.*

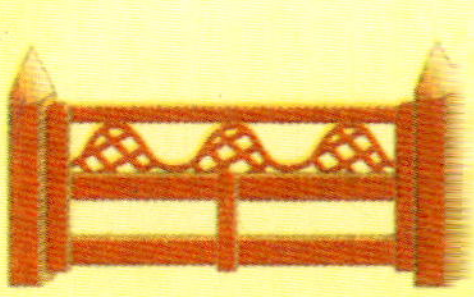

▲ *All the elements are suggested here, but the result is over-elaborate.*

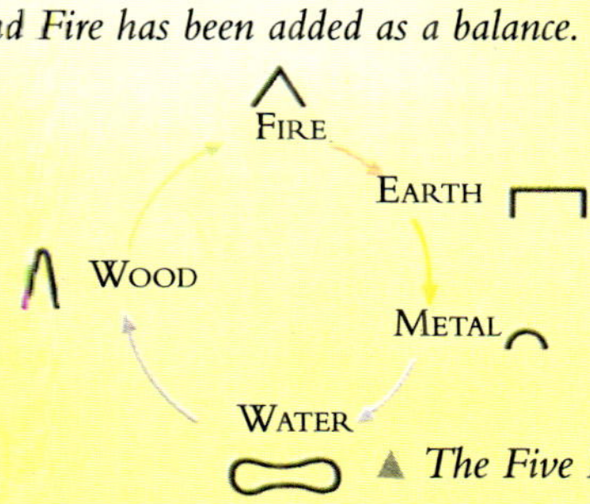

▲ *The Five Element cycle.*

WATER IN THE GARDEN

Water is of great importance in Feng Shui. In China it symbolizes the accumulation of chi, which is synonymous with wealth.

GARDEN PONDS

Any water feature situated near the home should be in proportion to the size of the house. Bigger is not better in this case, since large expanses of water will symbolically drown us. A pond which is too large will dampen our career prospects, and if a fountain is out of proportion we will find it exhausting. Everything in the garden should blend in with existing features and with the landscape. The materials we use are as important as the siting of the feature. Sharp angles could direct "poison arrows" at the house or outdoor seating area.

Whether we live in towns or in the country, our ponds will attract wildlife. Small animals that jump or fall into a pond may not be able to get out again, unless we provide them with some means to do so. If a pond has steep sides, we should make sure that there are rocks or ledges to allow creatures an escape route.

▼ *If you have a stream through the garden slow it down with overhanging plants.*

▲ *Ponds should fit naturally into a garden; irregular shapes with planting work best.*

If there are small children in the household it is important to ensure that ponds are completely safe. It may be better to install another type of water feature until children are old enough to take care.

The ideal shape for ponds is irregular, imitating natural ones. The more irregular the shape, the more plants and wildlife will thrive in and around it.

Round ponds tend to carry the chi away too quickly and square ponds create "poison arrows". Regular shapes are easier to construct, however, and can be softened and shaped into a more natural form by careful planting round the edges.

ROCKERIES

To balance the yin of a still pond we can introduce the yang energy of a rockery. This combination reflects the mountain and lake formations so important in Chinese philosophy and art and can represent the Tortoise, Dragon and Tiger formation, with the pond in front. The rules for rockery building are:

- ◆ Use an odd number of stones
- ◆ Bury the stones by at least a third in the soil
- ◆ Place stones the correct way up as indicated by the graining
- ◆ Use a flat stone next to an upright one on its concave side
- ◆ Line the other stone up with the "toe" of the first
- ◆ Do not place a round stone by a jagged stone
- ◆ Choose the most weathered, front "face" of the rock to face forwards
- ◆ Use the yin and yang theory to create a complementary arrangement

▼ *Rockeries should mirror the natural world and reflect the shape of mountains.*

▲ *The straight sides of this formal garden pond are softened with overhanging plants.*

Water Placement

Ancient Chinese writings set great store by the patterns on the surface of the water, probably as a way of determining the direction of the wind. The Water Dragon Classic, an ancient text, gives details of beneficial places to build and various shapes of water courses. The direction of the flow determines the best places to plant certain types of crops.

The direction from which water enters or leaves a property is deemed to be crucial, but theories vary. One theory suggests that it should correspond to our auspicious directions. Another suggests that in houses facing north, south, east or west, the water should enter from the east or from left to right in front of the property. Conversely, if a house faces north-east, south-east, north-west or south-west, the water should enter from the west. Another theory favours east since this is the direction of growth. Since few of us have a river running in front of our homes or are in a position to do anything about the flow, we should look at more relevant reasons for siting water features in our gardens.

The major, common-sense rule for water placement is that it should not flow quickly towards you from a point higher than your house because of the danger of flooding. A house built on a flood plain or below sea level might well experience problems, particularly as the effects of global warming cause water levels to continue to rise. It is deemed to be auspicious if the water is gently trickling towards the house, symbolizing wealth rolling in. Trickling from the east and towards our beneficial direction is also auspicious.

We are at present in a period when it is considered auspicious to place a water feature in the east to signify good luck and wealth until 2003. From 2004 until 2023, the south-west will be considered auspicious.

There are many types of water feature available commercially and many more which could be created by an imaginative gardener. Whichever feature we choose should be in harmony with the surroundings in terms of design and materials and the elements around it should be balanced.

▲ *A water feature in the south-west of the garden can symbolize future prosperity.*

▶ *Water trickling towards the house symbolizes wealth rolling in.*

Garden Furniture and Structures

▲ *An octagonal table is auspicious and allows everyone to communicate.*

As we expand our living space outside, the furnishings we choose should reflect the intended functions of the garden – play, entertainment, relaxation – as well as personal preferences. We should employ the same principles in our gardens as we do in our homes and carefully select furnishings that meet the purpose, reflect our tastes and support us.

Chairs and Tables

Garden chairs should follow the classic Four Animals formation and provide firm support for our backs as well as having arm rests. The colours chosen can be dictated by our individual preferences, but only if the Five Elements are taken into account. Chairs should be comfortable but as they are usually made of wood or metal they tend to be hard, which is acceptable if the design is right but uncomfortable if they are not ergonomically correct.

Tables should be chosen according to their function. Square tables are containing and a small square table by our favourite chair in a quiet spot may tend to keep us there and prevent us from searching for things to do. Round tables make for lively discussion but do not contain people for long. Rectangular tables with rounded ends are a common shape for garden furniture and are useful for summer lunch parties, although those seated at either end may sometimes feel left out. Octagonal tables are excellent because they are an auspicious shape and each person can communicate with everyone else around the table.

► *A supportive shape, this chair looks like a very inviting place to sit and dream.*

▼ *A perfect seat, circles and squares, with the four protective animal positions in place.*

▼ *A comfortable chair in which to spend a leisurely afternoon in the garden.*

Barbecues

Choosing a good location for a barbecue is mainly a matter of common sense. The north-west of the garden, next to a neighbour's fence where the south-west wind blows the smoke straight towards their kitchen window, is not a sensible choice. Barbecues are often positioned near a wall, but it is far better to position the cooking grid where the cook faces into the patio or terrace and is able to join in the party. Green is the best colour for a portable barbecue as black and blue represent the Water element and red might just add too much fuel to the flames.

Garden Buildings and Structures

Our gardens can also be furnished with buildings. Where we position these will affect their use and make a great impact on the overall structure and harmony of the garden. The materials used should blend with the surrounding buildings and the shapes and colours are important if we aim to keep a balance of yin and yang with the Five Elements.

▼ *A wonderful children's tree house that also blends well with its environment.*

▲ *The structures we build should blend in with the character of the garden.*

It is important that the house sits well in its environment and that we create stability at the four "cornerstones" of the garden – south-east, south-west, north-west and north-east. Garden buildings and decorative structures are a useful way of achieving this, provided they follow the Five Elements balance.

Where we use garden buildings for a specific purpose, such as our work, for growing seeds, or craft activities, the work bench should face one of our best directions, as determined earlier. We should arrange the layout to ensure that we face the entrance when standing at the bench. If this is not possible, then we should take measures to ensure we are not surprised from behind. A wind chime will alert us to someone entering and something reflective on the bench will enable us to see behind us. Mirrors are not recommended because the combination of mirror and sun can start a fire.

Some garden buildings are purely for decoration. Gazebos, although attractive to look at, are not comfortable to sit in as they are open to the wind. Structures with open sides offer no support when sitting and are therefore not ideal places in which to relax. Carefully positioned, however, they can provide excellent private spaces where we can escape and enjoy the solitude. Facing east, a gazebo can be a good place to eat an early breakfast and enjoy the energizing impact of the rising sun. Facing west, a gazebo will provide a restful spot to relax and unwind at the end of the day.

When siting garden features, take care that the edges and corners do not shoot "poison arrows" at the house or seating areas. Where points exist, climbing plants will soften or conceal them.

Useful Shapes and Colours for Cornerstones

Directions	Shapes		Colours
South-east			Brown, Green
South-west			Brown, Red
North-west			White, Silver, Brown
North-east		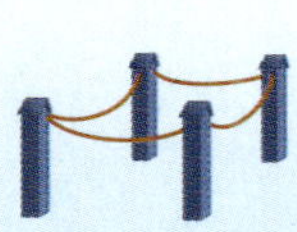	Brown, Blue

POTS AND ORNAMENTS

Containers of every conceivable size, colour and pattern are now available commercially, and they can be used to hold plants or as features on their own. Clay is the traditional material for pots and certainly plants look their best in them. Some pots are brightly coloured, which makes a welcome change and can look attractive, but they may clash with the natural colours in a garden. Consult the Five Elements table to check if the colours of the pots are compatible with the plants which will go in them. Shapes are also important and again the elements should be balanced.

Pots are imported from around the world, including many countries where frost is not a problem, so it is worth making sure that pots are frost-resistant if they are to stay outside during winter in colder climates. Frost may not be a problem when the pots are empty as it is the freezing and swelling of the water in the soil which causes pots to fracture. If plants are to remain outside in pots during the winter an extra-deep layer of drainage materials should be placed in the bottom at planting time and, when in position, the pots should be raised off the ground.

▲ *Pots of bulbs are useful throughout the year for a statement of colour. This one enlivens a dark corner.*

▲ *There is nothing dull about these pots of auriculas. They should be placed in a corner that needs bringing to life.*

Be aware of the impact the pots make. Highly decorative pots are generally suitable for formal gardens where they can be viewed from a distance but they may look out of place, or be an unnecessary expense, in a smaller garden, where they might be screened by other pots or where we will be looking down at them. We rarely notice pots at ground level and tend only to see the plants. Pots which are raised up are more noticeable.

Ornaments

Ornaments in the garden can be fun, particularly if they have been made by the owner. A garden can be a place in which to display our creativity and provides a wonderful backdrop for arts and crafts. Willow figures and wire sculptures are very popular and they have flowing lines which can bring a garden to life. Mosaics may be used as decorative features on pots and set into patios, pools and walls to bring vibrant colours into the garden. Stained glass is being increasingly used in windows and walls. Sundials are popular in gardens and can provide a useful learning aid for children.

◀ *Muscari never fail to please and are a welcome sight in Spring.*

▶ *Fire planting – use these colours to make a statement in the south or focus on Wealth in the south-east.*

▲ *A lovely corner in which to enjoy the fruits of our labours. Even a small town garden can have a similar restful space.*

▼ *Place animal ornaments with care so that they are in natural positions and with a background of the correct scale.*

Placing Pots and Ornaments

East: Wooden objects. Avoid metal, including wind chimes, and any pointed objects.
◆ Green and blue pots.

South: Wooden objects. Sundials.
◆ Green and red pots. Terracotta is included because of its reddish colour.

West: Terracotta or metal pots and ornaments.
◆ White or terracotta pots.

North: Metal ornaments. Avoid terracotta and wood.
◆ White or blue pots.

▲ *A spotless cherub in a beautifully maintained garden.*

▲ *With some imagination you can create unusual and original garden ornaments.*

▼ *Use discarded items from the home to make unusual garden features*

Think about how an ornament will look in its garden setting: is it reassuring or will its shape cause you to jump as it looms out of a mist or at dusk? Only choose images you like.

Objects placed in the garden should blend in with the overall design. We should be able to observe them one at a time rather than all at once, which can confuse the eye. A single object at the end of a path will have a completely different effect to one which we happen to notice at a turn in the path. We should choose objects for the former position very carefully if we are not to be disappointed at the end of our journey.

▼ *Be sure to position sundials where they will receive the sun all day long.*

STATUES

Garden suppliers offer an excellent array of statuary, making it possible to create anything from an historical garden to a Japanese garden or even a fantasy garden full of fairies. The same design principles apply to statues as to any other aspect of Feng Shui. It is a question of proportion, style and materials and whether they blend with their surroundings. Another consideration is the impact they make on us subconsciously in a positive or negative sense.

Statues usually take the form of people or animals and we need to feel comfortable with the images we have in our gardens: we need to like the faces of the people they portray. Statues of small children can be pleasing, but may make us feel sad if our own children have grown up and left home, or if we are unable to have children. Statues of animals may be fun so long as they do not become a constant reminder of pets that have died, or resemble species we dislike. Be aware of a statue's energy, whether it is grim and dour or pert and lively, it will affect how we feel in the garden.

▲ *A beautiful delicate statue that is perfectly framed by the well-balanced planting.*

▼ *Friend or foe? This magnificent beast could prove frightening at dusk.*

► *New garden statuary may take time to become weathered and antique-looking.*

Statues are made from a variety of materials and they should blend in with and not stand out from their surroundings. Unblemished grey concrete is not aesthetically pleasant until it has aged and weathered. Fake verdigris on modern metal statues clashes with the natural greens of the plants in the garden. Brilliantly white statues have a harsh appearance and do not age well.

The placement of statues is important and ideally we should happen upon them as we take a meandering route around the garden, but they should not appear to leap out at us as we round a bend. It is not a good idea to place the life-size statue of a person in an open space as the effect can be disconcerting at night. Proportion is also important and bigger is not always better. A huge, ornately carved fountain sits well in Versailles but not in a small urban garden.

GARDEN LIGHTING

▲ *Candlelight and the floodlights under this tree create a romantic setting.*

There are two types of lighting in the garden. The first is practical to enable us to make use of our gardens after dark, and the second is for special effects.

Lighting the Way

Particularly where there is no street lighting, it is important for occupants and visitors to gain safe access to the house.

Lights which line a path and those which are set into stair risers can make a homecoming much more welcoming than if we have to carefully pick our way through obstacles in the dark. One neglected area is the house name and number. How much more sociable for guests to be able to locate the house, the doorbell and, in the case of apartment buildings, the person's name. Floodlights are widely used, but ensure they are correctly positioned so that they are not triggered by every passing cat.

Garden lighting can extend the day. The key rule for lighting the garden is to keep it simple by accenting certain features to create a calm, yin atmosphere. Lighting placed below or nearby can light up a statue or rock and give it an entirely different night-time appearance.

◀ *Simple but effective – this lantern can prolong the time spent outdoors.*

▶ *The lights in this modern town garden also make interesting shapes by day.*

Lighting up Plants

We normally view plants from above, but placing lights behind and under them enables us to view them from a different perspective and the results can be stunning. Trees lit from below, particularly blossom trees and those with interestingly shaped branches, can make wonderful features. Placing low-voltage lights in trees creates dancing shadows below as the light is filtered through the branches. Tiny bulbs in a tree produce an energetic party feel.

Garden lighting is best placed below eye level to reduce dazzle and to avoid creating shadows which can be disconcerting at night. We should aim to create pools of light that lead us through the garden rather than attempt to light up the whole area. Careful attention should be paid to siting the lights or we may experience feelings of unease as we peer into the dark spaces beyond.

Safety is paramount when we use electricity in the garden. Ponds should not contain lights, though perimeter lights can be stunning.

CREATING THE GARDEN

With some knowledge of the principles behind Feng Shui, we will approach the creation of our gardens with a keener eye for detail. The plants we use – their colour, form, textures and smells – can feed our senses and create life-enhancing environments in which we can relax, entertain and indulge in our hobbies. Whether we have a minute basement or a rambling country garden, we can design our surroundings to support and nourish our senses.

THE HEALTHY GARDEN

A healthy garden is a place where we, the plants, and any food that we grow will thrive. Some plants are poisonous while others can adversely affect our health. Some gardening methods do not benefit us or the plants in the long term. There are alternatives to using chemicals in the garden, and our health and that of the wildlife will benefit if we turn to them where possible. If we follow the natural order then we, the plants, and the wildlife in the garden can live in harmony and support each other.

▲ *With careful planting we can obviate the need to use chemicals in the garden since nature can do the job just as well if we let it.*

Poisonous Plants

Many well-known garden plants are poisonous and some wild ones may also find their way in. While adults are comparatively safe with these plants, children may be attracted by their colourful berries and seeds, and we need to take preventative measures to exclude dangerous plants from the garden at least when young children are part of the household.

Poisonous Garden Plants

Laburnum, Lupins, Yew, Daphne

Common Poisonous Wild Plants

Lords and ladies, Deadly nightshade, Black nightshade, Buckthorn

Plants and Allergies

In recent years there has been an increase in the number of people suffering from allergies. We regard the garden as a healthy place, but some of the plants we love best can cause a great deal of distress for asthma and hay fever sufferers and a number of plants can cause dermatitis when handled. Some popular plants which cause allergic reactions are shown in the box (right). Common names have been used as these plants are familiar to most people, even if they are not gardeners.

Common Allergens

The Pollen of: Grasses, Yarrow, Marigold

The Leaves of: Chamomile, Ivy, Rue

The Sap of: Spurge, Christmas rose, Burning bush

The Scent of: Pelargonium, Carnation (below), Evening primrose

Mutual Support

In nature there are few devastating plant diseases, nor are many plants wiped out by insect damage. This is because plants regulate themselves and a variety of plants grow together in a mutually supportive way. Some species secrete chemicals that are required by neighbouring plants, or which repel predators. Others provide shade for their neighbours. By far the most natural way to plant a garden is to grow trees, shrubs and perennial plants which will build up a relationship with each other and the earth. Annual plants and vegetables can fill the gaps. The soil is fed with compost made from prunings,

▲ *Grow herbs in containers, with other herbs, or in the herbaceous border.*

Pest Deterrents

APHIDS: Fennel, nasturtiums, dill
FLEA BEETLES: Catnip, hyssop, tomatoes
COLORADO BEETLES: Coriander, onion, dandelion
NEMATODES: African and French marigolds (below), chrysanthemums

Sacrificial Plants

We can also use plants to attract pests away from those we want to protect.

MUSTARD: Wireworms
TOBACCO PLANT: Whitefly
BROAD BEANS: Red spider mites
NASTURTIUMS: Blackfly

Plants to Attract Beneficial Predators

WASPS: Celery, chamomile, sunflowers
HOVERFLIES: Fennel, solidago, ivy
LADYBIRDS: Stinging nettles, tansy, yarrow

Herb Companions

Herb	Supports
Basil	Tomatoes
Borage	Strawberries
Chives	Apples
Garlic	Roses
Parsley	Asparagus
Tansy	Raspberries

leaves and kitchen waste, so it is in effect recycled from the garden itself. By bringing in outside composts (soil mix) and chemicals we create an imbalance and potential problems. If we follow the example of nature we will not dig the soil because this damages its structure and disturbs the creatures which work there for us, breaking down the organic matter. Some plants are known to be particularly beneficial to other plants growing close by. Many herbs fall into this category.

Plants to Deter Pests

In a healthy garden chemical-based formulas should not used to control insect pests because in doing so we may kill beneficial insects as well as the birds and small mammals which feed on them. Plants that are grown monoculturally are more vulnerable to insect damage than they would be if they were grown together with plants of other species. We can help this natural process further by introducing plants which secrete substances to repel certain types of pest.

Plants to Attract Predators

There are some insects which we should positively encourage into the garden, since they are predators of common garden pests. Certain plants act as hosts to these beneficial insects.

CHOOSING PLANTS

The rules for planting in the Feng Shui garden are simple. Each plant should be chosen carefully with regard to the specific features we wish to introduce. You need to think in terms of the colour, size and form of each individual plant, and how they will look side by side.

The planting should also blend in with the topography of the surrounding area – unless we want to make a definite statement to the contrary. You might live in an area that has identical houses in gardens which have evolved a particular look. You may feel happiest following the established style of your area, but since change is a key feature of Taoism, in which Feng Shui has its roots, individual expression in garden design is to be welcomed or we will not develop. When planting, the needs of plants should be taken into consideration in terms of soil type, aspect, temperature and spacing. There is no point attempting to nurture a plant which needs alkaline soil and a southerly aspect in a space that has acid soil, facing north. There will be less difficulty and disappointment in the garden

Favourite Seasonal Plants in China

Spring: Magnolia and Peony
Summer: Myrtle and Locust
Autumn: Maple and Chrysanthemum
Winter: Bamboo (below) and Wintersweet

◄ *Native plants flourish in a medieval-style English garden. Indigenous species will always grow better than imported plants in the right conditions.*

▲ *Plants need the correct soil and growing conditions in which to thrive.*

▼ *Summer in the garden – roses and lavender make good companion plants.*

PLANTING FOR VISUAL IMPACT

FLOWERS: Camellia, Magnolia, Orchid, Peony, Forsythia

FRUITS: Crab-apple, Quince, Fig, Plum

LEAVES: Weeping Willow, Maple, Palm, Privet

SEEDS: *Clematis tangutica,* Physalis, Everlasting Pea, Eryngium (below)

▲ *Spruce trees should be planted alone.*

if plants are chosen wisely. Plants which are indigenous to an area will always grow best, since all the conditions will be right for them.

THE SEASONS

Gardens should have all-year-round interest and, more importantly, we should be able to see the changes brought about by the seasons through windows from inside the house and also from various vantage points in the garden.

Within each season it is considered desirable that each stage of a plant's development should be represented – flowers, leaves, fruits and seed.

TREES

Trees are used to enhance a space, to obscure unwelcome features and to balance other features in the garden. In ancient China, trees were regarded as having special powers. We are more aware now of the importance to our ecological system of trees and the way in which they act as the lungs of the planet.

Trees need to be planted meticulously to reflect a number of philosophical principles as follows:

◆ Trees should grow naturally, since their beauty is in their true shape.

◆ A single tree can be admired for its shape, bark, leaves and blossom.

◆ Groups of trees should be in odd numbers; threes or fives.

◆ Trees with branches growing horizontally, such as cedar or spruce, should be planted alone.

◆ Upright trees, such as bamboo or cypress, should not be planted alongside trees with horizontal branches.

◆ Weeping and pendulous trees, like willow or birch, do not mix with those bearing horizontal branches.

◆ Only trees with a canopy, such as oak or elm, are suitable for mass planting.

◆ Trees with distinctive shapes, such as yew and plane, should be planted alone.

▼ *The deeply furrowed trunk of the Dawn redwood. The bark of a tree can be as beautiful and remarkable as any flower.*

GARDENING FOR THE SENSES

We respond to our gardens through our emotions and senses. The scent of a favourite plant can bring on a feeling of euphoria, while stroking the hairy leaves of *Stachys lanata*, or lambs' ears, can be soothing.

SIGHT

When we think of sight it is usually in terms of the immediate visual impression made by a tree or a flower bed and whether or not we like what we see. In the Feng Shui garden, seeing is rather more than that. When we look at a tree we should see the shape of its trunk, observe the way the branches spread out and the intricate criss-crossing of the canopy. We should also perceive the veining on the leaves and the patterning on the bark and notice the small creatures busying themselves on it. We may think that it resembles an old man, slightly stooped, as it is highlighted against the glowing red of the evening sky. If we let our imagination run riot, he may appear to be wearing Aunt Hilda's sun hat with the large bunch of cherries on the side and if we were then to call the scene "Grandfather wearing Aunt Hilda's hat", we would be coming close to the way the Chinese perceive the world in their art and philosophy.

▼ *The magnificent show of colour provided by this Cotinus* obovatus *will encourage anyone to plant it for seasonal interest.*

▲ *There is immediate visual interest in this busy garden, but a single flower could make just as powerful a statement.*

Observing the seasons is important in the Feng Shui garden, and we should plant carefully to ensure that we maintain some interest all the year round. We can achieve this by:

- ◆ Arranging plants which have different flowering times in tiers.
- ◆ Positioning flowers of the same colour but with different flowering periods in successive tiers.
- ◆ Mixing plants which have different flowering times.
- ◆ Planting varieties with long flowering times and vivid colours.
- ◆ Planting trees first and filling the gaps with perennials.

What we see when we look out into our gardens is of the utmost importance, not only for the pleasure it gives us, but because of the subconscious impression it makes on us, which can affect us psychologically. Clutter around the garden, just as it is inside the house, will become a constant source of irritation.

WINTER INTEREST IN THE GARDEN

FOLIAGE PLANTS

Cornus alba, Vitis vinifera 'Purpurea', *Liquidambar styraciflua*

FLOWERING PLANTS

Hamamelis x *intermedia* 'Pallida', *Jasminum nudiflorum, Viburnum* x *bodnantense, Choisya ternata*

BERRIES

Cotoneaster horizontalis, Skimmia, Pyracantha (below), Holly

BARK

Acer capillipes, Pinus pinea, Prunus serrula

▲ *We can rely on wildlife or create our own sounds in the garden. This bamboo wind chime will resound gently in the breeze.*

Sound

It is rare in the modern world to be able to escape from the noise of machinery or traffic, even in the garden, although by planting trees and dense hedges we can cushion ourselves to a certain extent. The garden itself is not really silent, and we would wish to encourage the sounds of nature there. Birdsong is always welcome, except perhaps for the harsh cawing of crows or the repetitive cooing of pigeons. Through careful planting, we can encourage the small songbirds into the garden, by tempting them with berries, seeds and the small insects which will be there if we do not spray with chemicals. The buzzing of bees while they work is another welcome noise which we can foster by adding their favourite plants.

The sound of gurgling water is relaxing, and bamboo plants, willow trees and tall grasses all make gentle swishing noises in the breeze. Placing Aeolian harps and wooden or shell wind chimes near where we sit is a good idea, provided we keep them near the house so they do not interfere with the finely tuned hearing of the wildlife. In the early autumn we should not be in too much of a hurry to sweep up since children like nothing more than the simple pleasure of crunching through leaves.

Clutter

Unwashed flower pots
Leaves in corners
Plants which catch on our clothes
Plants which catch our ankles
Dead branches
Dead plants
Overgrown hedges
Any jobs left undone

CASE STUDY

Even a garden in a perfect setting requires careful planning. Harry and Ann had a back garden with a beautiful view but when they hired a garden designer they did not feel comfortable with the result. A Feng Shui consultant came up with the following solution.

This beautiful open garden has a river meandering along the bottom and hugging the house. In the Phoenix position is a large oak tree marking the boundary of the property and beyond that a wonderful meadow with wild flowers, where horses graze.

The designer incorporated a row of conifers from the river to the door, blocking the wide view and creating a "poison arrow" of harmful chi from the gnarled trunk of the oak, which had become a threat to the house. This was likely to make the people living in the house feel irritable and restricted. At worst, this could result in mental instability and put a strain on their marriage. Removing the conifers from the design enabled Harry and Ann to have the full benefit of the wonderful view from their house once more.

▶ *Bamboo is an integral part of Chinese gardens, art and culture and grows well in a Western gravel garden.*

Touch

Touch is a sense which is often neglected in the garden. We tend to venture forth with caution, wearing gardening gloves and alerted to the perils lurking in the soil, the chemicals we have sprayed on the leaves, and even the plants themselves. Certainly we should be aware of the dangers, but to forgo the pleasure of feeling the soil running through our fingers as we plant a precious seedling, of burying our faces in a conifer after rain to smell its heady resinous scent, or to run our hands over rosemary and lavender as we pass, is to lose our connection with the earth.

The leaves of plants provide a range of sensations – stroking the woolly leaves of verbascum, the cold smooth leaves of mesembryanthemums or the rough carpet of dwarf thyme each gives its own form of tactile pleasure. The texture of bark on trees ranges from perfectly smooth to the peeling bark of the paper birch. We can get pleasure from stroking the soft petals of an iris or lily, or the face of a sunflower, or running our hands over the surface of the grass.

▲ *When harvesting your own fruit and vegetables remember to enjoy the feel of the earth and its produce.*

Taste

Nothing tastes better than home-grown fruit and vegetables, and it is possible to

▲ *No shop-bought produce can beat the taste of home-grown vegetables freshly dug from the garden.*

◀ *Rosemary delights in many ways – the colour of the flowers, the bees it attracts and the feel and smell of its leathery foliage.*

▶ *Fruit does not have to take up a lot of space: cordons or espaliers grown on walls and fences can be very productive.*

Scented plants

Spring

Daphne odora, Viburnum fragrans, Osmanthus burkwoodii, Ribes odoratum

Summer

Deutzia, Philadelphus, *Cytisus battandieri, Lupinus aboreus*

Autumn

Lonicera fragrantissima, Rosemary, Lavender, Sage

Winter

Chimonanthus praecox, Sarcococca hookeriana digyna, Hamamelis mollis, Acacia dealbata

▼ *The herb garden below will be full of wonderful aromas.*

grow them in the smallest of spaces. Salad vegetables sown in succession in a border will feed us through the summer months. Fruit trees grown on dwarfing rootstocks take up little space. Those grown on a single upright stem can be grown in pots near where we sit, to give us pleasure and remind us of earth's bounty. The taste of a freshly-picked sun-warmed apple or of tomatoes plucked from the vine in passing takes some beating. Herb beds close to the house also offer tempting flavours and lemon balm, sorrel, chervil, basil and parsley can give us a wide range of taste experiences.

▼ *A traditional wattle fence provides the backdrop for this mixed herb bed.*

Smell

No manufactured perfume surpasses the smell of a damask rose or of wild honeysuckle. The joy of scent in the garden is its subtlety. When the smell of elderflowers fills the house on a damp evening we crave more, but that would mask the other smells which drift in from the garden. The scents of *Lilium regale* and wintersweet are pervasive. Others will need to be placed near paths where we can brush against them to release the fragrance of plants like *Choisya ternata* and eucalyptus. Some plants do not object to being trodden on occasionally, and the Treneague chamomile and most thymes are suitable for planting on or near to paths.

▲ *Roses, particularly the old-fashioned varieties, provide a heady perfume.*

▼ *Some lilies are very fragrant and a pot by the back door will scent the kitchen.*

COLOUR

We all respond to colour in different ways, as is evident in the way we dress and decorate our homes. Our response is emotional and psychological and sometimes colours which we do not like can even bring about a physical response. In the Feng Shui garden, colour is part of the way in which the planting fits in with the garden's immediate environment, and with the natural contours of the landscape. In the natural world, colour blends into the background hue of the place – green in woodland, sand and pebble colours on the coast, purple shades on mountain slopes. If we look at poppies in a field they appear to shimmer on the surface,whereas a formal planting of marigolds or salvias in a park forms a solid mass of colour.

▲ Our response to colour in the garden is emotional and psychological.

The way in which we group plants is a matter of taste but all too often it is a hit-or-miss affair. If we examine an artist's use of colour, it can give us clues as to the harmonies which exist between different colours.

When any two of the three basic colours, red, blue and yellow, are mixed they give rise to a secondary colour – orange, violet, or green. These six colours make up the basic colour wheel as adapted by Gertrude Jekyll, whose harmonious planting ideas have influenced

◀ Observe the impact of the poppies which appear to shimmer across the field behind.

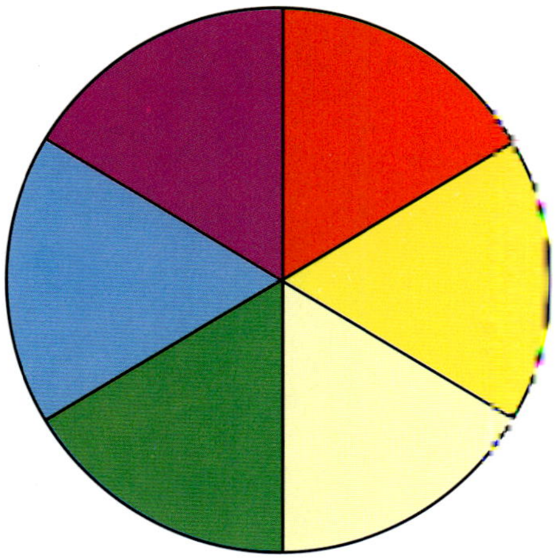

▲ *Use this simple diagrammatic colour wheel as a guide to basic colour harmonies and contrasts.*

gardeners all over the world. Three adjacent colours are known as harmonies. The others are contrasts. Those which sit diagonally opposite are complementary. Most of us respond positively to colours which are in harmony, and either complement or contrast with one another. In places where these rules cannot be applied, conflicting colours should be separated by neutral ones – white, grey or dark green.

In recent years research has been conducted into the use of colour in healing. Feng Shui practitioners believe that it is possible to determine a person's health or mood by the colours they use in their environment and that it is possible to alter perceptions by changing colours or by combining them in a variety of ways. It is fun to experiment and create gardens in which the colours are supportive and inspirational. Colours affect our mood; and it is worth remembering this when planning a garden in any climate.

▲ *White breaks up the vivid pink and orange plants in this bed.*

Colour is affected by the quality of the light. In Morocco and the Mediterranean countries bright colours look magnificent: brilliant red pelargoniums in Spanish courtyards are a sight to behold. Larger civic gardens and parks in these countries use green and abundant foliage to create cool shade, and a feeling of oasis-like sanctuary from the heat.

◀ *A stunning colour for a Mediterranean garden. The tone would need to be adjusted for it to work in a cooler climate.*

▼ *Vivid colours work well in hot countries because of the quality of the sunlight.*

PLANTING WITH A COLOUR THEME

▲ *Red plants like this* Euonymus alatus *'Compactus' make an impact at a distance.*

▲ *Yellow works well in this understated mixed planting.*

We have seen that colour alters our emotions and moods, but we can also use colour to focus on areas of the Bagua, depending on the elemental qualities of the area.

Red

Red plants will dominate a garden when planted in large patches and are not restful to sit near. They make excellent spot plants to draw the eye to a certain area.

Red trees and shrubs: *Acer rubrum, Berberis thunbergii* 'Atropurpurea', *Cotinus coggygria, Euonymus alatus* 'Compactus'.
Red herbaceous plants: *Ajuga reptans, Bergenia cordifolia, Paeonia lactiflora.*

◀ *White in a garden can soothe but also be strangely lifeless with no other colours near.*

White and Silver

All-white gardens appear fresh and clean and, in the evening light, luminous. Although calming, there may be a deadness to a large all-white garden unless it is carefully planned with many different shades and shapes of green to vary it.
White trees and shrubs: *Pyrus salicifolia, Drimys winteri, Skimmia japonica* 'Fructu Albo'.
White herbaceous plants: *Eremurus himalaicus, Aruncus dioicus, Astilbe* 'Irrlicht'.

Yellow

Yellow is usually associated with spring and late summer. It is a rich and cheerful colour, but, in its paler forms or when combined with white, it can feel uncomfortable and demoralizing.

▼ *A collection of hostas showing just how many shades of green there are.*

Yellow trees and shrubs: *Laburnum x watereri* 'Vossii', *Acer japonicum* 'Aureum', *Hypericum* 'Hidcote'.
Yellow herbaceous plants: *Phlomis russeliana, Rudbeckia fulgida* 'Goldsturm', *Achillea filipendulina* 'Gold Plate'.

Green

Spot planting, using pots of coloured plants and bulbs, is very effective against the backdrop of a green garden. In itself, the green garden, containing various shades and shapes of foliage, can be a

▲ *Muscari brings this gravel garden to life.*

restful, tranquil place. Green is the predominant colour in the Chinese garden.

GREEN TREES AND SHRUBS: *Juniperus chinensis, Chamaecyparis lawsoniana, Thuja occidentalis.*

GREEN HERBACEOUS PLANTS: Hostas, *Phyllostachys nigra,* Euphorbia.

BLUE

Blue borders have a sedative effect but unrelieved blue can be gloomy. Blue plants can be mixed with white and silver foliage and with soft pink flowers.

BLUE TREES AND SHRUBS: *Picea glauca* 'Coerulea', *Ceanothus impressus, Abies concolor* 'Glauca Campacta'.

BLUE HERBACEOUS PLANTS: *Echinops bannaticus, Gentiana asclepiadea, Salvia patens.*

PURPLE

A purple border can be sumptuous and restful at the same time. Mix purple with blues, whites and soft pinks for calm.

PURPLE TREES AND SHRUBS: *Jacaranda mimosifolia,* Syringa, *Hydrangea macrophylla.*

▼ *Purple and red make a powerful combination in this tub.*

▲ *Pink is a warm colour. This pink works remarkably well with the black pansies.*

PURPLE HERBACEOUS PLANTS: *Verbena patagonica,* Iris, *Salvia nemorosa* 'May Night'.

PINK

Pink is a warm colour and draws people to it. The gentler shades are preferable.

PINK TREES AND SHRUBS: *Magnolia campbellii,* Prunus, Spiraea.

PINK HERBACEOUS PLANTS: Lavatera, Peony, Geranium.

ORANGE

Orange is a rich, warm, happy colour, but difficult to place. It is probably best against a dark green background.

ORANGE TREES AND SHRUBS: *Spathodea campanulata,* Berberis, *Leonotis leonurus.*

ORANGE HERBACEOUS PLANTS: Rudbeckia, *Lychnis chalcedonica,* Chrysanthemum.

▼ *The colours work well together here since the shades are subtle and not harsh.*

THE COURTYARD GARDEN

Depending on the style of the property, courtyard gardens can be formal or great fun, giving expression to the artistic talent latent in everyone. With walls or fences to paint, floor surfaces to experiment with and only a tiny space to fill, courtyards can allow us unlimited scope for expression.

Often the difficulty in designing a small garden is in deciding what not to include. Gardens packed full of plants, using several different materials and textures, can appear fussy and make the space look even smaller than it is. On the other hand, the impact of one architectural plant with some pebbles and moss can look stunning in a tiny space, although gardens which are too minimal emphasize their small size.

A wide variety of materials is available now and, cleverly combined, they can become a work of art in themselves. Beware of surfaces which are likely to become slippery in damp areas: decking can look stunning when sun-baked by a pool, but in a dark shady area it can become stained and unpleasant. Often such spaces create their own microclimate where we can grow plants which will not normally grow outside. If a courtyard is overlooked, overhead wires supporting a vine will afford privacy while letting in light, creating an exotic Mediterranean feeling in the middle of a town.

Every feature in a small garden needs to earn its keep and it is self-defeating to hold on to a plant which has outgrown

▲ *Careful planting at a variety of levels creates a haven of peace and beauty in a tiny courtyard.*

► *A restrained use of colour stops a small space from looking too fussy.*

◄ *Wall-mounted pelargoniums are common in Mediterranean courtyards.*

Architectural Plants for Impact

Cordyline australis, Acer, *Fatsia japonica*, Fatshedera, *Juniperus scopulorum*, Box (below)

Plants for Shade

Euonymus fortunei 'Silver Queen', *Choisya ternata*, Philadelphus, Skimmia

Plants to Hide Walls

Campsis radicans, *Actinidia kolomikta*, Ivy, Jasmine, Roses (below)

its space or is past its prime. It constitutes clutter if it is a problem. We need to make the best use of trees and interesting features outside our own gardens and borrow them for our own design. Those we do not want – ugly walls, unsightly pipes and other features – we can blot

▼ *Climbers and baskets can be useful where ground space is limited.*

Combinations of Materials

- Wooden decking and pebbles
- Shingle and granite slabs
- Stone and moss
- Coloured concrete and mosaics
- Paving slabs and brick

out. Coloured trellis can work wonders on an unsightly wall. The plants we choose should be those which will fill the space when they reach maturity. They may take longer to grow than fast-growing species, but will ultimately be more rewarding since they will not cause maintenance problems later.

Some houses have enclosed spaces, with access only from a window, but if we design with care, we can use the colour and textures of different materials to create interesting and energetic spaces there. Some plants thrive in the most unlikely places. With just a chink of light in the darkest cave, a fern will usually grow, and the ivy family is invaluable in awkward corners. In small spaces, plants may even be incidental if we use materials, water and illusion to design what is essentially another room. Ornaments, sculptures and pots, strategically placed mirrors and brightly coloured walls can create stunning environments which will energize and stimulate us.

▼ *Strategically placed pots can enliven any space and are useful in paved courtyards.*

CASE STUDY

Moira and her family had just finished renovating an old house. Moira loved the spaciousness of their new home and the feeling that the family were doing things together, but she craved a space for herself where she could pursue her hobby – watercolour painting. The renovations had left a small courtyard at the back of the house.

1. The lean-to greenhouse was renovated to enable Moira to store her art materials and overwinter some plants.

2. The basement staircase was made safe by installing a gate. A trellis (Earth shape in the north-east) gave some height to the planting. A blue *Clematis alpina* scrambles over it.

3. Planting has been kept to a minimum so that watering does not become a chore, and because the space is small. Single plants, if they are large, can give a feeling of lusciousness and so a *Prunus stiloba simplex* was positioned here.

4. A cordyline was placed in this corner to liven it up and in front, a small pebble water feature was also added.

5. A terracotta wall feature of an upright jug was placed here to raise the view above the staircase and lifts the energy of the north-east.

6. Moira's chair and easel are here. A

canopy above the window shields them when it is hot. Since the window leads into the house it was not felt to be a problem behind the chair.

7. This table and storage unit for Moira's painting equipment can be wheeled into the greenhouse.

8. An ivy covered ball brings a playful energy to this corner

9. Moira plans to have a mosaic wall here with a blank space above the table for her still life arrangements.The space opens up ideas from the rising energy of the east, which Moira can draw on from her position opposite.

10. Moira hopes to sell her paintings one day. Taking her chair as the mouth of chi, and aligning the symbolic Bagua with it, this wall is the Offspring area. Moira plans to paint murals on this wall, which she can change over the years.

ROOFS AND BASEMENTS

▲ *Wooden decking creates an indoor feel to this well designed outdoor space.*

In urban areas where space is at a premium, living areas extend upwards and downwards. For people living in the centre of a city, a roof garden is a haven from the bustling life below. For those who live below street level in basements, sometimes their only view is of walls and of feet passing overhead. Both these spaces are difficult when planning a garden. The roof garden is totally exposed and unsupported, with little chance of capturing chi unless some structural alterations are made. In the basement garden chi becomes trapped and stagnant since it cannot circulate, so careful planning and planting are needed.

▼ *This country cottage-style garden is actually on an urban roof.*

Roof Gardens

Roof gardens are unique in that they encompass a number of problems which are not found all in one place in a conventional garden. Structure and load-bearing capacity are the first priorities, followed by drainage.

High winds will be a problem. Open trellis is preferable to a solid screen which creates wind turbulence. Winds cause damage to young shoots and causes soil to dry out quickly so maintenance is high, watering systems are an advantage. A light gravel layer on top of the pots will help to conserve moisture. Light free-draining compost (soil mix) in the pots and containers is preferable to heavy garden soil. Feeding will be necessary.

Temperatures may be higher than average in big citites. Pergolas can be used for shading, but great care should be taken that the structures are secure. Overhead wires are another option.

In such an unnatural environment plants will eventually outgrow their space and the only option will be to replace them. Sickly plants create stagnant chi and should be renewed quickly. It is possible to grow vegetables and fruit on roofs, either in pots or in growing bags.

▲ *On this secluded roof you would never dream you were in the city.*

▼ *Quarry tiles can be a hard-wearing and practical surface for a roof garden.*

Plants For Roof Gardens

Climbers

Clematis alpina, Hedera helix, Passiflora

Trees

Rhus typhina 'Laciniata', Ficus, *Acer negundo*

Architectural plants

Cordyline, Magnolia (below), Salix

Shrubs

Hebe, Lavender, Santolina

Herbs

Parsley, Basil, Chives

Vegetables

Tomato, Asparagus pea, Salad vegetables

Lighting is a consideration on the roof since there may not be sufficient light generated from within the building. Uplighters are useful since they show off the plants but avoid causing glare which could disturb neighbours.

Basements

At the other end of the scale, basements can be confined places with restricted amounts of natural light available. However, these conditions can be alleviated. If the outlook from the windows is bleak and the basement area is damp and fills up with wind-blown rubbish and leaves it is important to summon up the energy and initiative to clear up and take control of the space. Living without much natural light can drain personal energy so, in the basement garden, the object is to raise the chi of the space and the spirits of the occupants.

▲ *This* trompe l'oeil *effect seems to double the perceived size of the basement area.*

▼ *This could have been a dismal basement area but it has been transformed by the addition of scores of potted plants.*

Light-coloured walls are essential in a basement, and dark walls should be painted white. If the walls are high use a trellis to support climbing plants, rooted in the ground, if possible, or in large pots. As the plants grow and climb upwards they will raise the energy. Choose plants which are evergreen or have fairly large leaves, or clearing up will be a problem. Lush simplicity is preferable to fussy planting where space is restricted.

If there are stairs which are wide enough, pots of colourful plants can be placed at intervals to light the way. Avoid trailing plants, like ivy, which will have a depressing effect. Gertrude Jekyll suggested that even in the smallest space there should be a distinctive feature – an ornament, fountain or raised bed to create an interesting focal point.

Lighting is important in basements, and uplighters, shining through climbing plants, can improve the energy. Visual illusion can be used to good effect with murals or *trompe l'oeil*, or even strategically placed mirrors, and the area can be cheered by a bright floor surface – tiles and mosaics can be used if they blend in with the surrounding architecture.

Plants for Basements

Shrubs

Fatsia japonica, Fatshedera, Arundinaria, Cornus

Climbers

Wisteria sinensis, Chaenomeles speciosa, Hydrangea petiolaris, Parthenocissus quinquefolia

Ferns

Dryopteris dilatata, Polypodium vulgare, Phyllitis scolopendrium, Polystichum aculeatum

TERRACES AND PATIOS

Terraces, or patio areas, feature in both urban and rural gardens. They can be as simple as a few rows of paving outside the back door, or elaborate balustraded affairs running the length of grand country houses. Whatever their size, they enable a range of activities to take place and the emphasis will change over time as children arrive, grow up and eventually leave home, when parents can return to a more leisurely lifestyle. With careful planning, paddling pools and sand pits can be transformed into flower beds.

The size of the terrace will be determined by the size of the garden and should be in proportion. Those less than 2m (6ft) wide do not really allow enough room for much activity to happen there. Privacy may be a problem. Depending on the direction the terrace faces, some protection from the wind may be needed. Overhead shading may be required in the form of a plant-covered pergola, giving a dappled light effect, or a canopy to give more complete cover.

Patios can become extremely yang places in the height of summer, with the sun blazing overhead, the hard surfaces giving off heat, pools and metal objects

▲ *A dream terrace in an idyllic situation where the planting complements the view.*

▼ *A shady retreat from the hot sun, this terrace blends in well with the house.*

▼ *Tomatoes grow well in pots and are ideally close for picking if grown on a terrace.*

▲ *A delightful terrace with the view framed like a picture between the planting.*

and tables reflecting the glare. By introducing some height in the form of shading, and with plants around the edges as well as in containers, we can create a balance and make a cool and relaxing place to sit.

Terraces need easy access from the kitchen if eating or entertaining is to take place there. In north-facing gardens it is advisable to place terraces at a distance from the house, where they will have some sun and can be reached via a hard path so that trolleys can be wheeled along and people can carry dishes safely. On small terraces, built-in seating will save space and can look attractive if the materials used blend into the overall plan and with the house. On the other hand, built-in seating with raised beds behind it can be uncomfortable if insects are attracted to the area by the plants. Often on terraces, chairs are not backed by a wall, so if we want to keep our guests there for any length of time, we should provide them with high-backed chairs.

If the terrace is used for reading or quiet reflection we should place our chairs to face one of our auspicious directions. We can also align sun-loungers in the same way, depending on which way the terrace faces.

A paved area or deck may be a large space that is required for a variety of different family activities. Young children may like to have a sand pit and paddling pool there, though if you do have both, it is a good idea to keep the two well apart. Be mindful of the Five Elements when positioning the paddling pool. It is advisable to cover both the sand pit and the pool when not in use, especially if you have cats that are fond of using the former as a litter tray. Covering the pool will ensure that the water remains clean and hygienic.

► *Many fruit varieties are now grown on dwarf rootstocks suitable for growing in pots.*

Small children may want to ride trikes in the garden, so the patio or deck should be level with the adjoining grass area to prevent accidents. Where the area is raised and there are steps, secure barriers should be erected. Swings should never be placed on hard surfaces; if they are not on grass, bark chippings or another soft surface should be placed underneath.

The area near the house may also need to accommodate a number of items such as dustbins (trash cans), wood piles, sheds and washing lines. Keep these separate from any seating, hidden behind plant-covered screens or fences if possible.

Plants for the Terrace

Climbers

Clematis, *Lathyrus grandiflorus*, Vitis, Gourds, Wisteria

Small Trees for Shade

Catalpa bignoniodes, *Corylus alternifolia* 'Argentea', Acer, Prunus, Magnolia

Plants to Train on Walls

Malus, Ceanothus, Pyracantha, Jasmine, Chaenomeles

Herbs for the Barbecue

Rosemary, Sage (below bottom), Thyme, Oregano (below top)

Fruit and Vegetables for Pots

Tomatoes, Peppers, Aubergines Strawberries (below), Apples

RURAL GARDENS

In the rural garden the possibilities for design would appear to be greater than in the urban garden. Yet, in many ways, the design is more restricted by convention and the need to blend in with the natural landscape. In the Feng Shui garden, we capture the landscape and draw it into our gardens while, at the same time, ensuring that the garden is an extension of the house, linked physically but also by style.

Boundaries in the rural garden can be hidden by planting linked into a hill or group of trees beyond, which we can frame and use as our own. We can create boundaries within the garden using trellis, gateways and gaps in hedges to lead our eyes on and suggest new experiences beyond. Even a closed door in a wall will suggest possibilities, and adds an air of mystery. Proportion is important and can make all the difference to the feel of a garden. Tall narrow openings are far less inviting than wide ones. Since rural gardens are often larger than their city counterparts, it will not always be necessary to disguise the boundary or block out an ugly view. Rather than planting at the edge, a tree in the lawn with space to move behind will add depth and more interest to the garden.

Within the plot we can create special areas: places to be alone, to entertain, for the children to play and so on, always bearing in mind that the elements need to be balanced with regard to colour and shapes and that we need to maintain a balance of yin and yang, combining hard landscaping with soft planting, and in the height of plants or the shapes of their leaves.

Paths should meander through the garden, opening up new vistas at each turn and allowing us to happen upon things such as statues, rocks, pots or prize plants. A path can take us directly to the shed or greenhouse, which should ideally be situated fairly near to the house for

◀ *The "rooms" in this medieval-style garden mimic field divisions in the landscape beyond and are in harmony with it.*

▲ *A few pots at the base of the tree act as a stop before the eye moves on to travel around the garden.*

◀ *A variety of heights, shapes, forms and colours in planting schemes will ensure that the yin-yang balance is maintained.*

▲ *Produce which is harvested once a year can be positioned at the end of the garden.*

◀ *The plants in this garden have built up a relationship with their environment.*

convenience, and from there to the vegetable patch or fruit-growing area. We may like to consider the possibility of cultivating crops which take longer to grow and take up a lot of space, or are harvested infrequently – such as potatoes, asparagus and rhubarb – at the bottom of the garden, and those which we need on a daily basis – like herbs and salad vegetables – near to the house. A path, or even stepping stones in the lawn to the vegetable garden, will enable us to pick produce even on the wettest day. Picking a lettuce is less fun if you need to find boots and wet weather gear first.

Water makes a difference in any garden, but remember that all the creatures in the garden and surrounding area will be attracted to it. If you are not willing to share your terrace with hundreds of baby frogs, a fox, mice and the odd visiting rat, site the pond away from the house and, if you stock it with fish, be prepared for herons.

We should allow plants to breathe by enabling the wind to blow through them; spacing them well will mean less disease. We should extend this principle, by opening up the centres of each area and enabling the chi to circulate and move on. Above all we should respect the spirit of the place and choose plants and materials which are at home there, remembering that there are many things which human beings have to learn about the natural world and that the less we tamper with it and poison it, the better it will be for us, our families and the generations to come.

Rural Garden Plants

Plants for Hedges
Aucuba, Berberis, Euonymus, Ribes, Ilex, Mahonia

Plants for Shady Places
Arundinaria, *Aucuba japonica*, *Fatsia japonica*, Eleagnus, Mahonia, Skimmia

Shrubs for Interest
Chaenomeles, Cotoneaster, Hebe, Philadelphus, Pyracantha, Viburnum

Ground Cover Plants
Ajuga reptans, Bergenia, *Euphorbia amygdaloides*, Helleborus, Hosta, *Hypericum calycinum*

Trees for Small Gardens
Acer, Betula, Eucalyptus, Malus, Prunus, Sorbus

Plants for Pool Sides
Astilbe, Hosta, Iris, Ranunculus, Rheum, Trollius

Scented Plants
Oenothera (below left), Lavender (below right), Jasmine, Honeysuckle

WATERSIDE GARDENS

Water, in the form of pools, waterfalls and streams, is an important element in the Feng Shui garden. When the garden is situated beside a large river or lake, or by the sea, its design needs some special consideration.

COASTAL GARDENS

Coastal gardens are among the most difficult to cultivate. The effects of the salt-laden winds can spread as far as 8km (5 miles) inland, bending plants and trees double and scorching the leaves. However, given some shelter, these can also be the most rewarding gardens since they are virtually frost-free and rarely have snow. The climate lends itself to growing many plants which will not grow elsewhere.

The quality of the light in coastal locations is more vibrant than it is inland and planting can be brighter, although very colourful planting can seem harsh on dull days. Seaside resorts in temperate northern climes can come alive in summer when brilliant pelargoniums grow against whitewashed walls and give a Mediterranean feel. In winter it is often a matter of battening down the hatches, and hanging baskets and pots have to be secured against the elements. There is no better illustration of yin and yang than the vibrant yang bustle of a summertime resort in contrast with the yin stillness of the calm sea in the bay. When the holidaymakers have departed in the winter, the resort becomes quiet and yin while the sea is churned up and becomes yang.

Beach gardens can be fun and look attractive adorned with driftwood and other items washed up by the sea. Few plants flourish in such locations, but some grasses and plants which grow naturally there, such as horned poppies and thrift, do well. Windbreaks should fit in with the look of the area and bamboo or rush permeable fencing will help to fend off the wind. There are a number of shrubs that are useful as hedging in such areas. Higher up are the cliff-side gardens

▲ *Low planting is less likely to suffer wind damage than taller plants.*

▼ *Bright Mediterranean colours – of plants and paint – look good in a seaside garden.*

▲ *Many tropical plants will also grow in temperate conditions in protected locations.*

▼ *The results of beachcombing make a natural seaside garden.*

Plants for Coastal Gardens

Windbreaks

Atriplex, *Crataegus monogyna* 'Stricta', *Escallonia rubra, Griselinia littoralis*

Shrubs

Hebe, *Halimium libanotis, Tamarix ramosissima, Hippophae rhamnoides* – Sea Buckthorn

Rock Plants

Dianthus alpinus (below), *Pulsatilla vulgaris, Sedum spathulifolium, Sempervivum arachnoideum*

Plants to Try

Phormium tenax, Cordyline australis 'Atropurpurea', *Livistona chinensis, Dodonaea viscosa* 'Purpurea'

which fringe many coastal towns. Planted on the cliff face and linked by meandering paths, they escape the worst of the weather and can reveal some gems of plants, more suited to tropical climates.

Riverside Gardens

Riverside locations can be idyllic, particularly in summer. Homes bordering a river tend to be orientated towards it and occasionally the mouth of chi, the entrance, becomes the rear of the house. Fast-moving water is felt to dissipate energy and certainly the banks of fast-moving rivers are not home to the variety of plants which thrive by those which meander gently through the garden. Waterside gardens can incorporate a range of plants which do not thrive in other conditions: lush green carpets of bay arums provide a perfect foil for the dancing swards of sweet flag and the narrow stems of irises and rushes. Equally magnificent, delicate weeping willows vie

▼ *A slow-moving river at the bottom of the garden can be auspicious.*

▲ *This garden has incorporated the river as part of its design.*

for attention with the massive leaves of gunnera. It is not advisable to block the view of the river but to set a small shrub or rock as the boundary in the Phoenix position, and frame the river with some planting to block its coming and going at the boundaries – symbolic in China of wealth coming in then running away.

In urban and inner city areas, where heavy industry has moved out, housing developments often spring up around rivers and in dockland areas. Huge buildings dwarf most planting schemes and where possible, large trees should be introduced to create some yin energy.

犬

雞

鼠

龍

猴

THE FENG SHUI OFFICE

MANY OF US SPEND A LARGE PART OF OUR LIVES AT WORK AND OUR SURROUNDINGS THERE ARE AS IMPORTANT AS THOSE IN OUR HOMES. WE USUALLY HAVE LITTLE CONTROL OVER THE BUILDINGS WE WORK IN, BUT AWARENESS OF PROBLEMS THAT CAN AFFECT US WILL ENABLE US TO TAKE COUNTER-MEASURES AND MAY ENCOURAGE THE CREATION OF STIMULATING AND NURTURING ENVIRONMENTS.

豬

INTRODUCTION

The Feng Shui principles are "First, luck; second, destiny; third, Feng Shui; fourth, virtues; fifth, education". While we have no control over our luck or our destiny, we can have an impact on the quality of our lives by applying ourselves to the other three areas. Education in childhood may vary in quality but as we get older we are able to take more responsibility for it. We are privileged if our early education is of a high standard and enables us to acquire the knowledge and skills needed to enhance our careers,

▼ *The energy of an office is dependent on the people who work there, and the relationships they form with each other.*

▲ *In this clutter-free and airy office, there is room for personal space and a central meeting point.*

▶ *In this modern office, meeting areas again combine with individual spaces to give a harmonious working environment.*

but we should also take steps to improve our knowledge and expertise when we are adults. The term "virtues" applies to the way we relate to people and situations. How we relate to people is, to some extent, written in our horoscopes, but our own personal energy also plays a large part. We can also apply Feng Shui to create an environment which will support us and enable us to make progress.

The energy of any office can be dramatically improved if its occupants respond to each other in a positive way and co-operate with one another. If the office environment is unsatisfactory, it is possible to offer to paint it and to move in plants and images which will improve it and make it a better place to work. If the management is considered to be unreasonable and deadlines are unrealistic, there should be a way of approaching a situation positively to avoid conflict. Negativity breeds negativity so forward planning and planning work programmes holistically, rather than on a day-to-day basis, will reduce stress.

Our relationships with our colleagues will influence our happiness and performance at work. Astrology plays a part in determining our characteristics and those of the people we have positive and negative relationships with. Understanding this will benefit us and help us to create harmony in the office or workspace.

The location of the office is not normally something over which we have control but its internal layout can make a great difference to the way people feel and behave. It is now thought that some buildings are "sick" and an awareness of the causes can improve the lot of those who work there. When we employ Feng Shui in an office environment we can assist the movement of the energies and at the very least we can take positive steps to keep our personal workspace clear of an accumulation of clutter which will affect our performance.

It is accepted that the energies of home and workplace are not independent of each other and if something is not working well in one, it will affect the other. If relationships at home are not happy, it could be because of a problem in the office, which could be caused by a lack of harmonious relationships there, or the problem could simply be a blockage of chi resulting from the position of a desk or workstation.

Feng Shui can help in the office environment in two ways. It can help to make the business function efficiently and prosper; to gain an advantage over competitors, as it is widely used in the East; and to give individuals the edge over rivals in career development – all yang aspects. The second, yin, application is to improve job satisfaction, foster harmonious working relationships, and provide a stress-free environment in which personal careers can develop and the company can thrive.

Feng Shui in Practice

The plans for the famous Hong Kong and Shanghai Bank in Hong Kong, designed by British architect Sir Norman Foster, required modification before it was considered suitable by a local Feng Shui consultant. Detail on the outside of the building was altered so that the symbolic arrows point up and not down as on the original plan. The escalators were realigned to draw chi into the building from an auspicious direction and the large stone lions which protect the entrance were placed in position at an auspicious time.

▲ *The Hong Kong and Shanghai Bank stands in a prime position facing Victoria harbour and is protected behind by the Peak, one of the Dragon Hills that protect Hong Kong.*

The bank's main rival, the Bank of China, erected a new building soon afterwards and started a Feng Shui war. The new building's design was such that its corners directed "poison arrows" of negative energy at its rival, who had to ward it off by installing mirrored glass to symbolically direct it back again.

Another aggressive measure in the East is to point cannons at rivals, who respond by installing larger ones to point back.

EXTERNAL FACTORS

The buildings we inhabit are part of a wider environment that can have a profound effect on how we operate within them. Their location, what they are surrounded with and even their shape can make us feel comfortable, or it can jar and can have a great impact on our clients. The energy emanating from different directions suits some businesses more than others and we can design our office space in order to encourage these different energies. When we move to a new building, or travel, the timing is crucial to the success of the venture.

LOCATION

When you are searching for suitable business premises there are important questions to ask even before finding out about access and other practical matters. A walk around the area will indicate if it is thriving or not and what type of activities are located there. The fortunes of the previous occupants can provide a clue to how successful the new undertaking will be, and it is worth making enquiries as to their activities and how they fared before committing yourself to a building or area.

The maxim, "Location is everything" applies to offices as well as houses. A prestigious address may be taken as a sign of success by clients who may not realize that your office is little more than a cupboard on a floor shared by three other companies, but a company operating in such a space would not thrive for long unless other factors were right. Some areas are traditionally associated with certain types of business – for example, lawyers. Support networks spring up, contacts are made in cafés during lunch breaks and in bars after office hours, and other enterprises which are not associated will feel isolated. One question which needs to be asked by organizations on the move, or those setting up, is whether or not the area really needs the services it is offering. There are only so many solicitors, estate agents or expensive boutiques that one area can support, and in many cases the success of a business is down to market research and is not something that Feng Shui can cure.

Sometimes we have an impractical dream of setting up a business or opening a shop offering a service or products which the area does not need. For example, a sushi bar in a district predominantly

▲ *The varied skyline of downtown San Francisco indicates a thriving and successful city, full of business opportunities.*

▼ *The water and greenery around this building, appropriately home of a building design company, help to energize its environment.*

populated by low-income families with small children will not thrive since the food tends to be expensive, such families have to budget carefully and young children are notoriously unadventurous when it comes to diet. A themed diner-type establishment offering burgers and fries and catering for children's parties would probably thrive in such an area. Similarly, a shop selling modern craftwork and ethnic jewellery is unlikely to do well in an area where the population is elderly. Market research is well worth doing before establishing a business and a little research initially may prevent problems later.

It is true that the fortunes of locations run in cycles but, even so, an area which is run down, where vegetation does not thrive, and where there are many empty or vandalized buildings is best avoided. It is often possible to read patterns into the energy of an environment or a particular building. If a building has had a fire, then it pays to be wary. If the previous occupants of a building were in a similar line of business and went bankrupt, or had to reduce their activities drastically, warning bells should ring. It may have been due to poor management, but it could also be associated with the building and its environment. In either case, potential clients may associate the two businesses so it would be better to steer clear. It is recognized in Feng Shui that certain types of business thrive in certain types of building and location. Choosing the correct ones for a business is the first step on the road to success.

▲ *Water is good for communications, but some Wood and Fire energy is also needed for this book-supplying company. At present the Earth element dominates.*

The Five Elements and Buildings

Buildings and environments associated with each of the Five Elements support different types of business activity.

Element	Type of Building, Environment and Energy	Suitable Businesses
Wood	Wood buildings are tall and narrow in shape, or are made of wood. Wood environments are ones where there are trees and vegetation. The energy suggests new ideas and new beginnings.	Woodcrafts, Garden centres, Artists, New businesses, Producers
Fire	Fire buildings have pointed roofs and spires. Fire environments may have chimneys. The energy suggests production and dynamism.	Manufacturing, PR and marketing, Sales
Earth	Earth buildings are rectangular and have flat roofs. Earth environments tend to be flat and fenced. The energy suggests stability, nourishment and nurture.	Storage and warehousing, Agriculture, Housing
Metal	Metal buildings tend to be round or domed. Metal environments are those where fuels, minerals and gases are extracted from the earth. The energy suggests consolidation and profit.	Metal crafts, Jewellery, Mining, Finance
Water	Water buildings are those which have irregular shapes. Water environments are ones suggesting flow and making links. The energy is that of communication.	Communications, Electrical systems, Liquids, Healing

▼ *This restaurant will thrive – the colours and seating are designed for a quick turnover of people in a bustling city location.*

THE OFFICE SITUATION

Where offices are situated and the support they receive from other buildings are crucial. Open communication channels and access are also very important to the success of a business.

▲ *In Feng Shui terms, round-edged buildings are more sociable than square-edged buildings.*

▼ *This building would benefit from having railings right across the front and lowering the wall to give an even view.*

The Four Directions

The first consideration when choosing an office location is support and we can apply the Four Animals arrangement here. Although it is not considered good Feng Shui for an office to be dwarfed by surrounding buildings, it is useful if there is a taller building to the rear to act as the Tortoise, with supportive buildings on either side: the Dragon, to the right when facing the building, should be higher than the Tiger on the left. Alternatively, trees or (for lower buildings) walls and fences, can fulfil these roles.

In the Phoenix position, at the front of the building, it is important to mark the front boundary of the business in some way, with a low wall or fence, or with a sign carrying the company name. If a tall barrier is needed for security reasons, choose railings rather than a solid wall or fence. This allows a view from the building whereas a solid barrier would be restricting. Since it enables others to see in, it will also offer more security against break-ins.

Having found a good position to locate your business, it is important to check for any threatening features in the environment. The corners of adjacent or opposing buildings, glare from glass buildings and satellite dishes, and flag poles or decorative features pointing at the office are all of concern since they appear to attack us.

Access

In ancient times, rivers were the main routes of access. Today roads and other transport links serve the same purpose

▲ *Hong Kong harbour accumulates chi for the island and helps to create prosperity for the many businesses located there.*

and their importance in the siting of business premises will depend on the nature of the business, the numbers of visitors, deliveries and so on. A company which uses technology as its main communication channel will not be so dependent on roads. Whatever the nature of the business, it is important that its communication channels are kept open. Poor service from network providers and computer engineers to such a business is the equivalent of unreliable rail links and road systems to others.

Businesses situated on urban freeways will suffer if they have frequent visitors and deliveries but do not have adequate parking facilities. Those situated by roundabouts rarely do well since traffic, or chi, is constantly passing by, unable to stop or collect there. Buildings located at crossroads, on the other hand, are considered to have good Feng Shui, since traffic approaches them from two directions. However, this is diminished if there are other buildings pointing at them from the diagonally opposite corner. A mirror, or other reflective surface, will direct the negative energy back at itself.

Buildings at the end of a T-junction, with traffic travelling straight towards them, are seen to be under threat and those in a peninsula position are considered to be unstable. A cul-de-sac location is not generally considered to be good Feng Shui, since parking will almost certainly be restricted and the energy will become stuck.

Wherever possible, attempt to create a well-maintained garden or green area around the building, which will be attractive to workers and visitors alike and will provide a barrier between the office and the road.

▲ *Stunning foliage helps to provide a vibrant energy for an international western company in this Malaysian suburb.*

▲ *The Johannesburg Stock Exchange depends entirely on efficient communication channels and can only thrive if these are working well.*

▼ *The green area around these office buildings provides some protection from the Lyndon Johnson Freeway in Dallas, USA.*

HARNESSING THE ENERGIES

Feng Shui considers that different types of energies emanate from each direction. Since it is based on the cycles of nature, it is easy to understand that, for example, the energy of the east is represented by the rising sun and by spring and fresh young growth. If we employ this imagery we can see that the rising energy of the east would suit new companies; the south, dynamic activities such as marketing; the west, consolidation and financial activities; and the more static northern energy, activities indicating stillness such as storage or counselling.

The energy of your business is primarily determined by the direction in which the entrance faces.

▲ *This designer's home and studio symbolize the Wood element – it even looks as if a tree is growing through the centre.*

◀ *Libraries and archives are ideal in the north, which symbolizes storage and communication activities.*

Yin and Yang

We can utilize the principles of Feng Shui to help us determine the types of activities which will be suitable in each direction. The Bagua diagram indicates the elements associated with the directions, and which of them are considered to have yin qualities and which have yang attributes.

WOOD: Often known as "The Arousing" in its yang form, Wood signifies growth and movement. In its yang form it is more dynamic, suggesting brainstorming, new ideas and snap decisions. In its yin form, often referred to as "The Penetrating", it is more intuitive. Plans are carried forward and executed, ideas turned into designs.
YIN (–) SOUTH-EAST: Design
YANG (+) EAST: Development, ideas

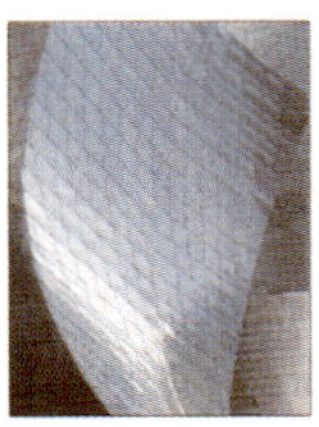

METAL: In its yin form, Metal is known as "The Joyous". It suggests pleasure and reflection, both in its inward and outward manifestations, mirrors and shiny objects, and contemplation. In its yang form, Metal is often referred to as "The Creative" and suggests strength and immobility as represented by large manufacturing machinery.
YIN (–) WEST: Small metal objects, e.g. knives, ornaments, finance, meditation
YANG (+) NORTH-WEST: Heavy engineering, machinery

EARTH: In its yin form, Earth is often known as "The Mountain", indicating stillness. Here we sow the seeds, prepare and provide support. In its yang form, Earth is often referred to as "The Receptive" and is productive – its output is turned into goods.
YIN (–) NORTH-EAST: Plant nurseries, printing and reprographic services
YANG (+) SOUTH-WEST: Quarrying, pottery, food production

FIRE: Fire is yang and does not have a yin form. It is also known as "The Clinging" and suggests activities concerned with bringing ideas and products to fruition and promoting them.
YANG (+) SOUTH: publishing, public relations, laboratories

▲ *Laboratories do well in the south, symbolized by the Fire element.*

WATER: Water is yin and does not have a yang form. It is also known as "The Abysmal" and suggests an area where the energy is not active, but where there is a regular flow.
YIN (–) NORTH: Storage and warehousing, secret negotiations, production lines

◀ *The Metal energy of the west is an ideal location for financial markets.*

▼ *This diagram of the Bagua shows the Five Elements with their yin and yang characteristics and the directions which represent them. We can use this to arrange our workspaces to make best use of the energies of each area within them.*

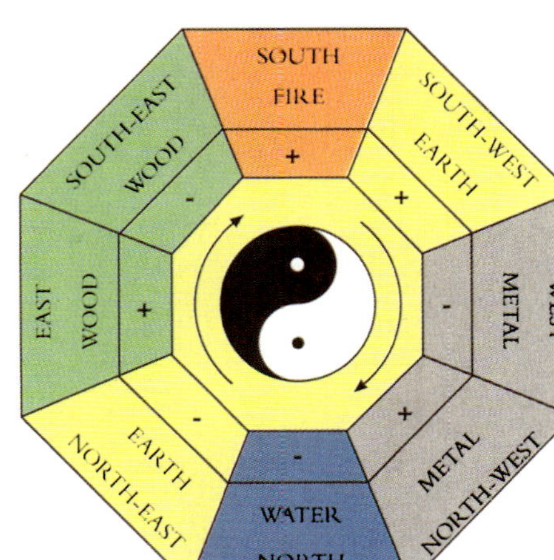

WHICH DIRECTION?

If you are setting up a new business or moving office there are considerations to be taken into account. Ideally, the entrance to an office or business should be orientated so that it faces one of the owner's best directions. Where we work for others, we should arrange our desks to face a supportive direction. We can ensure that our career is not harmed if we move jobs or buildings if we take the direction of our move into consideration.

Choosing a Location

When relocating or setting up a new business it may be possible to choose a building with an entrance in one of our best directions. Within the building we can hopefully ensure that our desk faces one of these directions. At the very least we should attempt not to sit facing our two worst directions.

Directions to Avoid Each Month

Every month there is a type of energy which will have a detrimental effect on an office or business. Each month is represented by one of the twelve Chinese animals and, it is the direction ruled by the animal which sits directly opposite ours that we should try to avoid moving towards.

▲ *It is important to feel comfortable at work, and facing our desk in a favourable position, whatever our position in the company, helps.*

▼ *With so much competition in the financial world those who use Feng Shui in the East seem to be able to win an advantage.*

Good Directions

Magic Number	1st Choice	2nd Choice
1	South-east	North
2	North-east	South-west
3	South	East
4	North	South-east
5-Male	North-east	South-west
5-Female	South-west	North-east
6	West	North-west
7	North-west	West
8	South-west	North-east
9	East	South

Worst Directions

Magic Number	2nd Last	Last
1	North-west	South-west
2	South	North
3	North-east	West
4	West	North-east
5-Male	South	North
5-Female	East	South-east
6	North	South
7	South-east	East
8	East	South-east
9	South-west	North-west

Checking the Monthly Directions

1. Locate the animal which rules the month in which you are planning to move on the "Favoured Months and Directions" diagram (opposite).

2. Locate the direction of the animal directly opposite yours. Try to avoid moving office to this direction in that month and delay the move until the following month.

Favoured Months and Directions

This diagram shows the element which rules the nature of each of the 12 animals and the months and directions ruled by each.

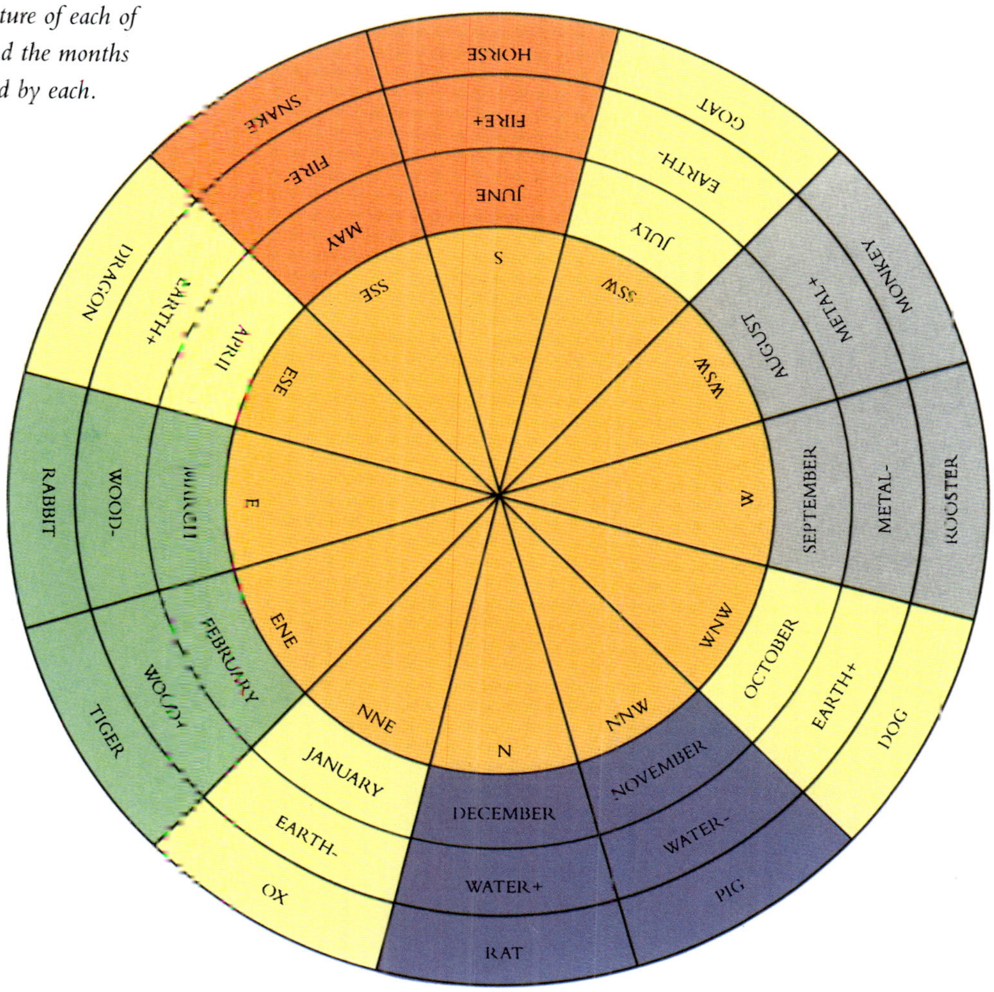

Find Your Favoured Directions

1. Check your Magic Number.

2. Look at the table opposite to find out the first and second choices of directions for your office to face.

Yearly Directions

1. Find the animal which rules the year when you are planning to move. Check the dates – the Chinese year begins in January or February.

2. Locate the direction of the animal directly opposite this animal. Avoid moving in this direction in that year.

◄► *When moving office, the direction the entrance faces is an important consideration.*

FIRST IMPRESSIONS

▲ *A large, clear sign, a car park and an attractive green outlook welcome visitors to this office building.*

First impressions of people or buildings are likely to colour our subsequent dealings with them. The ease with which we find the premises, the surrounding environment, the reception area and the greeting we receive are all indicative of the overall character and energy of a company and contribute to its success. Feng Shui can help to improve some aspects, but often it depends on the personalities involved, who will frequently determine whether we want to work with a particular organization or not.

Identification

On arrival at a business or office, visitors should be able to establish instantly that they have arrived in the right place. If the business occupies the whole building the company sign or logo should be prominently placed where it can be seen from the road. This may be on a signboard, but it should also be repeated on the building itself, in proportion to its size.

If the company shares a building with other businesses, a nameplate should be placed prominently outside the building and again inside to indicate which floor it is on. A notice inside the lift indicating which companies occupy each floor will make life easier for visitors, as will instructions on the wall facing the lift on each floor directing visitors to the company they are looking for or, if there is sole occupancy, to the reception desk.

Communication

Effective communication systems are crucial to the running of a successful business. The first point of contact is usually a telephone call and this can be the first stumbling block when approaching a business.

Business cards, stationery and brochures are another point of contact which needs to be considered. Names and addresses on stationery should be clear, and if a business is in an awkward location, a small map should be included.

The Company Name

Great importance is attached to the name of a business or retail premises. In the Chinese language, many words sound similar to others and only the intonation indicates the difference. For this reason,

▼ *A good telephone manner can make all the difference. The telephone is often the first point of contact with the company.*

Business Stationery

The first impression made by a letter is very important and business stationery should conform to the auspicious measurements. The colours used on the type should conform with the company colours and it is best if the name and address are in an easily readable font. The company logo should be featured and good-quality paper should be used to give a good impression.

▲ *This attractive reception area receives plenty of natural light, and drinking water is provided for staff and visitors.*

▼ *This powerful building is well signed. The name and the logo work well together and can be clearly seen.*

words which are similar to those that have undesirable meanings are not used for business names.

Signs

The importance of signs with a distinguishable company logo cannot be over-emphasized. Lettering should be legible. Colours are important and should be balanced according to the Five Elements. Three or five are the preferred number of colours; three representing growth and five, fulfilment. Signs along shopping malls and high streets which jut out at right angles to the building can be useful for drawing people in, especially if they are eye-catching. Signs should be firmly attached to a wall or other solid surface and should be in proportion to the whole of the building.

Logos

The images portrayed on a logo are important. Unpleasant and sharp images should be avoided. Points are normally not used, although an upward-pointing arrow symbolizes growth. Squares and circles are recommended, as well as images which denote upward energy. Again, colours should follow the Five Elements cycle and be balanced.

▼ *Vertical signs that jut out into the street are very eye-catching. Well-known companies will always dominate so you need to compete.*

THE WORKING OFFICE

How we function at work depends on a number of factors, some within and some beyond our control. We are usually able to organize our personal workspace so that it supports us and enables us to work efficiently. Other factors such as lighting, furnishings and layout we may not be able to change ourselves, but if we do not feel comfortable we may be able to influence the decision-making processes in order to achieve a balanced and harmonious environment to support us and ultimately benefit the company.

DRAWING THE PLAN

Having determined which directions our businesses are best suited to, we can look at the internal design and layout. The various departments in an organization should be positioned in locations where the energy supports the tasks they perform.

You Will Need

- ◆ A compass with the eight directions clearly marked
- ◆ A protractor – a circular one is best
- ◆ A ruler
- ◆ A lead pencil and five coloured pencils – green, red, yellow, black/grey, dark blue
- ◆ A scale plan of your office space
- ◆ A tracing of the Bagua with the suggested information marked on it

Taking a Compass Reading

- ◆ Remove watches, jewellery and metal objects and stand clear of cars and metal fixtures.
- ◆ Stand with your back parallel to the entrance and note the exact compass reading in degrees.
- ◆ Note the direction faced by the entrance, in this example 95° East, and mark it on to your plan as shown in the diagram. You are now ready to transfer the compass readings on to your Bagua drawing.

To Draw a Plan

Using graph paper and a tape measure, take measurements for each of the following floor-markings:

- ◆ External walls
- ◆ Internal walls
- ◆ Alcoves
- ◆ Staircases
- ◆ Doors
- ◆ Windows
- ◆ Permanent fixtures

This will enable you to design the final layout using the principles discussed later to position desks, furniture and other features in positions which will benefit those working there.

◀ *This reception area in a restaurant enables customers to relax while they wait for their table, while being part of the atmosphere.*

Transfer the Compass Reading to the Bagua

1 Place the circular protractor on the Bagua diagram so that 0° is at the bottom at the North position. Mark the eight directions.

2 Find the compass reading for your office and check you have the corresponding direction. If not, you may be reading the wrong ring.

3 Mark the position of the entrance.

4 Double-check the direction, using the table opposite.

Transfer the Directions to the Plan

1 Find the centre of the plan. Match the main walls across the length of the plan and crease the paper lengthways.

2 Match the main walls across the width

Directions

North	337.5–22.5″
North-east	22.5–67.5″
East	67.5–112.5″
South-east	112.5–157.5″
South	157.5–202. 5″
South-west	202.5–247.5″
West	247.5–292.5″
North-west	292.5–337.5″

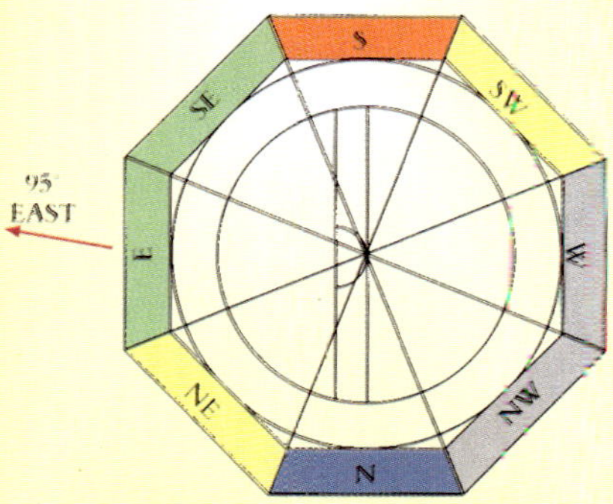

and crease the paper widthways. Where the folds cross each other marks the centre of your office.

If your office is not a square or rectangle, treat a protrusion less than 50% of the width as an extension to the direction. If the protrusion is more than 50% of the width, treat the remainder as a missing part of the direction.

3 Place the centre of the Bagua on the centre point of the plan and line up the entrance position.

4 Mark the eight directions on the plan and draw in the sectors.

5 Transfer the colour markings.

▼ *Once the Bagua is in place over the plan, we can see the direction of each room and the element that represents it. The location of the rooms can now be allocated.*

▲ *In a small building this reception area would probably feel oppressive. In a large office it offers the contrast of a cosy space with access to the larger space beyond.*

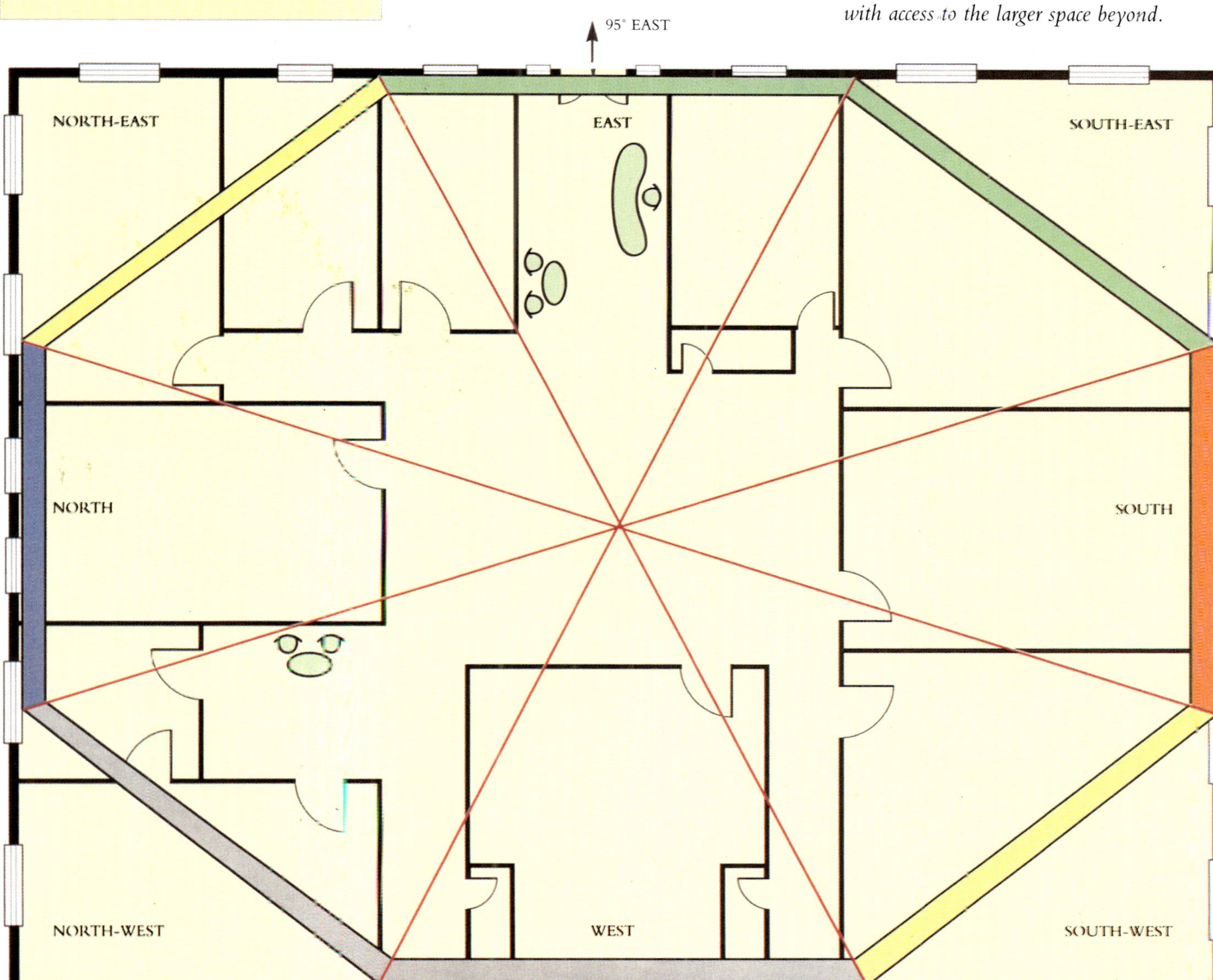

DESIGNING THE LAYOUT

Taking into account the types of energy associated with each of the eight major compass directions and the types of activities suited to each, we can investigate how to design our office space accordingly. Some features – toilets, car parks and eating areas – which are more suited to some directions than others can be repositioned.

It is important to give some consideration to what visitors will see when they enter the office. Ideally, they should not be able to see directly into the main working area. Every organization has times of stress, but visitors and potential clients should not be aware of the daily traumas of office life or be able to overhear any heated conversations that may be taking place. Doors should therefore be positioned out of the line of sight of visitors, who should receive an impression of calmness and efficiency in congenial surroundings.

Entrances

Entrances are auspicious if they face the favourable positions of the owner of the company, as determined by his/her Magic Number. If it isn't in our power to effect this – and usually it isn't – we can place our workstations or desks in a favourable direction instead. Entrances which face east encourage the energy of growth, while west-facing entrances foster stability. Whichever direction we face we should ensure the elements are balanced.

▼ *This modern office building in Singapore is distinguished by a traditional Chinese entrance, complete with guardians on either side.*

▲ *These impressive entrance doors have been carefully designed to be in proportion to the building and its surroundings.*

▶ *A loo with a view, but the large building opposite is threatening the office with a "poison arrow" of negative energy.*

▲ *An attractive staff kitchen does wonders for office morale, and must be kept clean and tidy.*

Bathrooms and Toilets

Always difficult to place, toilets should never face the office entrance. They should preferably be placed on an outside wall or if internally sited, ventilation must function efficiently. Bathroom doors should be closed at all times and should be designed so that even when open the toilets are not visible within. These areas should be kept clean and pleasant.

▲ *An indoor garden gives support to the fragile staircase in this light and airy reception area.*

▲ *This entrance has a lovely view but the reception desk is cut off and has beams over it.*

Staff Kitchens and Restaurants

Favourable areas for kitchens and restaurants are the east, south-east, south and south-west. Cleanliness and good ventilation are most important to ensure that the air is fresh and pleasant at all times.

Staircases

Ideally staircases of any kind should not be positioned in the north, north-west or the centre of the building.

Car Parks

Company car parks are best situated in the east, south-east and the north-west.

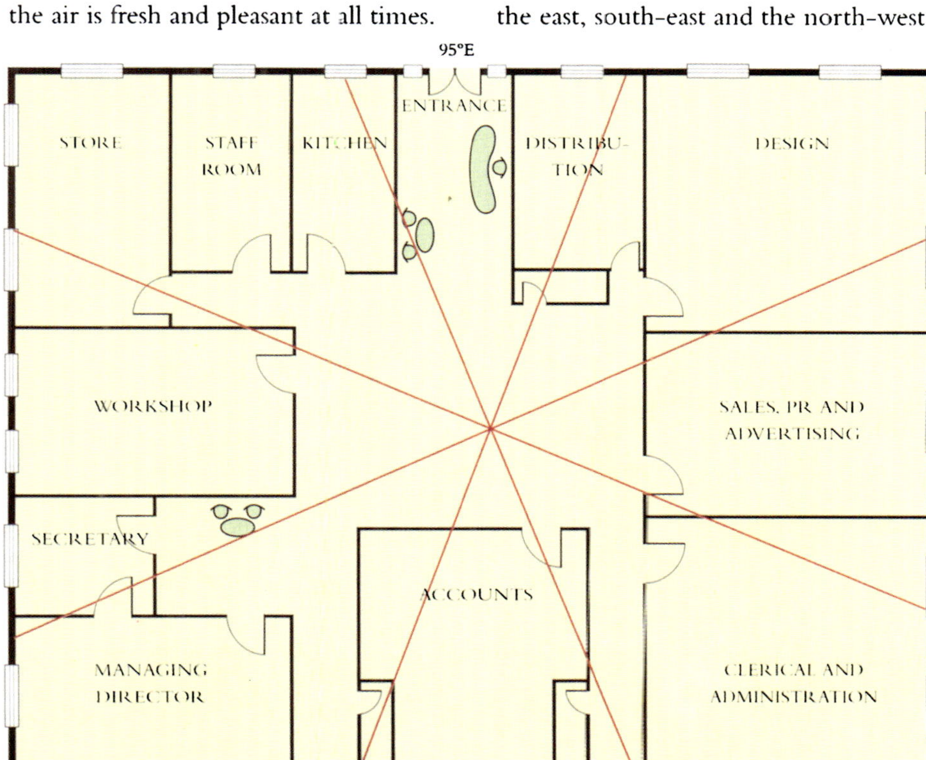

▶ *This model office has been designed so that all the functions are in suitable directions. Work-flow has been taken into account and the doors are positioned away from public sight, while giving the widest possible view for people entering on business.*

YIN AND YANG

The forces of yin and yang act together to create movement and keep a balance in the world. In the office yin and yang can relate to physical matters like layout and decor, but analysis of them also applies to the various activities which take place and to the interaction of those who work there.

Most offices tend to be more yang than yin. The straight lines of the desks, bright fluorescent lights, computer screens, shiny floor surfaces and metal cabinets, the bustle and the noise are all indicative of a yang environment. The chairman's room and the boardroom are usually remote from the hurly-burly of daily office routine and they have a more yin decor, often housing art works and other pleasing reflections of a company's wealth. In a busy office, plants can soften the harshness of the yang environment and water features can draw wealth in symbolically to the reception area, and other areas too.

▲ *This chairman's office is a yin space, decorated with paintings and with a general air of calmness.*

▼ *The straight lines and shiny surfaces of this office are yang, toned down with plants, pictures and wooden surfaces.*

Office activities also fall into yin and yang categories. Day-to-day administrative tasks are yin, and the yang energy is where the action is – decision-making and implementing policies. For example, a typical brainstorming session will involve several people sitting around a table in a well-lit, virtually empty room and it is almost possible to see the vibrant energy circulating around. Every now and again, a lull, a yin space, occurs when the chairman sums up the outcome before tossing another point in to build up the energy again. We can contrast this largely yang process with that of putting the ideas into practice. Programming a computer, for example, requires hours of yin time

▲ *This decision-making room is very functional. There are no distractions and the chairs are not too comfortable.*

compared with an occasional frustrated outburst of yang energy when things do not go according to plan. Yin is always present within yang and vice versa.

People also fall into yin and yang categories. Some people are outwardly more dynamic and energetic, but are sometimes prone to nervous disorders and illnesses caused by physical exhaustion. However, people who proceed slowly and calmly can often surprise their colleagues by giving vent to built-up frustration. An energetic, high-powered manager may need a calm and efficient assistant, and decision-makers often need people who work in a complementary way to them to put their ideas into practice.

In an office, a balance of yin and yang is necessary for the smooth running of the organization. An office atmosphere which is too yang may mean that jobs do not get done and can result in stressful situations. If it is too yin productivity may be low and the company could remain static, failing to move forward and keep up with trends. As we have seen, people have either yin or yang natures and these can become evident in the workplace. Recognizing that other people work and behave differently to us is essential to a harmonious office environment.

▲ *In a hectic office the constant yang energy often results in staff becoming over-stressed.*

Yin and Yang Offices

Yang offices contain:	Yin offices contain:
Machines	Paper
Telephones and faxes	Carpets
Rectangular desks	Curtains
Blinds	Art works
Metal cabinets	Dark furniture
People traffic	One person
Conversation	Wooden cabinets
Light decor	Wallpaper
Reflective surfaces	Textured surfaces

Yang activities include:	Yin activities include:
Brainstorming	Administration
Deadlines	Creating
Marketing	Producing
Selling	Packaging
Promoting	Reviewing

Yang people are:	Yin people are:
Enthusiastic	Receptive
Energetic	Creative
Quick-thinking	Imaginative
Precise	Methodical

► *These two very different office spaces both show a balance of yin and yang, with straight lines and reflective surfaces softened by colours and fabrics.*

UNSEEN ENERGIES

It is now widely accepted that some buildings can create or exacerbate health problems for their occupants. Sick Building Syndrome has become a commonly accepted term for a number of problems in modern buildings which can cause minor and, occasionally, more serious illnesses or viruses. Most of these problems stem from the fact that modern buildings are virtually sealed units in which air, introduced and circulated by machines, becomes stale and a breeding ground for bacteria or viruses. This stale air is continually recirculated by air-conditioning units and the germs are constantly reintroduced to the atmosphere. A toxic mixture of chemicals from manufactured materials can also build up.

▲ *The heating and lighting systems of office blocks burn huge amounts of energy.*

▲ *Office buildings with windows looking out on to green areas make better places to work.*

▼ *The air-conditioning in this office is very much in evidence, and very oppressive.*

The Air We Breathe

Modern buildings are designed to keep the less desirable aspects of the weather out and to regulate the temperature at what is considered to be a comfortable working level. Sealed double-glazed units

HARMFUL SUBSTANCES CAN BE FOUND IN:

FURNITURE: Particleboard, Chipboard, Plywood, Stains and varnishes, Upholstery

FURNISHINGS: Carpets, Curtains, Plastics, Paint, Wall coverings

EQUIPMENT: Photocopiers, Printers, Duplicating machines

STATIONERY: Pre-printed paper, Correction Fluids, Plastic folders, Adhesives.

▼ *We need time out from the constant pressures of modern office life to recharge our energy and also protect our health.*

keep out the damp and the cold, but at the same time they also prevent fresh air from circulating around a building. Some buildings have insulation in the walls which also prevents air from entering. In such buildings, air-conditioning keeps the air circulating. Dry air circulation can create throat irritation, respiratory problems, tiredness and headaches, with a resultant loss in working performance. Air that has been passed through cooling towers to add moisture to it can suffer from a build-up of bacteria and viruses in the water.

MATERIALS

Human beings function best when they are in the same range of vibrations as the Earth, which has a frequency of 8–12 hertz. Most large buildings have either steel frames or foundations made

▲ *In a sealed and overcrowded office the lack of fresh air can easily cause a range of illnesses, resulting in poor productivity.*

from concrete reinforced with metal rods. This metal, along with that in air-conditioning pipes and ducts, may disturb the Earth's vibrations within the building and, in consequence, have a negative effect or even harm us.

The materials which are generally used in offices are made from manufactured substances and not from natural materials. Even if the curtains are made from cotton, they are usually treated with a fire-retardant substance which releases toxic chemicals into the air. There is also an increasing incidence of allergic reactions to a variety of substances.

Where we have control over our workspaces, it is desirable to use natural materials or, if this is not possible, at least to ensure that there is a supply of fresh air. Scientists at NASA, investigating air quality inside spacecraft, discovered that some plants are useful in extracting harmful substances from the atmosphere. At the very least position one of these on your desk, especially by a computer.

PLANTS WHICH CLEAN THE AIR

Lady palm (*Rhapis excelsa*)
Dragon Tree (*Dracaena marginata*) (right)
Rubber plant (*Ficus robusta*)
Dwarf banana (*Musa cavendishii*)
Peace lily (*Spathiphyllum*)
Heart leaf philodendron
Croton (*Codiaeum variegatum pictum*)
Dumb cane (*Dieffenbachia* 'Exotica compacta')
Golden pothos (*Epipremnum aureum*)
Boston fern (*Nephrolepis exaltata* 'Bostoniensis')
Syngonium (*Syngonium podophyllum*) (below)

STRUCTURAL DETAILS

▲ *The barriers between these desks do not block people sitting near to them.*

Often there is little we can do about the overall structure of an office building, and we have to work with and around the layout. Old buildings with small rooms are difficult to change, but if the building is open-plan, we can introduce screens and furniture to create our own layouts. Our working conditions make a great impact on how we feel about our jobs and on our performance. Being aware of problematic features enables us to design remedies to make our working lives more comfortable.

BEAMS

Beams are not recommended in Feng Shui. They can be oppressive when positioned over a desk and can suppress the chi of those beneath them. They are necessary to support a building, and concrete beams are often a feature in offices. Desks and seating areas should not be placed underneath beams. In open-plan offices, partitions can be placed under the beams to make the best use of the space. Otherwise, filing cabinets and bookcases should be placed there, or large plants which lift the energy.

COLUMNS

Straight-sided columns are difficult to deal with. Where the edges point at chairs, the people sitting in them will feel uncomfortable. We should take measures to disguise or soften the corners of the columns by rounding them off in some way, or by disguising them with plants and other items.

BARRIERS

Where several small rooms have been converted to one large office, there are occasionally parts of walls left for structural reasons. It is important that both eyes have the same-length view, as Feng Shui consultants recognize a pattern of illnesses which result if the view from

▼ *A staircase directly opposite the entrance will channel chi away from the office.*

▼ *The flow of chi in this room appears to have nothing to contain it.*

▲ *The chi rushes straight through these wide doors and is unchecked by anything inside.*

▼ *Patterned rugs or hanging lights would slow down the energy in this long corridor.*

▼ *The giant curve slows down the movement of chi in this corridor.*

▲ *A large plant at the bottom of this light, attractive spiral staircase would give it more stability and reduce the corkscrew effect.*

one eye is blocked. Barriers can create individual workplaces, often leaving people's backs exposed. Facing another person can cause conflict, and facing the back of a computer can cause illness.

Staircases

Staircases and escalators should not face the front entrance or the chi energy will be unable to circulate properly. Spiral staircases act as a corkscrew through a building and are not comfortable. Where they exist, place large plants at the bottom in terracotta pots to add stability.

Corridors

Long, narrow corridors funnel chi very quickly. Slow it down by strategically placing mirrors or plants, or using other means to create a meandering route – for example, changes in floor covering or pattern. Hanging light-fittings are another option. Where there are many offices along a straight corridor, the occupants often feel isolated. If the doors are opposite one another there may be rivalry and bad feeling. A plant by each door may help and leaving doors open will enable people to feel part of the community. If doors are not aligned, this can also cause problems and it is recommended that mirrors or landscape views are placed to fill in the spaces on either side of the doors.

LIGHTING

▲ *These adaptable tilted reading stands are an ingenious way to get the light to fall on the page at the right angle.*

◄ *Natural daylight is the best source of light but in strong sunshine there is too much glare on these highly reflective glass surfaces.*

▼ *Coloured glass creates a wonderful energy in this entrance door, generating the feeling that this is a successful company.*

Adequate lighting is essential in the workplace for health and safety reasons and to ensure maximum efficiency. Offices should be well-lit and it may be necessary to introduce a variety of lighting to support the various functions which are carried out there.

Natural Daylight

By far the best form of lighting in an office is natural daylight. Our bodies rely on light not only to enable us to see but also for Vitamin D, which comes from the sun and is absorbed through the skin. In countries that receive relatively little sunlight during some parts of the year people may suffer from SAD, or Seasonal Affective Disorder, brought about by an excess of melatonin, a hormone produced by our brains during the hours of darkness. People who work in offices that are artificially lit will almost certainly not be as healthy as those who benefit from natural light. Depression and lethargy are typical symptoms, but working in such conditions can produce a range of problems from headaches and nausea to poor eyesight, stress and fatigue, particularly where the lighting is fluorescent.

However, precautions should be taken where computer screens and desks are close to windows since the glare of the

▲ *A range of different kinds of lighting is used in this studio. Shadows may fall in different areas at different times of day.*

▼ *In this colourful staff restaurant, elegant uplighters by the side of each table create the impression of individual spaces.*

sun can also create problems. Measures can be taken to filter the light through vertical blinds, plants or movable screens.

Artificial Light

The quality of light is important. Full-spectrum lighting was designed to copy natural daylight as much as possible but unfortunately contains slightly higher levels of ultraviolet radiation than ordinary light sources. Fluorescent lights are still the primary light source in offices because they are easy to install and cheap to run, but this type of lighting emits higher electromagnetic fields than other sources, which can be detrimental. The flickering from fluorescent lights can cause stress and headaches and can even bring on fits in epilepsy sufferers.

Incandescent light bulbs offer a range of options, giving an even light throughout the office, and can also be used for task lighting on desks. Desk lamps should always be positioned on the opposite side to the dominant hand to prevent shadows falling across work.

▲ *Interesting lighting effects enhance this attractively-designed eating area.*

Uplighters can be useful in offices where ceilings are low and where it is not desirable to have spot lighting on desks. Reflected lighting, directed on to walls and ceilings, offers an additional lighting source; the colour of the decor will influence its effectiveness. Tungsten and halogen lamps are useful for this. Too bright to be used for task lighting and close work, they give a white light which is close to daylight and the low-voltage variety can be used for accenting. These bulbs are also energy-efficient.

DECORATION

When we use colour we are working with light, as light contains all colours, each with its own frequency. The colours we use in offices will be affected by the amount of natural daylight there and by the secondary light sources we use. The materials will also have a bearing on the overall effect of the office. Upholstered chairs and curtains in dark colours have a yin quality while smooth, hard surfaces and light and metallic surfaces have yang attributes. The materials we use in decorations and furnishings have the ability to absorb or transmit light and their colours will affect the energy in the office.

▲ *Plenty of natural daylight and lively colours make this staff dining area an energetic space.*

COLOUR

Colour is vibration and we each respond to it consciously and unconsciously in different ways. In our own individual offices, it is best to choose wall and floor colours that we like and feel comfortable with, but in communal offices a neutral colour to suit all tastes is preferable. Colour can be introduced in furnishings and other items – paintings, storage boxes and upholstery. The psychological effects of colour are numerous but there are some Feng Shui guidelines that we can follow. Normally offices are yang, and yang colours (red, purple, orange and bright yellow) will add to the yang energy. Yin colours (green, blue and black) will create a less dynamic feel. The colours in public areas should be neutral, with the accent colours reflecting the nature of the company, or the colours of the logo if it is one which is well-known.

THE FIVE ELEMENTS

The colours associated with the Five Elements evoke the quality of the energy of each element. We can use these colours in the office to highlight the

▼ *The colours of this curved reception area suggest that the company is not dependent on quick decisions or aggressive marketing.*

▼ *In this office the use of bright but muted colours and some awkward angles give the space a disturbing feeling.*

▼ *Interesting colours and shapes have been used in this design studio, where the chi moves unimpeded round the curves.*

Qualities of the Five Elements

Green (Wood): new businesses, growth and development
Red (Fire): dynamic, outgoing, forward-looking
Yellow (Earth): intellectual, rational
Brown (Earth): stability
White (Metal): fresh start
Black (Water): secret research

nature of the business or the qualities we wish to invoke there.

The colours which correspond to the Five Elements should be in balance in any office. Where one element is dominant, or lacking, then it may have an effect on the energies at work there. The table below shows the relationships of the elements and can be used to strengthen a weak energy or deplete the impact of one which is too dominant. We can use the colour, shape or material related to each element to balance an environment.

If we decide to decorate our office walls in strong colours, it is usually best to choose neutral colours for furnishings or to blend the colours. However, sometimes a clash of colours is a way of moving energy, especially useful in a company where rapid decisions are called for.

Materials

If we opt for a neutral colour on office walls and floors, we can introduce the qualities of the Five Elements through the furniture and fittings, soft furnishings, pictures and plants.

Hard, shiny materials, such as metal and glass, are yang and move energy on quickly. The use of these materials in staff canteens and meeting rooms will ensure that the activities there do not go on too long. Denser materials such as non-shiny metals, dark wood and upholstered chairs are more containing and the energy associated with them is slower.

Synthetic materials are not really recommended because of the associated health risks and although it is inevitable that we have these materials in the office, on computer casings, furniture trims and other office items, it is preferable for them to be kept to a minimum, particularly on desks at which people spend considerable amounts of time.

▲ *The green tree balances this atrium coffee bar in the centre of the building. Colourful pictures and furnishings on each level offset the white background.*

◀ *Bright Fire colours in shades of red and orange are very appropriate for a dynamic business such as this advertising agency.*

The Relationships of the Five Elements

Element	Helped by	Harmed by	Weakened by	Weakens
Wood	Water	Metal	Fire	Earth
Fire	Wood	Water	Earth	Metal
Earth	Fire	Wood	Metal	Water
Metal	Earth	Fire	Water	Wood
Water	Metal	Earth	Wood	Fire

ELECTRICAL EQUIPMENT

Another potential hazard in the workplace is the electromagnetic radiation from electrical equipment, particularly computers. Electromagnetic fields, or EMFs, from high-voltage power lines and electrical appliances, are thought to be injurious to health. It is believed that they impair the cell regeneration process and could be responsible for the increasing numbers of people with impaired immune systems. It is wise to sit as far as possible away from equipment and not to surround ourselves with wires. A particularly bad spot for a desk to be situated is where the mains power enters a building – desks should be moved away from that area.

▲ *Computers are an essential part of office life but it is essential to take regular breaks if our health is not to suffer.*

◀ *The impact of electromagnetic radiation on people working in this office block will be harmful.*

Computers

Computers are virtually indispensable in the office, yet we place ourselves at risk from a number of illnesses, ranging from eye problems to repetitive strain injury, if we spend too long in front of them. Many countries now have legislation

▼ *In such a hi-tech environment a* Cereus peruvianus *cactus might help.*

▼ *Wherever possible, use a laptop in preference to another computer.*

▲ *This office should be rearranged so that no-one sits behind a colleague's computer monitor.*

◀ *Shield the back of the monitor if people are sitting behind it.*

which limits the number of hours each day which can safely be spent in front of a screen. In some American states, pregnant women are not allowed to operate computers since prolonged exposure may lead to miscarriage. Screen filters help to some extent, and laptop machines do not have cathode-ray tubes which are a major cause of such problems. Wearing natural fibres also helps because they do not create static electricity.

Most of the electromagnetic radiation comes from the back of the computer monitor and when designing offices this should be taken into consideration so that no-one is sitting facing, or with their backs towards, the rear of a monitor. It is thought that some plants can help to shield us to some extent, particularly the cactus, *Cereus peruvianus*, which was adopted for that purpose by the New York Stock Exchange.

Photocopiers and Duplicating Machines

Photocopying and duplicating machines give off chemical emissions – the duplicating machine from the ink, and the photocopier from the toner – which are known to be carcinogenic. These machines should not be located in offices where people work all day, particularly if they are in constant use. Ideally, they should be located in a separate, well-ventilated room. Certainly, no one should sit close to a photocopier.

Mobile Phones

Ear and brain tumours have been attributed to the use of mobile phones. The US Food and Drug Administration advises that they should be used only when absolutely necessary and that calls should be kept short. Where it is essential to use them, ensure that the antennae do not touch the head. The use of mobile phones in cars may increase the danger, particularly hand-held models.

▼ *Mobile phones have serious health implications – use a conventional telephone whenever possible.*

CLUTTER IN THE OFFICE

▲ *This efficient storage system is in the centre of the office, where energy should circulate freely, so it is important to keep it tidy.*

Office clutter accumulates rapidly and there are few people who would not benefit from discarding extraneous items from their workplace and streamlining their procedures. Office clutter is not just things left lying about, but also the paper we hoard, out-of-date journals and uncleared hard disks.

Storage

There is no excuse for clutter. There are many storage options, ranging from cupboards which hide computers and printers to simple cardboard storage boxes. These are widely available in the local high street, or by mail order. Before tidying everything away in boxes or files, it is worth asking the question, "Do I really need this?"

Journals

Professional journals are invariably hoarded but rarely read. Many of these are now available on-line and professional organizations hold a complete set in their libraries if an article is needed. If we skim through journals when they arrive and note the issue and page numbers of interesting articles in a diary, we can file them.

Desks

Desk drawers harbour a considerable amount of rubbish, but if we throw away old pens and pencils which no longer work, and have special places for rubber bands and paper clips, we will feel more efficient and save time spent searching for things. It is advisable only to have a single-tier in-tray, otherwise the temptation is to categorize things into urgent and not-so-urgent, and the latter will never be dealt with. A satisfying feeling

◀ *These full-length storage cupboards help to keep the office free of clutter.*

▶ *The top shelf of a set of shelves is rarely used and should be "weeded out" frequently.*

at the end of each day is to know that the in-tray is empty and that all mail has been dealt with; it can be energy-draining to begin the morning confronted with the debris from the day before. Even if you haven't been able to finish the work, tidy your desk so that you at least give the impression that all is under control. Clearing the day's mail is an excellent habit to get into and if everyone dealt with bills promptly the world would be a far less stressful place.

Computers

Computers store an amazing amount of information and if we keep the hard disks clear of out-of-date files and back up our working files regularly, we will always have rapid access to the data we need.

It can take time to set up databases to print labels for a mail shot, but it is worth the initial effort for the time saved. Random thoughts as well as notes for lectures and workshops should be recorded to help us prepare well in advance and save time and anguish at the last minute. Old hard-copy files do not have to be stored in the office and are best removed to a storeroom or cupboard elsewhere to prevent a build-up of stagnant energy.

▲ *A well-organized, uncluttered desk leads to clear thinking and reduces stress.*

▼ *The storage in this reading room is good but its proportion overwhelms the table.*

▼ *This well-designed workspace has both individual and communal storage areas.*

Organizers

One of the most useful items in an office is a revolving card file by the telephone. Invaluable for instant access to addresses and telephone numbers, it can also be used to cross-reference suppliers, record birthdays and other information which, although it can now be stored on computers and electronic personal organizers, actually takes more time to access in these formats. Personal organizers are extremely useful items for both the home and the office, but major difficulties arise if we lose them.

Books

Many people find books difficult to discard, yet the speed of technological change renders information out-of-date rapidly and some books, such as directories and unread reference books, should be regarded as disposable items.

FURNITURE AND MEASUREMENTS

◀ *This manager's office is ideally furnished but the glass panel allows no privacy.*

▲ *Floor-to-ceiling shelves overwhelm this already small office.*

The importance of well-designed, ergonomically correct office furniture cannot be overstated. Life can become a struggle if we have to battle with stuck doors in confined spaces on a daily basis and we can cause ourselves physical harm if we sit on chairs with wobbly seats and no back support, or type on keyboards at the wrong height.

Office furniture is often neglected, particularly in offices not visited by outsiders. In small offices occupied by several people, it is important that procedures are streamlined so that storage cupboards and filing cabinets can be kept to a minimum. Positioning desks in accordance with the workflow can also help, by keeping the movement of people through the office to a minimum.

The corners of all furniture should be rounded to help movement through the office and so that the corners do not point at anyone working close by, which can be uncomfortable. Catching a hip on the corner of a desk every time we go to a cupboard, or being unable to open a door without difficulty because someone's chair is in the way, will be frustrating and may lead to tensions.

Health and Safety

Repetitive Strain Injury (RSI) is the result of spending a long time performing the same task and can cause great discomfort for sufferers. Wrist supports and other methods of easing the condition are available. Office managers should be sympathetic to sufferers and provide suitable furniture and equipment to alleviate the problem and to prevent it occurring in the first place.

Storage units should be at a suitable height for the items contained in them so that staff do not have to bend or stretch excessively to reach them. Shelving above head height can be oppressive and create insecurity. The edges of shelves near a chair can create "poison arrows" of energy, which can cause discomfort to those sitting nearby. Where possible, cupboards are preferable to open shelves near seating and make the

▲ *Furniture has to be the correct height in studios, where people bend and stretch.*

▼ *This efficient workshop has furniture at the right height and tools to hand.*

office look less cluttered. Floor-to-ceiling shelving is particularly overpowering in small offices, and the more shelves we have in an office, the more likely we are to fill them up with things we do not really need. Mirrors can be placed in small offices to create an illusion of space, but do not place them where people can see themselves as they work, otherwise, depending on their personality, they will feel uncomfortable or be preening all day.

Auspicious Measurements

(Yes = Auspicious, No = Inauspicious)

CM	INCHES	
0–5.4	0–2⅛	Yes
5.4–10.7	2⅛–4¼	No
10.7–16.1	4¼– 6⅜	No
16.1–21.5	6⅜–8½	Yes
21.5–26.9	8½–10⅝	Yes
26.9–32.2	10⅝–12¾	No
32.2–37.6	12¾–14⅞	No
37.6–43	14⅞–17	Yes
43–48.4	17–19⅛	Yes
48.4–53.7	19⅛–21¼	No
53.7–59.1	21¼–23⅜	No
59.1–64.5	23⅜–25½	Yes
64.5–69.9	25½–27⅝	Yes
69.9–75.2	27⅝–29¼	No
75.2–80.6	29¼–31⅞	No
80.6–86	31⅞–34	Yes
86–91.4	34–36⅛	Yes
91.4–96.7	36⅛–38¼	No
96.7–102.1	38¼–40⅜	No
102.1–107.5	40⅜–42½	Yes
107.5–112.9	42½–44⅝	Yes
112.9–118.2	44⅝–46¾	No
118.2–123.6	46¾–48⅞	No
123.6–129	48⅞–51	Yes
129–134.4	51–53⅛	Yes
134.4–139.7	53⅛–55¾	No
139.7–145.1	55¾–57⅜	No
145.1–150.5	57⅜–59½	Yes
150.5–155.9	59½–61⅝	Yes
155.9–161.2	61⅝–63¾	No
161.2–166.6	63¾–65⅞	No
166.6–172	65⅞–68	Yes

For dimensions in excess of these, the cycle repeats.

▲ *A round-edged table is ideal for meetings and prevents passers-by knocking into it.*

Measurements

Furnishings are usually purchased from office suppliers. If they are specially designed, it will be advantageous to follow the preferred Feng Shui dimensions. It is felt in China that some dimensions bring good luck but others are not advantageous. By using the correct dimension for signs, windows, doors, desks, chairs, bookcases and other furnishings, we can ensure that we are in a strong position to develop our businesses successfully.

The measurements are taken from eight divisions of the diagonal, roughly 43 cm (17 in), bisecting a square based on the Chinese foot, which is virtually the same as an imperial foot. This corresponds to the "Golden Section", "Divine Proportion" or pi in Eastern architecture, and is based on proportion in nature. It can be found in the growth patterns on shells and the markings on plants, among other phenomena.

The three main dimensions of office desks should be in accordance with the auspicious Feng Shui dimensions, as should the height and back width of the chairs, although the ergonomics of the furniture obviously has to conform to today's standards. Other furniture, such as bookcases and display cabinets, can also be designed according to these principles.

▼ *These modern chairs look attractive but do not offer enough support for the back.*

▼ *The manager's chair is larger than his visitor's, giving him the edge in negotiations.*

DESKS AND WORKSTATIONS

▲ *Both desks have a view of the door, with plenty of time to see someone approaching.*

As we spend a considerable amount of time at work, it is important that we position ourselves where we feel comfortable and where we can tap into the beneficial energies of a supportive direction. This is easier to achieve if we are the sole occupant of an office, but even where an office is shared with other people it should be possible to find a supportive space.

◄ *This desk would be better placed sideways to avoid having one's back to the window.*

The most important rule in Feng Shui is to feel comfortable and this cannot be achieved if we sit with our backs to a window or door, since we will feel uneasy and nervous. The glare of the sun through a window onto computer screens can cause headaches. A useful remedy is to place plants on the windowsill, or position a piece of furniture there, as long as this will not restrict our space.

The best place for a desk is diagonally opposite the door so that we can see anyone entering the room. This is certainly the place for the most senior person in the room if it is occupied by several people, as they will be bothered less by day-to-day tasks than those closer to the door. Those who sit facing the door will

► *Low barriers give a view of the office and do not hem people into their own space.*

Desk Positions

Most of us spend a considerable amount of time at our desks so it is important to feel comfortable and well supported. This will be affected by the position of the desk in the room. Try sitting in a position that allows a view of the room while being removed from the bustle at the door, and compare it to the way you feel when you are sitting in a vulnerable position next to the door.

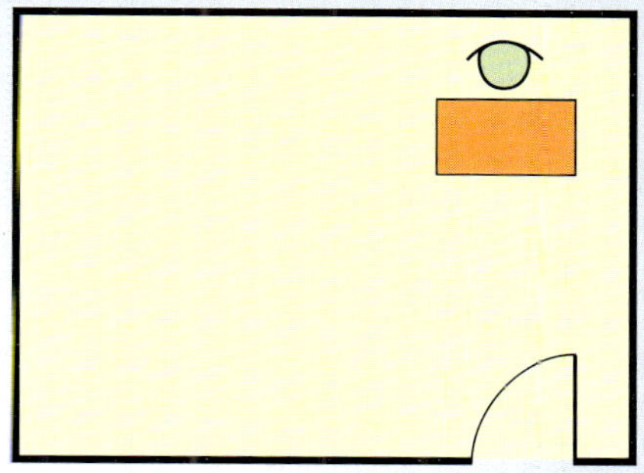

3. This position for a desk will make the occupant feel directly in the firing line.

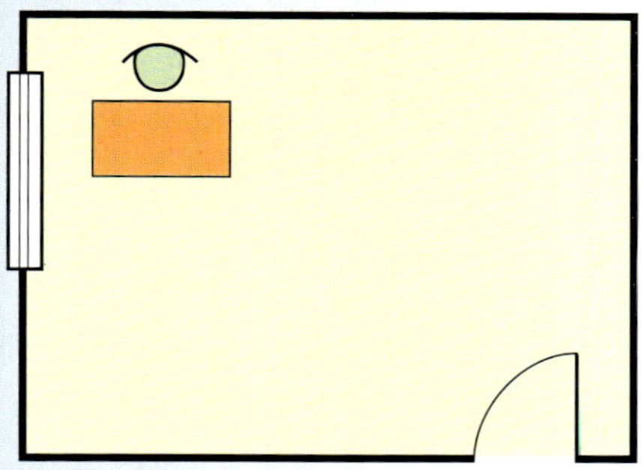

1. This is the best Feng Shui position, facing but not in front of the door..

4. This is the worst position in which one could feel comfortable.

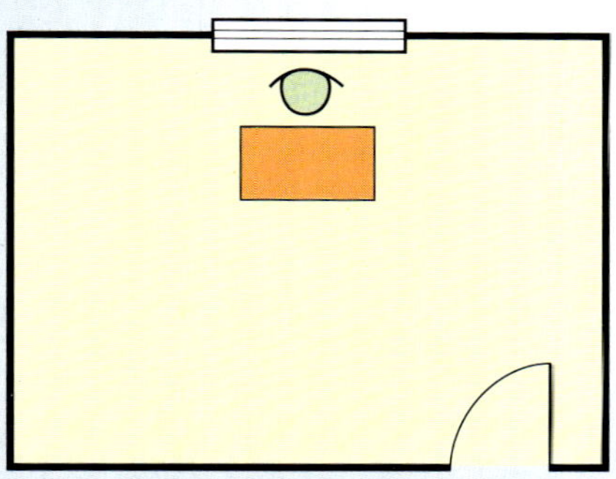

2. This is disconcerting; some plants on the windowsill as a barrier would help.

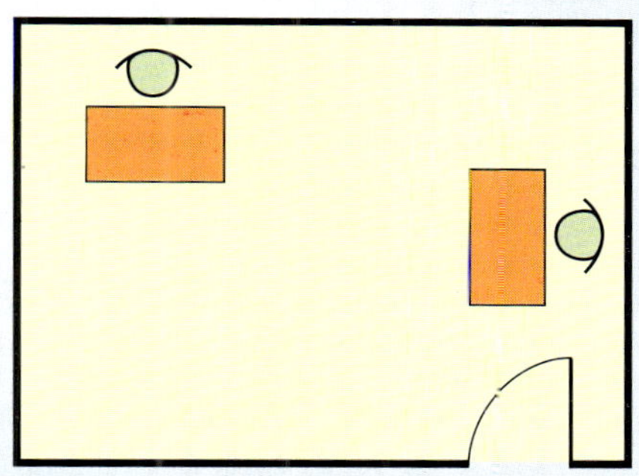

5. The person near the door will be disturbed more than the person opposite.

be in the firing line for anyone entering and those closest to it will have less job satisfaction than those further away because they will be constantly interrupted in their work by people coming in and out. People who sit in these positions rarely stay long in a job. It is their pens and equipment that visitors borrow and their papers which get knocked off the desk.

Open-plan Offices

In open-plan offices, desks and workstations are often in small booths and the occupants' backs face into the room. In this position, there is an element of surprise when someone approaches from behind and it is not a comfortable position in which to work. The remedy is to place a mirror on the wall.

The size of our desk should be in proportion to our position in the company. It is usual for the chairman to have a large desk and he/she would not retain much credibility if it was the smallest desk in the office.

In Feng Shui, desk shapes are important. Square and rectangular desks are considered suitable but are best if the corners are rounded so that they do not point at anyone or catch them as they

▲ *This is a lovely desk but the chair is not supported behind. A large plant or low screen would help*

pass by. L-shaped desks are perceived to resemble meat cleavers, with the shorter side being reminiscent of the blade, which will cut off communications and authority. If possible, separate the two parts of the desk and use the smaller one for a computer. Round desks will not encourage anyone to sit and work at them for long, but are ideal for meetings, which should be kept short.

Workstations can be a problem in that they come with trailing wires. These should be secured in some way or run in channels for safety reasons. It is detrimental to health to sit facing the back of a computer monitor and every attempt should be made to design the office so that this does not occur.

▼ *Wide desks ensure that people are not sitting too close to the computer screens.*

RECEPTION AREAS

The entrance to a building sets the tone for the whole company and its importance cannot be overstated. A clean, bright, welcoming entrance area will encourage clients to think well of an organization and will create a positive atmosphere for employees. A dark and scruffy area, on the other hand, will indicate a failing or shoddy company to clients and deplete the energy of employees before they start the day.

Entrances

The main entrance door or doors should be in proportion to the building. If there are double doors, both should be open or the flow of chi into the building will be restricted, resulting in a dark and stale area behind the closed door. Revolving doors help to circulate energy at the entrance but are only suited to large office buildings.

Doors should open easily and not be too heavy or they will deplete personal energy. If a company takes deliveries, or if clients bring portfolios or large sample cases, there should be some means of propping the door open to enable easy access otherwise the whole entry process will symbolize a struggle, which may continue throughout the visit. If there are windows immediately opposite the door, plants should be placed in front to prevent the chi from passing straight through without circulating around the building.

The Reception Desk

Visitors should be able to see the reception desk from the entrance but it should not be too close to it, or opposite, or the receptionist will be exhausted by the activity there. It is important that the receptionist has a comfortable chair and is backed by a solid wall so as not to be startled from behind. Receptionists should be occupied with work that will not clutter the desk and should be trained to put visitors' needs before those of

▲ *An impressive entrance, but the second door symbolizes chi escaping. It would be better turned into a window.*

▼ *This well-designed desk enables the receptionist to keep in contact with colleagues as well as greeting clients.*

▼ *This amazing sculpture is out of proportion to the entrance and exerts great pressure on it.*

▲ *The glass wall of this reception area acts as a barrier in what would otherwise have been a vulnerable position.*

◀ *The stained glass doors in this comfortable reception area add interest. Each door can be recognized by a different design.*

▼ *Care has been taken over the design of this reception area, decorated with a vase of fresh flowers.*

other employees and the demands of the telephone. Procedures should be in place to remove all deliveries from the reception area as soon as possible after arrival so that the area will not be cluttered.

Reception areas

Chi flow in reception areas is important and employees should be able to move quickly through to their work areas via lifts and staircases. It is important that reception areas are fresh and that the air is circulated, so fans, plants and water features can play a useful role. Any water features outside the building can be reflected by mirrors in the reception area. Mirrors should be positioned to one side of the entrance so that the chi will not be reflected back through the door.

Fish tanks are often placed in reception areas. In China, fish symbolize wealth and often there are nine fish in the tank – eight gold ones and a single black one to soak up any negative energy. Tiny darting fish create an active energy useful in commercial companies, whilst larger, slower-moving species create a calm atmosphere, which can be useful in health practices. Aquariums should be large enough to enable the fish to move freely and should recreate as natural an environment as possible.

The Ideal Reception

This reception area contains various features to help the flow of chi:

1. A water feature with a fountain and plants lifts the chi in the reception area.

2. A well-designed reception desk supports the receptionist and is positioned so that he/she is in contact with employees and visitors.

3. Plants help to keep the air fresh and add to the Wood energy, symbolizing growth.

4. The round table indicates that energy will spin around this area quickly, suggesting that visitors will not be kept waiting long.

5. The company logo opposite the entrance adds prestige to the reception area.

6. Employees pass through this pleasant, energized area on their way to the lifts.

7. The delivery area is located close to the lifts for convenience and so that the reception area is kept clear.

COMMUNAL AREAS

◀ *Everything is incorporated in this cleverly designed office – individual spaces, meeting and eating areas, kitchen and training – and it works quite well.*

The communal areas of the office are important not just for visitors but also for staff morale. It is false economy to neglect staff areas since a contented staff that feels valued and appreciated will produce more, represent the company better and feel happier at work. Consequently there will be less absenteeism. Office and desk conditions are important but refreshment, washroom and rest room facilities are equally so.

The Entrance

Even if an office building does not have visitors on a regular basis, it is important that the entrance to the office is clearly marked and well maintained for the sake of the people who work there.

What the staff see as they arrive each day is important. Waste bins should not be placed by the entrance and deliveries should be put away immediately as they arrive. Uncollected mail and any other clutter should not be allowed to accumulate. Make sure there is someone responsible for this area. Positive images encourage staff as they arrive each day and are a "feel good" factor as they leave.

Stairs and Corridors

Poor decoration and maintenance within the building are depressing. Shadowy corners and ill-lit passageways will not encourage staff to linger in the evening, or stay late to finish projects. Fresh paintwork and clean flooring help to create an air of efficiency and, together with positive images on the walls, suggest to employees that they are valued.

▼ *In this typical meeting room the round table encourages the circulation of ideas.*

Offices

Cramped working conditions lead to cramped minds. We feel resentful if we constantly knock ourselves on colleagues' desks and cupboards. Mirrors can create an illusion of space and have a positive impact provided they do not reflect a cluttered environment. Open-plan offices can leave people feeling vulnerable so it is important that they personalize their spaces and are not surprised from behind. Strategically placed mirrors will deal with this but make sure that they are not positioned so that members of staff can see their reflections from their desk.

Staff Rooms

Staff rooms are where employees meet, discuss work and air grievances and the Feng Shui of these rooms is important if

▼ *A grand boardroom; the chairman sits at the head of the oval table and takes charge.*

staff are to be positive, though they should not be too comfortable or breaks will be extended. If the staff room has a kitchen area, it should be clean and conform to health and safety standards and provision should be made for clearing up at busy times. Notice boards are important and act as a communication medium between staff and employer. Notices should be up-to-date and changed regularly, and there should be a balance between work and social information.

▲ A staff dining room with a pleasant view will help to recharge energies for the afternoon session.

Meeting Rooms

Meeting rooms range from a small area where two or more people can meet to discuss a specific issue to large boardrooms. Where "Hot Desking" is practised, meetings take place standing up at hard shiny, yang tables set at "leaning height", so employees do not get too comfortable and quick decisions are made. In more conventional meetings everyone should sit facing their best direction where possible. Table shapes can affect meetings. Boardroom tables are best if they are oval. Round tables are useful for brainstorming sessions and rectangular shapes for meetings with a leader who sits at the head. Boardrooms should be well furnished and the chairperson's seat should be larger than the rest, backed by a wall with a view of the door.

▲ *There are only two safe spaces at this table, and all will feel very vulnerable in this glass box exposed to everyone in the office.*

▼ *This office design allows for individual workspaces and the opportunity for people to come together for discussions.*

▼ *A well-designed kitchen area, however small, will boost staff morale and make them feel valued.*

OFFICE ENERGIES

Feng Shui considers the movement of chi through a building and how it effects the working environment. It also takes into consideration the personal energies of the individuals who work there. In this section we investigate different approaches used in office communication systems, and observe how our personalities determine the way we react in certain situations, and how we respond to our colleagues. We also look at how Feng Shui can help us at interviews and on business trips, and how our home and office are linked.

OFFICE ENERGIES

▲ *A happy office is a productive one. Staff need time out in a congenial space to unwind and interact with colleagues.*

As we have seen, Feng Shui is largely about ensuring that there is a free flow of movement around a building and arranging the space accordingly to ensure that the energy, or chi, flow does not become blocked, get stuck or stagnate. Moving furniture and redesigning space is comparatively easy and when the benefits are pointed out, there are few who cannot see the advantages, but a crucial factor that is overlooked in most organizations is the mental energy of the people who work there.

Where psychology is employed in a business, it is usually intended to bring advantages to the organization and to increase levels of production. While this is understandable, production will always automatically increase where staff are happy and one aspect which is generally overlooked is the fact that not everyone is the same, nor do they work in the same way. If we can accommodate a variety of working styles, then we will create a contented work force and thus generate greater productivity.

The Collaborative Office

"Hot Desking" is an office design revolution that originated in architectural colleges. It is based on the idea of an open-plan office and its purpose is to encourage people to be more creative by interacting and networking in order to foster the exchange of ideas. The characteristics of this approach are:

- ◆ No personal space
- ◆ Communal desks and equipment
- ◆ A variety of workspaces – communal and intimate around a central hub
- ◆ No internal telephone calls or memos
- ◆ Stand-up meetings which reduces their length
- ◆ No departments
- ◆ No clutter – anything lying around is thrown out; staff have personal lockers
- ◆ No receptionists or secretaries
- ◆ All staff can do all jobs

This system has already been adopted by several companies working mainly in the area of PR and advertising. The work ethic of these types of companies is already yang and staff tend to be young and dynamic, and work under pressure.

▼ *In this typical "Hot Desking" office, the layout does not encourage people to stay long in one place.*

▲ *A central place for meetings and discussions ensures that ideas come from all directions.*

Such organizations need some yin in their furnishings but their efficient, clean lines suggest this is not happening, in which case the staff may feel even more pressured and eventually burn out.

At the same time as "Hot Desking" was being introduced and companies were reporting profits up by two-thirds, a report published in the *British Journal of Psychology* of a research project at Reading University suggested that open-plan offices are bad for business since their noise can affect staff, reducing their performance by 60%. It is probable that the type of people who are attracted to fast-pace media-type jobs are those who are also attracted to "Hot Desking", but it is a hard way to live for very long.

▼ *In a "Hot Desking" office different activities, such as working on a computer and discussion, are conducted side-by-side.*

The Personalized Office

Enclosed offices with no natural light will inhibit creativity, and in this type of environment, false windows, landscape pictures, mirrors and bright colours should be used to give the illusion of spaciousness. Employees should also be encouraged to make their own area a pleasant place to be in.

Marking territory lies deep in the evolutionary part of all living things. Animals scent their space to lay claim to it and repel invaders. Similarly, office workers personalize their space in some way with photographs, ornaments and other items. As a result they feel more stable and committed. Research has shown that those who do not do this tend not to stay long in any organization. A business that takes all working styles into account and provides space for different approaches and activities will have a happier, less stressed and more stable work force.

▲ *Many people in traditional offices personalize their desks with a photograph or ornament.*

▼ *A bunch of flowers is a distinctive way of making an office desk look individual as well as attractive.*

CHI FLOW

▲ *Chi flows around each floor of these open-plan offices. The sculpture in the centre also creates energy.*

How the energy circulates in an office is important for the smooth running of the organization and also in encouraging job satisfaction and harmonious working relationships. Chi energy moves in the physical environment but its effects are subtle and affect us psychologically. Where movement, either around the building or in our dealings with colleagues, is slow or becomes stuck, this can greatly affect our performance and sense of well-being.

Chi and Positioning

If we consider the model office discussed earlier in "Designing the Layout" we can see that the departments likely to import and export bulky goods are placed near the entrance. The workshops are next to the store so that products do not have to be transported through public areas and the administrative offices, accounts, sales, PR and advertising areas are all in close proximity for convenience. The managing director's office is removed from the hub of activity but is near enough to be in contact. It is linked to his/her secretary's office for speedy communication and there is a separate reception area here for important visitors, to remove them from the busy reception area.

Difficulties often arise in rooms occupied by several people and a lot of office equipment. Inevitably, some people are better positioned than others and tensions may arise. The top diagram opposite shows a badly designed office in a large

◀ *Cramming desks and people into an awkward space restricts the flow of chi.*

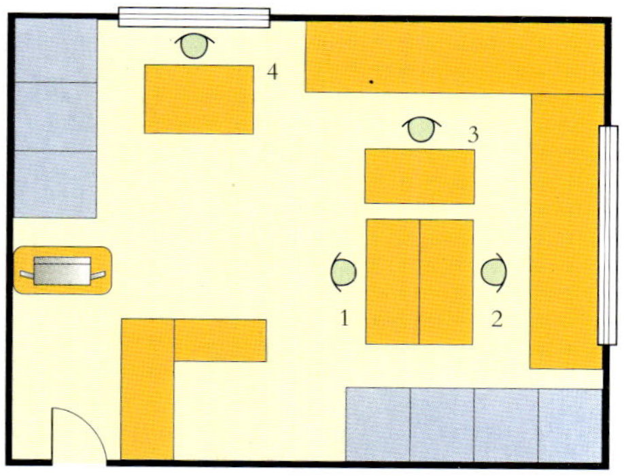

▲ *In this office layout the flow of chi is blocked, affecting working relationships and preventing harmony.*

▼ *The same office has been redesigned with a few simple features to give a more efficient work flow.*

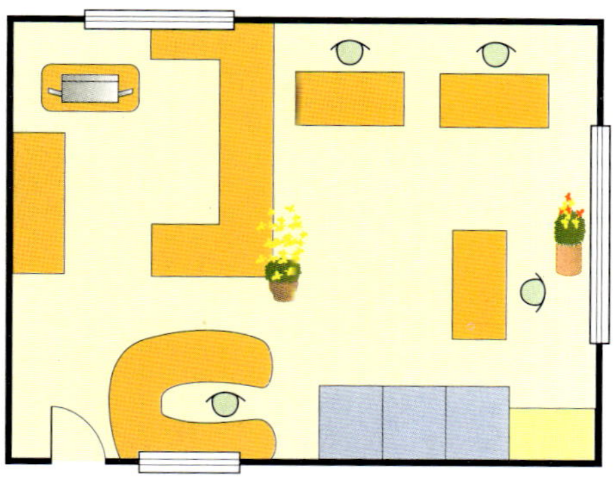

organization. The occupants were irritable and visiting staff needing stationery, photocopies or advice also became irritable because the entrance was restricted and there was always a queue for the copier. If they needed stationery they had to make their way through the office and thus the occupants there had constant disruptions. The staff were often ill; the employee who sat at desk 4 suffered from headaches from the sun glaring on her computer screen as well as the fumes from the photocopier. The occupants of desks 1 and 2 faced the backs of each other's VDUs. The employee seated at desk 1 was always short-tempered as she was also in charge of the reception area and was constantly having to get up.

The next diagram shows how a few simple adjustments can make life easier and healthier. A glass screen isolated the copier, which was repositioned near the window for ventilation and reduced congestion in the door area. All the stationery required by those not working in the office was placed near the copier so the office staff were no longer interrupted.

A reception window was cut into the wall which reduced the number of people coming into the room and the reception desk was made into a working area for the receptionist, who no longer had to keep moving from one position to another. Clutter was removed from the office and this reduced the amount of storage required, enabling the staff to have a small kitchen area with a refrigerator and a kettle. With the desks facing into the room and an empty central area, the office felt larger and less restricted and the staff were much happier.

Communication

Day-to-day communication among staff members is of paramount importance in a successful organization. Bulletin boards in communal areas may be useful as a reinforcement, but face-to-face communication is preferable, and a short briefing meeting during the day enables staff to be informed and to air their views. These are best not held first thing in the morning. People's internal clocks vary and many take time to adjust to the working day, particularly after a bad journey. Last thing in the afternoon is equally bad as staff will be anxious to get away and may already be planning the evening's activities in their minds. By around 11am most people will be settled, attentive and willing to communicate. An informed workforce which feels that its views are valued will be a productive one.

▲ *Chi cannot flow properly on a narrow desk where you have to sit too close to the computer screen.*

▼ *Choosing the right time of day is important if staff communication is to be meaningful for everyone concerned.*

OFFICE PERSONALITIES

We all know individuals who greet us with a smile, radiate enthusiasm for the task in hand and volunteer their services unsolicited. Conversely, there are those who never volunteer and always find a reason why an idea will not work. Personal chi, or karma, is nothing to do with Feng Shui yet it has a great impact on the office environment.

▲ *An office meeting will include people of very different dispositions.*

Compatibility

Our personalities are partly determined by the year in which we were born, and Chinese astrology indicates that we are compatible with some people and not others. We can use this information to maintain harmony in the workplace.

People often become unhappy at work because they are affected by the people around them. With some knowledge of the characteristics belonging to each animal sign, it is possible to arrange the workplace so that individuals working in close proximity are compatible.

Strengths and Weaknesses

Each of us has characteristics that lend themselves to performing certain tasks. If we can harness particular strengths and avoid placing people in areas of work which they are not suited to we can generate a happy and fulfilled workforce. The following pages describe the characteristics of each animal, and which kind of activity they do best.

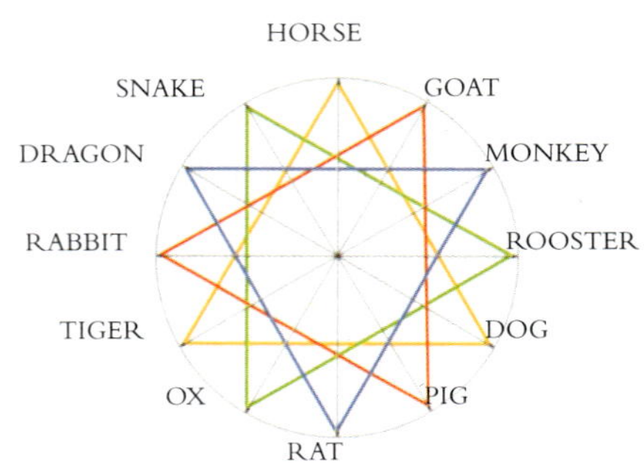

► *Each coloured triangle links animals with harmonious relationships. Those immediately opposite each other are antagonistic and should be kept apart.*

Compatibility Table

	Rat	Ox	Tiger	Rabbit	Dragon	Snake	Horse	Goat	Monkey	Rooster	Dog	Pig
Rat	+	=	+	–	★	=	–	–	★	–	+	+
Ox	=	+	–	=	+	★	–	–	+	★	–	+
Tiger	+	–	+	–	+	–	★	+	–	=	★	=
Rabbit	+	+	–	+	=	+	–	★	–	–	=	★
Dragon	★	–	+	=	–	+	–	+	★	+	–	=
Snake	+	★	–	+	=	+	–	=	–	★	+	–
Horse	–	–	★	–	=	+	–	=	+	+	★	+
Goat	–	–	=	★	+	+	=	+	+	–	–	★
Monkey	★	+	–	–	★	–	–	+	=	+	+	=
Rooster	–	★	+	–	=	★	+	=	–	–	+	+
Dog	+	–	★	=	–	+	★	–	+	–	=	+
Pig	=	+	=	★	+	–	–	★	–	+	+	–

Key: ★ Excellent = Good + Workable – Difficult

The Rat at Work

Rats make good bosses, team builders and leaders. Their quick minds enable them to weigh up situations at a glance and home in on important points. They do not respond well to a "nine to five" approach and work best in flexible situations.

Wood Rat
Positive: Energetic. Full of ideas. Inspirational, Popular.
Negative: Inflexible.

Fire Rat
Positive: Competitive. Flexible.
Negative: Dislikes routine. Lack of diplomacy. Low boredom threshold.

Earth Rat
Positive: Stability. Loyalty. Even temper.
Negative: Resistant to change. Intolerant.

Metal Rat
Positive: High standards. Money-handling skills.
Negative: Stubborn.

Water Rat
Positive: Sociable. Shrewd. Knowledgeable.
Negative: Conservative. Indiscreet.

The Ox at Work

Loyal, hardworking and honest, Oxen systematically undertake any task, often working beyond the call of duty to complete it. They do not easily tolerate what they perceive to be slacking in others.

The Tiger at Work

Tigers are dynamic and can carry others along by sheer enthusiasm. They are always very eager to launch themselves into new ventures. On the other hand, they often make rash decisions and can be very critical of the others. They enjoy a challenge and have good leadership skills.

Wood Ox
Positive: Leader. Spokesperson. Confident. Hard-working.
Negative: Quick-tempered

Fire Ox
Positive: Determined. Honest. Protects staff. Perceptive.
Negative: Outspoken. Inconsiderate.

Earth Ox
Positive: Loyal. Accurate. Shrewd.
Negative: Slow. Uninspiring.

Metal Ox
Positive: Energetic. Reliable.
Negative: Outspoken. Selfish.

Water Ox
Positive: Integrity. Persistent. Respects the views of others.
Negative: Sensitive.

Wood Tiger
Positive: Team player. Positive. Tolerant. Innovative.
Negative: Short attention span. Aloof. Temper. Ego.

Fire Tiger
Positive: Popular. Resourceful. Optimistic.
Negative: Restless. Loner.

Earth Tiger
Positive: Analytical. Practical Objective.
Negative: Lacks humour. Insensitive. Pushy.

Metal Tiger
Positive: Assertive. Competitive. Risk taker. Staying Power.
Negative: Aggressive. Headstrong. Self-centred.

Water Tiger
Positive: Intuitive. Objective. Understanding.
Negative: Vengeful. Procrastinator.

The Rabbit at Work

Rabbits are polite, considerate and dislike conflict of any sort. They wilt under criticism and dislike being backed into a corner and will always find a means of escape. Flexible, they refuse to panic. Artistic and intuitive, rabbits never miss anything. They keep close counsel and advance by weighing up situations and methodically taking advantage of them until they achieve their goals, often to the surprise of others. Rabbits have strong wills and an inbuilt sense of self worth.

Wood Rabbit
Positive: Generous. Accommodating. Flexible.
Negative: Indecisive. Lenient. Impersonal. Vain.

Fire Rabbit
Positive: Fun-loving. Progressive. Intuitive. Diplomatic.
Negative: Temperamental. Outspoken. Neurotic.

Earth Rabbit
Positive: Persistent. Trustworthy. Rational. Prudent.
Negative: Calculating. Materialistic. Introverted.

Metal Rabbit:
Positive: Intuitive. Dedicated. Thorough. Ambitious.
Negative: Moody. Cunning. Intolerant.

Water Rabbit
Positive: Supportive. Good memory. Friendly.
Negative: Over-sensitive. Emotional. Indecisive.

The Dragon at Work

Dragons are entrepreneurs and leaders. They have an irrepressible energy and an unswerving confidence in their abilities. Dragons find it difficult to keep secrets and will not accept criticism, and a crossed dragon is a sight to behold.

Wood Dragon
Positive: Innovative. Generous.
Negative: Proud. Condescending. Outspoken. Pushy.

Fire Dragon
Positive: Objective. Competitive. Inspirational. Enthusiastic
Negative: Demanding. Inconsiderate. Aggressive. Impetuous.

Metal Dragon
Positive: Honest. Charismatic.
Negative: Intolerant. Inflexible. Ruthless. Critical.

Water Dragon
Positive: Methodical. Resourceful.
Negative: Autocratic. Impersonal. Pragmatic.

Earth Dragon
Positive: Sociable. Fair. Initiator.
Negative: Bossy. Distant.

The Snake at Work

Snakes have an inner wisdom which, combined with intelligence, make them formidable. They usually follow their own path and leave the mundane tasks to others. If attacked they find subtle ways of revenge. Snakes are intuitive and are not easily fooled; they have a dry sense of humour.

Wood Snake
Positive: Intuitive. Far-sighted. Logical. Staying power.
Negative: Vain. Aloof. Big spender.

Fire Snake
Positive: Confident. Perseverance. Charismatic. Ambitious.
Negative: Self-centred. Suspicious. Jealous. Uncompromising.

Earth Snake
Positive: Trusting. Calm. Reliable. Shrewd.
Negative: Conservative. Frugal.

Metal Snake
Positive: Generous. Co-operative. Self-sufficient. Opportunistic.
Negative: Suspicious. Scheming. Uncommunicative. Domineering.

Water Snake
Positive: Intuitive. Practical. Organized. Determined.
Negative: Secretive. Vindictive. Calculating.

The Horse at Work

Horses have low boredom thresholds and attention spans. They like action and short, to-the-point instructions. Capable of work-ing tirelessly to meet a deadline, they adhere to their own timetables and like flexibility. They are perceptive and have lightning brains and can come to conclusions in an instant, although they may occasionally come to the wrong one. They work on hunches and are great improvisers. Their tempers are quick to flash, but they soon forget the cause.

Wood Horse
Positive: Logical. Inspirational. Intelligent. Friendly.
Negative: Restless. Highly strung. Lacks discernment.

Fire Horse
Positive: Intellectual. Flamboyant. Passionate.
Negative: Volatile. Troublesome. Inconsistent.

Earth Horse
Positive: Methodical. Adaptable. Logical. Amiable.
Negative: Indecisive. Overstretches.

Metal Horse
Positive: Intellectual. Intuitive. Logical. Enthusiastic.
Negative: Headstrong. Unfinished tasks. Foolhardy.

Water Horse
Positive: Adaptable. Spontaneous. Cheerful. Energetic.
Negative: Indecisive. Inconsiderate.

Wood Goat
Positive: Compassionate. Peace-loving. Trusting. Helpful.
Negative: Clinging. Resistant to change.

Fire Goat
Positive: Courageous. Intuitive. Understanding.
Negative: Spendthrift. Volatile. Impatient.

Earth Goat
Positive: Sociable. Caring. Optimistic. Industrious.
Negative: Sensitive. Conservative. Self-indulgent.

Metal Goat
Positive: Artistic. Adventurous. Self-confident.
Negative: Possessive. Moody. Vulnerable.

Water Goat
Positive: Articulate. Friendly. Popular. Opportunistic.
Negative: Silky. Dislikes change. Impressionable. Emotional.

The Goat at Work

Goats get on well with everyone. They cannot bear confrontation and wither when disciplined. Schedules and deadlines are not for Goats, who thrive when allowed complete freedom. Goats are idealistic and often impractical and yet they usually seem to bring others to their way of thinking by their charm and persistence. When it doesn't happen, they will sulk. Survivors, Goats worry a lot and need approval to function effectively.

The Monkey at Work

Naturally sociable, the monkey will always have a following. His quick wit and leadership skills ensure he is never isolated. Monkeys are capable of great achievement and know it. They do not suffer from false modesty, neither do they boast. Monkeys are problem-solvers. Entirely flexible, they manipulate situations to achieve their goals. They learn quickly and their fine memories mean that no one gets the better of them. On the rare occasion that this happens, monkeys will bounce back.

The Rooster at Work

Roosters are proud and opinionated and are prone to offering unsolicited advice. They are however, on their good days, outgoing and amusing and make good company. They never miss anything and are real sticklers for detail, Roosters exel at accounts and will not miss even the smallest error. If the mistake is yours you will never hear the end of it.

The Dog at Work

Dogs are sociable and fair, they are also reliable. If there is a cause to fight for, or if someone they know needs some help and support, the Dog will be there. Dogs work well with those they like but can ignore or dismiss those they don't get on with. If crossed, their tempers are quick, though they do not bear grudges. They will reluctantly accept, but are not really happy in, the limelight. Dogs keep a clear head in a crisis and inspire confidence in others. Their preference for a quiet life can give the impression of moodiness.

The Pig at Work

Pigs are the stabilizing force in an office. Amiable and always willing, pigs rarely attract dissent, although they can waste time in pursuing unlikely schemes. Pigs are never crafty and have an endearing innocence which attracts others to them. Competitive is not a word known to pigs who may occasionally be ridiculed for their slow reactions. Pigs are responsible and accurate workers. If there are any problems, pigs will take up the cause and carry others with them. Rarely do they flare up but when they do it will only be fleeting, then all will be forgotten.

Wood Monkey
Positive: Intuitive. Resourceful. Persistent. Inventive.
Negative: Restless. Dissatisfied. Rash.

Fire Monkey
Positive: Self-confident. Truthful. Self-motivating.
Negative: Domineering. Mistrustful. Jealous. Confrontational.

Earth Monkey
Positive: Reliable. Generous. Scholarly. Honest.
Negative: Moody. Rude. Unlawful.

Metal Monkey
Positive: Self-reliant. Loving. Creative. Hard-working.
Negative: Proud. Uncommunicative. Inflexible.

Water Monkey
Positive: Kind. Flexible. Persuasive.
Negative: Touchy. Secretive. Evasive.

Wood Rooster
Positive: Enthusiastic. Reliable.
Negative: Easily confused. Regimental. Blunt

Fire Rooster
Positive: Independent. Organized. Dynamic.
Negative: Fanatical. Inflexible. Temperamental.

Earth Rooster
Positive: Hard-working. Efficient. Careful.
Negative: Critical. Dogmatic.

Metal Rooster
Positive: Industrious. Reforming.
Negative: Opinionated. Uncompromising. Inhibited.

Water Rooster
Positive: Persuasive. Energetic. Practical.
Negative: Fussy. Bureaucratic.

Wood Dog
Positive: Likeable. Calm. Honest.
Negative: Hesitant. Ingratiating.

Fire Dog
Positive: Leader. Innovator. Honest.
Negative: Rebellious. Strong-tempered.

Earth Dog
Positive: Fair. Efficient. Stable. Kind-hearted.
Negative: Secretive. Demanding. Show-off.

Metal Dog
Positive: Dedicated. Decisive. Charitable.
Negative: Secretive. Demanding. Extreme.

Water Dog
Positive: Sympathetic. Fair. Calm. Democratic.
Negative: Distant. Indulgent.

Wood Pig
Positive: Organising. Promoter. Orator.
Negative: Manipulating. Gullible.

Fire Pig
Positive: Optimistic. Risk taker. Determined.
Negative: Bullying. Underhand.

Earth Pig
Positive: Patient. Reliable. Diligent.
Negative: Unyielding.

Metal Pig
Positive: Sociable. Direct. Enduring.
Negative: Domineering. Tactless. Resentful.

Water Pig
Positive: Persevering. Diplomatic. Honest.
Negative: Over-indulgent. Slapdash. Gullible.

HOME-OFFICE LINKS AND THE BAGUA

When there are problems with no obvious cause in the home, a Feng Shui consultant will often look to the office, and vice versa. However good the Feng Shui of the home and the office, karma is paramount, as of course is destiny. There are steps that can be taken to improve life, even where the odds appear to be stacked against us. Healthy lifestyles and positive attitudes help and Feng Shui can tip the balance.

▲ *Supple, healthy bodies enable the chi to flow unobstructed through them.*

A Positive Attitude

Negative attitudes are self-destructive and a sure way of provoking a negative reaction from others. Negative people are far less likely to get a contract or promotion than those who are always willing to try something and appear enthusiastic. Being positive is easier if we are fit and healthy and if our lives outside the office environment are happy and fulfilled. Using Feng Shui is just part of the package that will enable us to achieve what we want in life. If we live in a chemical and electromagnetic soup, eat food that is contaminated by chemicals and spend our leisure time slouched behind closed curtains in front of a TV screen, we will not be as healthy or able to cope with our increasingly complex society as someone who eats fresh food, exercises the body and the mind and is open to a wide range of people and experiences.

◀ *If we spend our days like this, then our leisure activities should offer exercise and time away from electrical equipment.*

▼ *We should only use the Bagua for ourselves. It would be difficult to use on this shared desk without affecting other people.*

Sleep and Health

We can use Feng Shui to make sure we are sleeping in a direction that supports us. The best direction – the one in which it is best to site our doors, desks and beds – is the one to use if all is well. There is another direction, known as the Celestial Doctor, which is useful if we are ill. It is used to tap into the energies of the universe and aid recovery. Refer to the table to the right.

Using the Bagua

The Bagua is a tool we can use to focus on various aspects of our lives. We can align it to the compass directions and position it on a plan of our homes and offices, or on our desks. We can also use it to represent a symbolic journey of our lives by aligning it to where we sit at our

Bed Directions

Magic Number	Best Direction	Celestial Doctor
1	South-east	East
2	North-east	West
3	South	North
4	North	South
5 (Male)	North-east	West
5 (Female)	South-west	North-west
6	West	North-east
7	North-west	South-west
8	South-west	North-west
9	East	South-east

(NB: These are the directions of the bedroom in the house and are also to be faced by the top of the head when lying down.)

desks or to the front of our houses. Most people want to focus on two areas – the Career path and Wealth. Equally as important are the Helpful People who will make success possible.

The Career Area

This area represents the start of our journey. It sits in the north direction, represented by the Water element. A water feature here will support the energy of the area and Metal will give it a boost so a wind chime or other metal object here would be helpful. A black-and-white picture representing both Water and Metal would also be useful. If we are using the Bagua symbolically, we will need to check that anything we place will not clash with the elemental energy there. We may prefer to use a brochure of the organization we wish to gain employment in or the business card of the company whose account we are hoping to take on. We can enhance the Career area in our homes, but we would need to have a private office to do this at work or we will be taking responsibility for the careers of colleagues as well.

▲ *Using the principles of Feng Shui in the home will have the combined effect of improving life at work; the two worlds are inextricably linked.*

The Helpful People Area

By stimulating the Helpful People areas in our homes or in our offices, we encourage the support of others. This is a Metal area and Metal is supported by Earth. Therefore a rock, terracotta pot or crystal here will stimulate the energy. Again, if using the Bagua symbolically, the element of the direction should be checked and the elements should be balanced. Be careful when hanging crystals; anything harmful reflected in them will be magnified by their many faces and break up rather than encourage beneficial energies.

▼ *The Bagua can be positioned on to your workstation or desk, just as you would place it over a plan of your house.*

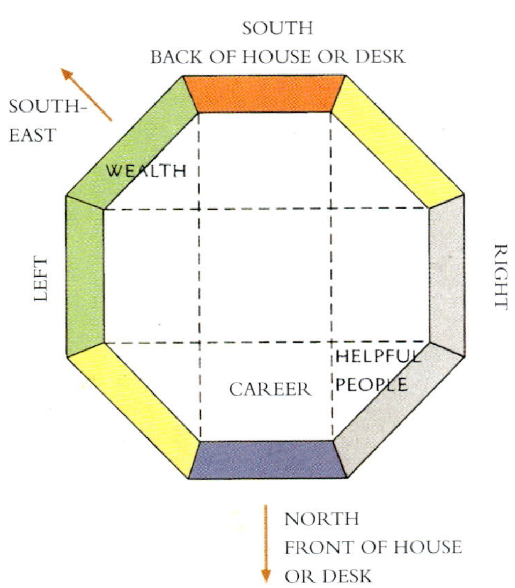

Wealth

Many people are attracted to Feng Shui by the promise of wealth, as represented by the Wealth corner of the Bagua. If only it were that simple! We have seen that Feng Shui is only part of the picture and that other forces such as destiny and personality come into play. If there is no demand for your services, Feng Shui cannot help. The Wealth area is a Wood area and a plant will support the energy. Other options are an empty pot placed ready for the wealth to pour in, some coins in a dish or a bowl of spring water that has been placed in moonlight and is changed every day.

▼ *We can align the Bagua to our desks and activate an area. This desk is well organized but cluttered. A small trolley to hold equipment would be useful.*

INTERVIEWS

Interviews are often gruelling and many factors besides professional competence play a part in the selection procedure. There is nothing we can do about our compatibility with members of the selection panel, but we can make use of some Feng Shui techniques to give us the best possible chance of acquiring a job. Other factors which will play a part are punctuality, awareness of the impact of our body language and maintaining eye contact.

▼ *Gestures and facial expressions tell us a lot about other people.*

Clothes

Research has shown that given the choice of three women candidates, one in a business suit, one in a suit but with the addition of a scarf or a piece of jewellery, and one in floral dress, most interviewers opt for the candidate in the business suit (a yang outfit) with some (yin) additions on the grounds that it looks professional but not as if the woman is trying to emulate a man. Obviously it is not always necessary to wear such an outfit and a business suit might even be inappropriate in some areas of employment. Feng Shui can help by suggesting which colours suit us and the jobs we are seeking so that we can use them either in accessories or in the outfit we wear. This does not just apply to women; men can use their suitable colours in ties, shirt patterns and socks.

Women in a predominantly male profession may feel more confident if they introduce some yang colours into their clothing – reds, purples and oranges. If a

▲ *Faced with a panel like this, you can at least move your chair to face a good direction.*

▼ *Body language plays an important part in communicating with other people.*

man wishes to be employed in an occupation that is usually the domain of females, then some yin colours – blues and greens – will be appropriate.

Each of the Five Elements is associated with different types of professions. It may be useful to introduce something of the energy of the business into clothing or even into any files or pens we carry to the interview. The table below indicates the elements associated with some of the most common businesses.

Which Direction

Sometimes we will have the opportunity to choose where to sit. Many large organizations' selection processes now require candidates to mingle and dine with executives prior to formal interviews. If we take a small compass with us and familiarize ourselves with the orientation of the building, we may be able to sit in our best direction. If we have to give a presentation, we should aim to orientate ourselves to face one of our best directions. Even during a formal interview, it may be possible to move the chair slightly so we can gain the advantage of facing an auspicious direction. The table below is a reminder of our best direction based on our magic numbers.

▲ *If you need to give a presentation, it is important to face a direction that is auspicious for you.*

▼ *Each of the Five Elements is particularly relevant to different types of business. These are some of the most common.*

Wood	Fire	Metal	Earth	Water
Green/Jade	*Red/Purple*	*White/Grey*	*Yellow/Brown*	*Dark Blue/Black*
Horticulture	Marketing	Accountancy	Agriculture	Communication
Floristry	PR	Banking	Building	Electrical
Forestry	Advertising	Mining	Food	Fishing
Wood crafts	Fashion	Jewellery	Pottery	Transport
Publishing	Law	Engineering	Personnel	Travel
Media	Chemicals	Appliances	Clothing	Health

◀ *In an interview, Feng Shui can give us that "extra something".*

▼ *When you go into an interview, always remember your best direction.*

Magic Number	
1	South-east
2	North-east
3	South
4	North
5 (Male)	North-east
5 (Female)	South-west
6	West
7	North-west
8	South-west
9	East

BUSINESS TRIPS

We should follow the same procedures on business trips as we do in our homes and offices. If the trip is important and much rests on the outcome, then it is worth requesting a room in one of our best directions when we book the hotel. When packing for a business trip, always remember the compass. This will enable us to position ourselves in an auspicious direction when we are negotiating, and to align our beds to beneficial energies as we sleep.

Travel Arrangements

The energy of certain months suggests that we should not move towards a certain direction. In the "Favoured Months and Directions" diagram, we can see which of the twelve Chinese animals rules each month. It is inadvisable to move towards the direction opposite the animal which rules each month, during that month. For example, in November, which is ruled by the Pig, it would not be wise to travel in the south–south-east direction. Travelling in this direction may have result in misunderstandings and the break-up of negotiations. Although the indications are that this will only be of a temporary nature, it is obviously best to try and avoid such complications. If it is possible to alter the route of your journey so that you travel towards your destination from another direction, this will reduce the impact.

▼ *If you are in charge of a group, keep their instructions clear and precise.*

▲ *Business trips can be tiring and frustrating. It helps if you can arrange to travel in an auspicious direction.*

The Meeting

Whether we meet clients or colleagues in a public place or in their offices, we can attempt to gain some advantage for ourselves if we pay attention to where we sit. We should always try to be supported by a wall behind us and never sit with our backs to a door, or at a window. In addition, if we can manoeuvre ourselves so that we face our best direction then we will be in an advantageous position.

The Hotel Room

It will benefit us if our head faces one of our auspicious directions as we sleep. The position of the bed is important and we should attempt to ensure that we are supported by a wall behind and that we do not face the ensuite bathroom since negative energy will emanate from it. If the bed does face the bathroom, make sure

▼ *Laptops enable us to make use of travelling time. If possible, place them so that you face an auspicious direction.*

Packing Tips

- A compass
- Details of your best directions
- Something to cover a mirror
- Incense or oils and a burner
- A water spray
- The name of a good restaurant to celebrate success

▲ *When you want to dominate, choose the prime position for yourself and the vulnerable one for your client.*

that the door is closed at all times. A mirror facing the bed is not considered to be good Feng Shui and we will have a disturbed sleep if we do not cover it. Many hotel beds are surrounded by electrical cables for bedside lamps, telephones and radios. Some are even built into the headboard and there is little we can do about them. Switch off and unplug all appliances and move the bed away from them if possible.

Hotel rooms will have accumulated the chi energy from all those who have been there before us. It is obviously better for us if we can remove this energy and create a pleasant environment for ourselves. Opening windows to let in fresh air is an obvious starting point. It may be difficult, because of the noise involved, to raise the sound vibrations in the room by clapping, ringing bells and making other noises to perk up the energy, but we can silently improve the air quality by burning incense or aromatic oils and spraying water around the room to increase the negative ions.

Having created as much of a temporary home-from-home for ourselves as is possible, and tapped into our beneficial energies, we should place ourselves in the most advantageous position possible for our business discussions.

▲▼ *Unplug electrical appliances before you fall asleep. Cover a mirror or television screen as they will both reflect the bed.*

Entertaining

When we take clients out to a restaurant, we can place ourselves in suitable positions to make the negotiation process work to our advantage. We can ensure that those we wish to score points against are placed in a vulnerable position – for example, with their backs to the door or in the path of cutting chi from the corner of a pillar. If, on the other hand, we want to win someone over, it may be worth allowing them the supported position while we sit in our best direction.

PICTURE ACKNOWLEDGEMENTS

The publishers would like to thank the following picture libraries for the use of their pictures.
Abode UK: 101br; 108t; 109tl. A-Z Botanical Collection ltd.:41br(Mike Vardy); 134tr(Jean Deval), br(Robert Murray); 146t(Bjorn Svensson); 160br(Margaret Higginson); 182tr(J. Whitworth); 191tr(A. Stenning), b(J. Whitworth). Bruce Coleman: 127m(Werner Layer); 129bl; 130r(Paul van Gaalen), m (Stefano Amantini); 135r; 141bl(Dr.Stephen Coyne). The Garden Picture Library: 41bl(Morley Read); 132-3(Ron Sutherland); 135tl(Erika Craddock); 137tr(Erika Craddock), bl(Juliette Wade), br(Erika Craddock); 138tr(Ron Sutherland), bl(Ron Sutherland); 139tr; 140tr(John Glover); 150tr(Eric Crichton); 154-5; 158bl; 161br(Steven Wooster); 167tl(Ron Sutherland), bl(Sunniva Harte), br(John Glover); 178bl(Jaqui Hurst); 184tl(Ron Sutherland), r(Linda Burgess); 185tr(Linda Burgess), m(Vaughan Fleming); 190tr(Steven Wooster), bl(J. S. Sira; 256br. Robert Harding Picture Library: 105tl(IPC Magazines); 107tl(IPC Magazines); 108b(IPD Magazines); 109bl(IPC Magazines); 255bl. Holt Studios Int.: 128bl; 135br(Willem Harinck); 141tr(MichaelMayer); 158tr(Alan & Linda Detrick); 160bl(Primrose Peacock); 161tl(Bob Gibbons). Houses and Interiors: 40tr(Roger Brooks); 48bl(Roger Brooks), tr(Roger Brooks); 52tr(Mark Bolton); 53bl(Mark Bolton); 56tr(Roger Brooks); 85l(Verne); 88bl(Mark Bolton); 90tr; 114tr(Mark Bolton), bl(Mark Bolton); 186tr(Roger Brooks), bl(Roger Brooks); 187tr(Roger Brooks); 247tr(Mark Bolton); 255tr. Hutchinson Library: 8br(Robert Francis); 10tr(Merilyn Thorold); 13tr(Melanie Friend); 26bl(T. Moser), br(Lesley Nelson); 27tl(F. Horner); 28t(Edward Parker), bl (Sarah Errington), r(John G Egan); 29bl(Tony Souter); 34tr(Pern.), r(P. W. Rippon), bl(Robert Francis); 35tl(Tony Souter), bl(Carlos Freire), tr(G. Griffiths- Jones); 42t; 43tl (Phillip Wolmuth), t(L. Taylor), t, m, br(Andrew Sole); 68b(Sarah Murray); 69tl(Lesley Nelson); 71t(N. Durrell McKenna); 120bl(Nancy Durrell); 124tl(Tony Souter), br(Robert Francis); 125bl(Robert Francis); 136br(Hatt); 144bl(Tony souter); 195tr(Christine Pemberton); 198tr(Robert Aberman); 200(Leslie Woodhead)t; 201tl(Sarah Murray), m(Robert Francis), b(Tim Motion); 204bl(Robert Aberman); 205bl(Sarah Murray), br(Robert Francis); 206tl(Tim Motion); 207br(Robert Francis); 212bl(Juliet Highet); 224l(Robert Francis); 232m(Jeremy A. Horner). Images Colour Library:; 11b; 12b; 13bl, bl; 14tr; 15no. 2, no. 5; 25br; 29tr; 134bl; 136t; 143,; 144r; 145bl; 203; 248t, bl, br.The Interior Archive: 1m; 8tl(Schulenburg); 9tr(Schulenburg); 44tr(Schulenburg); 48r(C. Simon Sykes); 54bl(Schulenburg); 55t(Schulenburg); 67tr (Henry Wilson); 74 (Schulenburg); 76tr(Schulenburg); 77tl (Schulenburg); 80bl(Schulenburg), t(Simon Upton); 84bl (Schulenburg); 86b(Schulenburg); 87tr (Schulenburg); 89bl(Schulenburg); 90br(Henry Wilson); 92t(Tim Beddow); 94bl(Schulenburg); 97r (Schulenburg); 100tr(Schulenburg),b(Schulenburg); 102l (Schulenburg);105tr(Schulenburg);106bl (Schulenburg); 110tr(Henry Wilson), bl(Schulenburg); 111bl(Schulenburg), br(Schulenburg); 113tl (Schulenburg), br(Schulenburg); 119tl; 122br (Schulenburg); 123tr(Schulenburg); 229tr (Schulenburg). Peter McHoy: 159tl; 166tr; 174bl; 175tl; 180tl; 185tl. Don Morley: 124tr, bl; 125bl, tr. The Stock Market: 14br; 15no. 1(K. Biggs); 36tr, bl, br; 37b, t; 38tl, m; 39tl; 64t(David Lawrence); 66br; 67tl, tr; 68t; 115b; 143; 144tr; 145t; 192bl; 193br; 194bl; 201tr; 203bl(B. Simmons); 204t; 206r; 215tr; 217tr; 229r; 239br; 241br(Jon Feingersh); 246m; 249bl; 250br. Tony Stone: 66bl(Angus M. Mackillop); 225br(Laurence Monneret); 227tr(Tim Flach); 231br(Robert Mort); 239r(Bruce Ayres); 241tr(Tim Flach); 246tr(Jon Gray); 249tr(Dan Bosler); 250tr(Peter Correz), bl(David Hanover); 251t(Christopher Bissell). Jessica Strang: 120r; 123bl; 212br; 213tl, bl; 214r; 217l; 220br; 228tl, tr, br; 233l; 235tr, bl, br; 247br. Superstock: 22tr, m; 23br. View: 9m(Phillip Bier); 15no. 1(Dennis Gilbert); 43tr(Phillip Bier); 45l(Chris Gascoigne); 54tr(Phillip Bier), br(Phillip Bier); 55bl(Phillip Bier); 65tr(Peter Cook); 88tr(Phillip Bier); 94bl(Peter Cook); 96tr(Chris Gascoigne); 99tl(Phillip Bier); 115tl(PhillipBier); 120t(Chris Gascoigne); 121l(Peter Cook); 143; 192m; 193bl, tl; 194t(Chris Gascoigne), r(Chris Gascoigne); 196-7(Peter Cook); 198b(Dennis Gilbert); 199tr(Peter Cook), br(Chris Gascoigne); 200b(Dennis Gilbert); 202t, b(Peter Cook); 203tr(Chris Gascoigne); 207m(Dennis Gilbert),bl(Dennis Gilbert); 210bl(Chris Gascoigne); 211tr(Peter Cook);212tr(Dennis Gilbert); 214br(Chris Gascoigne); 215r(Peter Cook), br(Peter Romaniuk); 216tr(Chris Gascoigne), tl(Peter Cook), b(Dennis Gilbert); 218tl(Chris Gascoigne), bl(Peter Cook), br(Dennis Gilbert); 219tl(Dennis Gilbert), l(Chris Gascoigne), bl(Chris Gascoigne), tr(Chris Gascoigne); 220tl(Nick Hufton), tr(Peter Cook); 221r(Chris Gascoigne), bl(Chris Gascoigne); 222tr(Chris Gascoigne), br(Chris Gascoigne); 223bl(Nick Hufton), tr(Chris Gascoigne); 224tr(Chris Gascoigne), bl(Dennis Gilbert), br(Peter Cook); 225t(Nick Hufton), l(Chris Gascoigne); 226t(Nick Hufton), bl(Nick Hufton), br(Peter Cook); 227r(Chris Gascoigne), bl(Peter Cook); 228tl(Chris Gascoigne); 229b(Peter Cook); 230t(Nick Hufton), bl(Peter Cook), br(Chris Gascoigne); 231tr(Chris Gascoigne); 232t(Chris Gascoigne); 233tl(Chris Gascoigne); 234tl(Dennis Gilbert), m(Chris Gascoigne), br(Chris Gascoigne); 235l(Chris Gascoigne); 236-7; 238tl(Chris Gascoigne), br(Chris Gascoigne); 239tl(Peter Cook), bl(Chris Gascoigne); 240t(Peter Cook), b(Dennis Gilbert); 246bl(Chris Gascoigne); 251m(Peter Cook), b(Peter Cook); 254t. Elizabeth Whiting Associates: 42m; 43m, tr; 44br; 48r; 60tr, bl; 61tr; 64bl; 69r, br; 70bl; 76bl, l; 77tr; 84t; 89t; 91tr; 93tl; 102br; 116tr; 117r, bl; 118t; 119tr, bl; 192t; 208-9; 213tr; 214tl; 221t; 222bl, b; 232bl, br; 233b.

AUTHOR'S ACKNOWLEDGEMENTS

I should like to thank the staff at Anness Publishing Ltd: Helen Sudell for commissioning the book and Joanne Rippin for managing the project with courage and fortitude, despite the author, and Isobel for keeping her sane.

My family, as ever, deserve praise for their support and tolerance and the anonymous arm with the coffee mug at the end of it deserves a particular mention. Thanks to Tony Holdsworth and Jan Cisek for advice, and to all my friends for keeping off the telephone. A big thank you to Arto for being there and maintaining incredible patience – for a Fire Ox.

BIBLIOGRAPHY

Feng Shui (general)

Lau, Theodora, *The Handbook of Chinese Horoscopes* (HarperCollins, London, 1979)

Man-Ho Kwok, Palmer, Martin & Ramsay, Jay, *The Tao Te Ching* (Element, London, 1997)

Ni, Hua-Ching, *The Book of Changes and the Unchanging Truth* (Seven Star Communications, Santa Monica, 1983)

Palmer, Martin, *The Elements of Taoism* (Element, Shaftesbury, 1991)

Palmer, Martin, *Yin and Yang* (Piatkus, London, 1997)

Walters, Derek, *Chinese Astrology* (Aquarian Press, London, 1992)

Walters, Derek, *The Feng Shui Handbook* (Aquarian Press, London, 1991)

Wong, Eva, *Feng Shui* (Shambhala, Boston, 1996)

Understanding Feng Shui

Franz, Marie-Louise von, *Time* (Thames and Hudson, London, 1978)

Jung, Carl, *Man and his Symbols* (Arkana, London, 1990)

Lawlor, Anthony, *The Temple in the House* (G.P. Putnam's Sons, New York, 1994)

Lawlor, Robert, *Sacred Geometry: Philosophy and Practice* (Thames and Hudson, London, 1982)

Lindqvist, Cecilia, *China: Empire of Living Symbols* (Massachusetts, Reading, 1991)

Mann, A.T., *Sacred Architecture* (Element, Shaftesbury, 1993)

Pennick, Nigel, *Earth Harmony: Places of Power, Holiness and Healing* (Capall Bann, Chieveley, 1997)

Poynder, Michael, *Pi in the Sky* (The Collins Press, Cork, 1997)

Modern Feng Shui

Cowan, David & Girdlestone, Rodney, *Safe as houses? Ill Health and Electro-Stress in the Home* (Gateway Books, Bath, 1996)

Myers, Norman (ed), *The Gaia Atlas of Planetary Management* (Gaia Book Ltd., London, 1994)

Pearson, David, *The New Natural House Book* (Conran Octopus, London, 1989)

Thurnell-Read, Jane, *Geopathic Stress* (Element, Shaftesbury, 1995)

Gardens and Plants

Howerdew, Bob, *Complete Book of Companion Planting* (Kyle Cathie Ltd., London, 1993)

Hale, Gill, *The Feng Shui Garden* (Aurum Press, London, 1997)

Harper, Peter, *The Natural Garden Book* (Gaia Books, London, 1994)

Hu Dongchu, *The Way of the Virtuous, the Influence of Art and Philosophy on Chinese Garden Design* (New World Press, Beijing, 1991)

Huntington, Lucy, *Creating a Low Allergen Garden* (Mitchell Beazley, London, 1998)

Liu Dun-zhen, *Chinese Classical Gardens of Suzhou* (McGraw Hill, Inc., New York, 1993)

Riotte, Louise, *Astrological Gardening* (Storey Communications Inc., Pownal, 1994)

Wolverton, B.C., *Eco-Friendly House Plants* (Weidenfeld & Nicolson, London, 1996)

Zhu Junzhen, *Chinese Landscape Gardening* (Foreign Languages Press, Beijing, 1992)

Ki Astrology

Sandifer, Jon, *Feng Shui Astrology* (Piatkus, London, 1997)

Yoshikawa, Takashi *The Ki* (Rider, London, 1998)

Space Clearing

Kingston, Karen, *Creating Sacred Space with Feng Shui* (Piatkus, London, 1996)

Linn, Denise, *Sacred Space* (Rider, London, 1995)

Treacy, Declan, *Clear your Desk* (Century Business, 1992)

USEFUL ADDRESSES

UK

Gill Hale, M.Ed., Dip.ScGD., RCFSS Consultant for home, office and garden. Workshops, training.
Tel/fax: 0181 688 8516
E-mail: gillhale@mistral.co.uk

THE FENG SHUI ASSOCIATION
Consultations for home, office, garden, signboard and logo design, interior and garden design and building services, clearing intangible forces.
31 Woburn Place, Brighton BN1 9GA
Tel/fax: 01273 693844
E-mail: fengshui@mistral.co.uk
Internet Home Page:
http://www.mistral.co.uk/fengshui

THE FENG SHUI SOCIETY
The Society is an organization representing all the different approaches to Feng Shui, and serves as a focus for the exchange of information.
277 Edgware Road, London W2 1BT
E-mail Karen@fengshuisociety.org.uk

AUSTRALIA

THE FENG SHUI DESIGN STUDIO
PO Box 705, Glebe NSW 2037
612 315 8258

FENG SHUI SOCIETY OF AUSTRALIA
PO Box 1566, Rozelle NSW 2039
612 98101110

FENG SHUI INNOVATIONS
696 Darling Street, Rozelle NSW 2039
612 98101110

FENG SHUI ADVISORY CENTRE
Mosman NSW 2088
612 9751 1016

AUSTRALIAN SCHOOL OF ADVANCED CLASSICAL FENG SHUI
Double Bay NSW 2028
612 9362 8089

FENG SHUI CONSULTANTS
1 Napier Court,
Frankston VIC 3199
613 9776 5439

LIVING CHANGES FENG SHUI & GEOMANCY CONSULTANCY
1 North Court,
Surrey Hills VIC 3127
613 9830 2009

FENG SHUI CONSCIOUS ENVIRONMENT
9 Lima Grove, Northcote VIC 3070
613 9481 1129

USA

AMERICAN FENG SHUI INSTITUTE
108 North Ynez, Suite 202,
Monterey Park CA91754
626 571 2757

FENG SHUI INSTITUTE OF AMERICA
PO Box 488, Wabasso, FL 32970

THE FENG SHUI DIRECTORY AND MAGAZINE
PO Box 5701, Charlottesville, VA 22906
804 974 1726

THE FENG SHUI GUILD
PO Box 766
Boulder, CO 80306
303 444 1548

WESTERN SCHOOL OF FENG SHUI
437 South Hwy 101, Suite 752
Solana Beach, CA 92075
619 793 0945

INDEX

INDEX OF TABLES

Assessing a Location, 35
Auspicious Measurements, 229
Bagua and Desks, The, 121
Bagua and Family Seating, The, 95
Bagua or Pa Kua, The, 24, 203
Bed Directions, 246
Best and Worst Directions, 49, 204, 249
Boundaries and the Five Elements, 43
Building Positions, 11
Buildings and the Five Elements, 249
Businesses and the Five Elements, 249
Chinese Animals Table, 17
Colours, The, 22, 242
Directions, 50, 149
Energy of Numbers, 25
Favoured Months and Directions, 205
Five Element Features in the Garden, 143
Five Elements, The, 25, 249
Four Animals Formation, The, 10, 137
Magic Numbers, The, 25, 249
Magic Square, 24
Materials and the Five Elements, 59
Nature of the Animals, The, 16, 125
Placing Pots and Ornaments, 165
Planting Times, 145
Plants that Represent the Five Elements, 63
Qualities of the Five Elements, 223
Relationships of the Five Elements, The, 14, 42, 223
Symbolic Chinese Animals, 127
Tastes and the Elements, 94
Three Gates Bagua, 27
Useful Shapes and Colours for Cornerstones, 163
Where to Sit, 150
Yin and Yang Offices, 215
Yin/Yang, 13, 139

access, office location, 200-1

acupuncture, 13
air: breathing, 113, 216-17
  in cars, 125
allergies, plants and, 170
animals: Chinese astrology, 16-23
  Four Animal formation, 10, 11, 137, 200
  good and bad directions, 204
  office personalities, 242-5
astrology, 8-9, 16-23

babies, nurseries, 104-5
  paths, 156-7
Bagua, 24, 26-7
  Bagua mirrors, 61
  home offices, 121
  planning gardens, 149, 152-3
  planning homes, 51
  planning offices, 203, 210-11, 246-7
  seating plans, 95
  Symbolic Bagua, 78-9
balconies, 116-17
bamboo, 59
barbecues, 162
barriers, in offices, 218-19
basement gardens, 184, 185
bathrooms, 110-13, 213
beach gardens, 190
beams, 54-5, 218
bedrooms, 100-3
  children's rooms, 106-7
  en suite bathrooms, 112

  in hotels, 250-1
  nurseries, 104-5
  teenagers' rooms, 108-9
beds, 100-1, 106
black, 75, 223
blue, 75, 181
books, 76-7, 227
boundaries, gardens, 158-9, 188
breathing, 113, 216-17
bridges, 141
Bright Hall, 147
brown, 75, 223
buildings, in gardens, 141, 163
business trips, 250-1
cabinets, bathroom, 112
calendar, 16
candles, 92
car parks, 213-14
Career area, Bagua, 78, 247
cars, 124-5
ceramics, 59
chairs, 86-7, 93, 162
chemicals, in the home, 58
chi, 13
  flow in a living room, 53
  in gardens, 140-1
  in the kitchen, 97-8
  office energies, 238, 240-1
  roads and, 39
Chi Kung, 26
children: children's rooms, 106-7
  nurseries, 104-5
  Symbolic Bagua, 78
Chinese gardens, 134-5
cities, 38-9
clay, in the home, 59
clearing unseen energies, 37
clothes: interviews, 248-9
  storage, 102
clutter, 76-7
  in bathrooms, 112
  in bedrooms, 103
  in cars, 125
  in children's rooms, 106
  in gardens, 175
  in living rooms, 90
  in offices, 226-7
  in studies, 123
  in teenagers' rooms, 108
coastal areas, 41, 190-1
coir matting, 59
coloured glass, 69
colours: in bathrooms, 113
  business clothes, 248-9
  cars, 125
  in gardens, 178-81

  in the home, 74-5
  in offices, 222-3
columns, 218
communal areas, offices, 234-5
communication systems, offices, 206
companion planting, 170-1
compasses, 10, 24, 27
  planning gardens, 148-9
  planning homes, 50-1
  planning offices, 210-11
compatibility of astrological signs, 22, 242
computers, 66, 123, 224-5, 227
conservatories, 114-15
containers, in gardens, 164, 165
corners, 52
cornerstones, in gardens, 163
corridors, 219, 234
country locations, 40-1, 188-9
courtyard gardens, 182-3
crystals, 69
curtains, 89

desks: clutter, 226-7
  home offices, 120-1
  offices, 230-1
  reception areas, 232-3
  studies, 122-3
dining rooms, 92-5, 114-15
dinner parties, 95
directions, 246
  best and worse directions, 48-9
  East and West groups, 51
  gardens, 149
  and interviews, 249
  office location, 200-5
dog: Chinese astrology, 16-17, 21, 22, 23
  office personalities, 242
doors, 56-7
  front doors, 45, 84
  offices, 232
dowsing, 37
dragon: Chinese astrology, 16-17, 19, 22, 23

Four Animal formation, 10, 11, 137, 200
office personalities, 242, 244

earth: and buildings, 199
element, 14-15
in gardens, 143
and interviews, 249
office personalities, 243-5
in offices, 203
earth grids, 37
East Group, 25, 51
edges, 52
electrical equipment, 66-7, 102-3, 224-5
electromagnetic radiation, 66-7, 103, 224-5
elements, 14-15, 27
boundaries, 159
and buildings, 43, 199
in gardens, 142-3
and interviews, 249
materials in the home, 59
office personalities, 243-5
in offices, 202-3, 222-3
plants, 63
and tastes, 94
transformation, 143
en suite bathrooms, 112
energy: energizing our homes, 77
lighting, 65
office energies, 238-41
unseen energies, 36-7, 144-5, 216-17
see also chi
enhancements, gardens, 152-3
entrances: homes, 44
offices, 205, 212, 232, 234
environment, 10-11, 29, 34-5

fabrics, in the home, 59
Fame area, Bagua, 79
Family area, Bagua, 78
fences, 159
fire: and buildings, 199
element, 14-15
in gardens, 142-3
and interviews, 249
office personalities, 243-5
in offices, 203
fireplaces, 88
first impressions, offices, 206-7
fish, 70, 233
Five Elements see elements
flowers, 63
food: balanced eating, 94
tastes, 72
Form School, 10
Four Animal formation, 10, 11, 137, 200
front doors, 45, 84
front gardens: boundaries, 158
paths, 156
furniture: in gardens, 141, 162
offices, 228-31
see also individual rooms

Gaia, 29
gardens, 129-91
geopathic stress, 36, 37
glass: coloured, 69
in the home, 59
goat: Chinese astrology, 16-17, 20, 22, 23
office personalities, 242, 245
green, 75, 180-1, 223

halls, 84
healthy gardens, 170-1
hedges, 158-9
Helpful People area, Bagua, 78, 247
herbs, 171
home, 31-123
home office, 120-1
home-office links, 246-7
Hong Kong and Shanghai Bank, 195
horse: Chinese astrology, 16-17, 20, 22, 23
office personalities, 242, 245
"Hot Desking", 235, 238-9
hotels, 250-1

I Ching 10
insect pests, 171
interviews, 248-9
intuition, 10-11, 29
investigating your home, 80-1
Island of the Immortals, 139

kitchens, 96-9
in conservatories, 114
in offices, 213
Knowledge area, Bagua, 79

lakes, 40-1
Landform School, 10
ley lines, 36
life force see chi
lighting, 64-5
dining rooms, 92
in gardens, 167
living rooms, 88
offices, 220-1
living rooms, 86-91, 115
lobbies, 85
location: homes, 34-41
offices, 198-207
logos, 207
Lovelock, James, 29
luo pan, 10, 16, 24, 27

magic numbers, 25
Magic Square, 24, 27, 136
marble 59
Margulis, Lynne, 29
materials: for boundaries, 159
courtyard gardens, 183
in the home, 58-9
in offices, 217, 223
paths, 157
measurements, auspicious, 229
meditation, 26, 113
metal: and buildings, 199
element, 14-15
in gardens, 143
in the home, 59
and interviews, 249
office personalities, 243-5
in offices, 203
mirrors, 60-1
in bathrooms, 111-12
in bedrooms, 101-2
mobile phones, 66, 225
money plant, 63
monkey: Chinese astrology, 16-17, 20, 22, 23
office personalities, 242, 245
moon, 145
mountains, 10-11, 134, 137

names, offices, 206-7
natural world, 29
negative attitudes, 246
numbers: cars, 125
magic, 25
nurseries, 104-5

oak trees, 29
offices, 193-251
home office, 120-1
open-plan offices, 231, 238, 239
orange, 75, 181
organizers, office, 227
orientation: buildings, 43
homes, 43, 48
ornaments: in cars, 124
in dining rooms, 92-3
in gardens, 164-5
in living rooms, 90-1
ox: Chinese astrology, 16-17, 18, 22, 23
office personalities, 242, 243

Pa Kua, 24
paintings, 90, 92-3
parks, 38
paths, 44-5, 141, 156-7, 188-9
patios, 186-7
personalities, office, 242-5
perspective, gardens, 139
pests, in gardens, 171
Phoenix, Four Animal formation, 10, 11, 137, 200
photocopiers, 225
pictures, 90, 92-3
pig: Chinese astrology, 16-17, 21, 22, 23
office personalities, 242
pink, 75, 181
plans: gardens, 148-51

homes, 50-1
offices, 210-11
plants: allergies, 170
architectural plants, 182
basement gardens, 185
choosing, 172-3
cleaning air, 217
colours, 178-81
companion planting, 170-1
conservatories, 114
in containers, 164
courtyard gardens, 182
in the home, 58, 62-3
meanings, 135
and the moon, 145
in offices, 225
poisonous plants, 170
roof gardens, 185
rural gardens, 189
scented plants, 177
for terraces, 187
window-boxes, 116-17
yin and yang, 139
plastics, in the home, 59
"poison arrows", 45, 87, 98, 160, 195, 228
poisonous plants, 170
ponds, 160
pools, swimming, 118-19
pots, in gardens, 164, 165
purple, 75, 181

rabbit: Chinese astrology, 16-17, 19, 22, 23
office personalities, 242, 244
radiation, 37, 66-7, 224-5
radon, 37
railways, 39
rat: Chinese astrology, 16-17, 18, 22, 23
office personalities, 242, 243
rattan, 59
reception areas, offices, 232-3
red, 75, 180, 223
Relationship area, Bagua, 78
restaurants, 213, 251
"right time", 79
rivers, 10-11, 40-1, 191
roads, 39, 41, 200-1
rocks, in gardens, 140, 160
roof gardens, 184-5
rooms, position, 48-9
rooster: Chinese astrology, 16-17, 21, 22, 23
office personalities, 242
rural locations, 40-1, 188-9

scented plants, 177
seaside gardens, 190-1
seasonal plants, 172, 173
seating: dining tables, 95
living rooms, 86-7
selling houses, 35
senses, 68-73
and cars, 125
gardens and, 174-7
in nurseries, 104-5
shade, plants for, 182
shapes: gardens, 146-7
houses, 43
Sick Building Syndrome, 216
sight, 68, 125, 174
signs, offices, 207
silver, 180
sisal matting, 59
slanting walls, 53
sleep, 246
smell, sense of, 73, 177
snake: Chinese astrology, 16-17, 19, 22, 23
office personalities, 242, 244-5
sofas, 86-7
soil, 144-5
solar year dates, 25
sounds, 70, 105, 175
spirit of place, 145
staff rooms, 234-5
staircases, 85, 213, 219, 234
stationery, business, 206
statues, in gardens, 166
stereos, 89
stone, in the home, 59
storage, in offices, 226, 228-9
stoves, 96
streams, underground, 36, 144
studies, 122-3
studios, 122-3
suburbs, 38
sun, 145
swimming pools, 118-19
Symbolic Bagua, 78-9

tables: dining tables, 93-4
in gardens, 162
meeting rooms, 235
T'ai Chi, 13, 26
Tao, 12, 24, 29
taste, 72, 94, 176-7
teenagers' rooms, 108-9
telephones, 66, 103, 206, 225
television, 66, 89, 107
template, Bagua, 26-7
terraces, 186-7
Three Gates Bagua, 27
tiger: Chinese astrology, 16-17, 18, 22, 23
Four Animal formation, 10, 11, 137, 200
office personalities, 242, 243-4
toilets, 110-11, 213
Tortoise, Four Animal formation, 10, 11, 137, 200
touch, 71, 105, 176
transport, office location, 200-1
travel, business trips, 250-1
trees, 29, 135, 141, 173

underground water, 36, 144
unseen energies, 36-7, 144-5, 216-17
urban environment, 38-9
vegetable gardens, 189
vibrations, 14, 77, 217
vision, 68, 125, 174

walls: plants to hide, 182
slanting, 53
wardrobes, 102
water: bathrooms, 110
and buildings, 199
coastal gardens, 190-1
element, 14-15
in gardens, 140, 143, 160-1, 189
and interviews, 249
office personalities, 243-5
in offices, 203
rivers and lakes, 40-1, 191
sounds, 70
swimming pools, 118-19
underground, 36, 144
Water Dragon Classic, 11, 161
Wealth area, Bagua, 78, 247
West Group, 25, 51
white, 75, 180, 223
wildlife, in gardens, 160
wind chimes, 70
window-boxes, 116-17
windows, 57
winter interest, gardens, 174
wood: and buildings, 199
element, 14-15
in gardens, 142, 143
in the home, 59
and interviews, 249
office personalities, 243-5
in offices, 203
work: home office, 120-1
offices, 193-251
workstations, 231

years: animal rulers, 23
directions, 204
yellow, 75, 180, 223
yin and yang, 12-13, 138-9, 202, 214-15